*A Short History of
Modern Bulgaria*

For our sons, Will and Ben

A Short History of
Modern Bulgaria

R. J. CRAMPTON

Senior Lecturer in History, The University of Kent at Canterbury

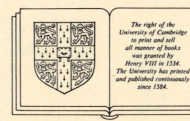

The right of the
University of Cambridge
to print and sell
all manner of books
was granted by
Henry VIII in 1534.
The University has printed
and published continuously
since 1584.

CAMBRIDGE UNIVERSITY PRESS

Cambridge
New York   Port Chester
Melbourne   Sydney

Published by the Press Syndicate of the University of Cambridge
The Pitt Building, Trumpington Street, Cambridge CB2 IRP
40 West 20th Street, New York, NY 10011, USA
10 Stamford Road, Oakleigh, Melbourne 3166, Australia

First published 1987
Reprinted 1989

Printed in Great Britain by the University Press, Cambridge

British Library cataloguing in publication data

Crampton, R. J.
A short history of modern Bulgaria.
1. Bulgaria – History – 1878–1944.
2. Bulgaria – History – 1944–
I. Title
949.7'702   DR85

Library of Congress cataloguing in publication data

Crampton, R. J.
A short history of modern Bulgaria.
Bibliography.
Includes index.
1. Bulgaria – History.   I. Title.
DR67.C73 1987   949.7'7   86–17528

ISBN 0 521 25340 3 hard covers
ISBN 0 521 27323 4 paperback

UP

Contents

List of tables   *page* vii
List of maps   vii
Preface   ix
Transliteration scheme   xiii

1 PRE-MODERN BULGARIA   1

The Bulgarian lands before the Bulgarians   1
The first Bulgarian empire, 681–1018   2
The second Bulgarian empire, 1185–1393   5
Bulgaria under Ottoman rule   7
The national revival   9
The political struggle and the settlement of 1878   17

2 FROM LIBERATION TO THE END OF THE FIRST WORLD
   WAR   21

The reign of Alexander Battenberg, 1878–86   21
The Stambolovshtina, 1886–94   31
The establishment of Prince Ferdinand's personal regime,
   1894–1900   37
Years of crisis, 1900–3   40
From the Ilinden–Preobrazhensko rising to the declaration of
   independence, 1903–8   47
Urban unrest, 1903–8   50
The development of agrarianism and socialism before the
   First World War   54
From the declaration of independence to the first Balkan war,
   1908–12   57
Years of war, 1912–18   59
Social and economic development, 1878–1918   71

3 REVOLT, RADICAL RULE, REPRESSION AND WAR, 1918–44 *page* 82

Revolt and Agrarian rule: 1918–23   82
The fall of the Stamboliiski and the September revolt, 1923   93
Tsankov, Liapchev, and the Democratic Alliance, 1923–31   100
The government of the People's Bloc, 1931–4   107
The coup d'état of 19 May 1934   111
Boris's personal regime, 1935–9   114
Foreign policy, 1935–41   119
Bulgaria during the Second World War, 1941–4   124
Social and economic development, 1918–44   135

4 BULGARIA UNDER COMMUNIST RULE   145

The seizure of political power, 1944–7   145
The socialisation of the economy and the rise of Chervenkov, 1948–50   166
The Chervenkov years and the beginnings of destalinisation, 1950–6   173
The April plenum and the rise of Zhivkov, 1956–62   179
The Zhivkov era from the early 1960s to the early 1980s   185
Bulgaria in the mid-1980s   200

Suggestions for further reading   210
Index   215

Tables

Distribution of land by size of holdings, 1897 and 1908   *page* 72
Distribution of land by size of holdings, 1926–46   136
Industrial growth in the 1920s   140
Relative income per category of workforce, 1934   142
Planned and achieved growth under seventh and eighth five-year
    plans   196

Maps

Bulgaria, 1878–1918   *page* xiv
Contemporary Bulgaria   22–3

Preface

British scholars have paid less attention to Bulgaria than to any other country of eastern Europe with the possible exception of Albania. Bulgaria, it is true, provided fuel for Mr Gladstone's copious passions, and a street in Sofia still bears his name, but the other British citizens commemorated in this or similar fashion are no longer familiar names in their own country: James Bourchier, the first non-royal British subject whose head appeared on a postage stamp, Noel Buxton, after whom a 'residential complex' in the Bulgarian capital is named, and Frank Thompson, who died at the hands of the Bulgarian police in the Second World War and whose name was given to a village near where he was captured. The two world wars and the division of Europe in the late 1940s all found Britain and Bulgaria on opposite sides, and estrangement bred indifference from which ignorance inevitably followed. Since the 1970s contacts have increased. Western tourists began to visit the Black Sea coast in the 1960s and now also take winter holidays in the newly developed ski resorts of the Bulgarian interior, whilst British consumers have come to appreciate a range of Bulgarian products, not least the excellent wine now so widely available.

At the time when the final stages of this book were being written Bulgaria was still an apparently quiet corner of eastern Europe with no record of upheaval or political originality to equal Yugoslavia, Romania, Albania, Hungary, Poland or Czechoslovakia. It may be that this quiescence will persist. On the other hand it may be that significant changes of personality and policy are imminent. It is time perhaps to attempt to learn more of the land from which we have been long estranged.

The present work is presented as a first step towards a closer acquaintance; it makes no pretence of being the final word. Although the title confines the study to modern Bulgaria it has been thought appropriate to make a brief outline of the country's more distant past, not least because the Bulgarians themselves have recently placed much greater emphasis on the continuity of developments not merely amongst the Bulgarians as a

people but in the lands which they now occupy. The author is fully aware
that such innocent-sounding phrases can carry a high political charge, for,
the Balkans being the Balkans, there are few areas where who or what
constitutes a nation are generally accepted. I have attempted objectivity
in all questions concerning competing ethnic claims, but am not sanguine
that everyone will agree that I have succeeded.

This outline of modern Bulgarian history is overwhelmingly political,
with some consideration of economic and social issues. Cultural developments have been included in the political narrative in the sections on the
national renaissance and on Bulgaria since the socialist revolution, because
in both cases cultural affairs were inseparable from politics. In the
intervening years the connection was less close, and for these years a short
passage on the main developments in literature and the arts has been
inserted. No-one is more conscious than the author of the distortions which
this causes, for it has not allowed any consideration of Bulgaria's
considerable achievements in the fields of history, archaeology, mathematics and sub-atomic physics, to mention but a few. Nor should the author,
who constantly enjoins upon his students the necessity for brevity, invoke
limitations of space as justification for his shortcomings, but the prime
consideration has been to provide an introduction to the main political
events in the history of modern Bulgaria. It is to be hoped that scholars
more expert in cultural affairs will soon provide a detailed treatment of the
subject, as the distinguished American economic historian, John Lampe,
has done for the economic history of the country.

Because this book is intended more for the interested general reader
than for the professional scholar, editorial policy has been to exclude
footnotes as far as possible and to confine the bibliography to accessible
works in English.

All writers dealing with countries and nations which use the cyrillic
alphabet are plagued by the problems of transliteration. I have tried to
adhere to the system outlined on another page but have been unable to
use Iugov rather than Yugov or *komitadji* rather than *comitadji*, and have
also been somewhat lax in the use of plurals, sometimes retaining the
Bulgarian 'i', 'a' or 'ove', and at others relapsing into the simple English
's'; I hope the Bulgarian-speaker will indulge me in these inconsistencies,
which I trust will not trouble those who are unfamiliar with the language.
I have generally used the Slav form of place names but have preferred
established Western usage when it is available and have used the form
appropriate to the period under discussion, thus Byzantium or Constantinople rather than Tsarigrad or Istanbul, and Adrianople rather than
Edirne. It would be pleasant if the difficulties of nomenclature could be dis-

posed of so easily, but in a region where Slav, Turkish, Greek, German, and perhaps even Magyar forms exist, and where names can change with the political climate, no author can hope to be exhaustive in his provision. I have usually given past and present forms of the Bulgarian name when it is first encountered and then used that which was current in the period concerned. An even more vexing problem is that of dates. Until 1916 Bulgaria, as an Orthodox Christian state, used the Julian calendar, which was twelve days behind the Western, or Gregorian, system in the nineteenth century and thirteen days in the twentieth century. I have given both dates when citing specific days or months.

Many people and institutions have contributed to this work. The British Library, the invaluable Inter-Library Loan service, the libraries of the University of Kent at Canterbury and the Kiril i Metodi library in Sofia have given essential help and support. The University of Kent has again been generous in allowing me sabbatical leave in which to write free of teaching and administrative commitments. Many colleagues in the British, Bulgarian, American and German academic fraternities have contributed more than they could know or I could say by their advice, their encouragement and above all their friendship, and I owe a special debt to John Lampe of the University of Maryland, for allowing me to see the pre-publication typescript of his recent book on Bulgarian economic history and secondly for providing enormously valuable and much valued comment upon the typescript of this book. Above all, as always, there is the enduring debt to my wife for her constant support and her tolerance of the author in travail.

Canterbury, January 1986   R. J. CRAMPTON

Transliteration scheme

а - a
б - b
в - v
г - g (always hard)
д - d
е - e
ж - zh (but дж has been trans-
    literated 'dj')
з - z
и - i
й - y
к - k
л - l
м - m
н - n

о - o
п - p
р - r
с - s
т - t
у - u
ф - f
х - h (but 'kh' in Russian words)
ц - ts
ч - ch
ш - sh
щ - sht (but 'shch' in Russian words)
ъ - ŭ
ю - iu
я - ya

The Russian ы has been rendered into 'y'. The hard sign has not been transliterated.

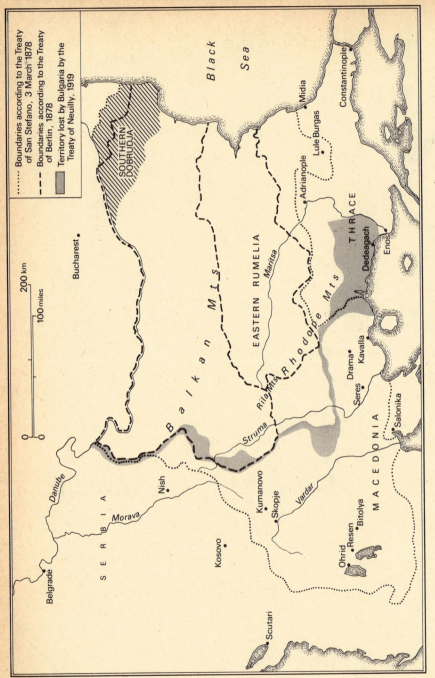

Black Sea

Constantinople

Midia

Lule Burgas

Adrianople

SOUTHERN DOBRUDJA

THRACE

Dedeagach

Enos

Bucharest

Maritsa

EASTERN RUMELIA

Rhodope Mts

Balkan Mts

Rila Mts

Drama
Kavalla

Seres

Salonika

200 km

100 miles

Struma

Danube

Nish

Kumanovo

Skopje

Vardar

MACEDONIA

SERBIA

Morava

Kosovo

Ohrid
Resen
Bitolya

Belgrade

Scutari

Map 1 Bulgaria, 1878–1918

1

Pre-modern Bulgaria

THE BULGARIAN LANDS BEFORE THE BULGARIANS

The first evidence of human occupation in the Bulgarian lands dates from the middle paleolithic era, *c.* 100,000 to 40,000 B.C. By neolithic times the improvement in the climate had enabled man to leave the caves for the plains where settlement had taken place and cultivation had begun. By the third millenium B.C. non-food crops such as flax were also being grown, metal-working was known, and dwellings such as those excavated at Kodjadermen in eastern Bulgaria showed sophisticated construction techniques.

The Bronze Age saw the Bulgarian lands for the first time loosely united within a common civilisation, that of the Thracians, an Indo-European race which established a social, economic and cultural system as advanced as those of their contemporaries in Greece and Asia Minor. From the end of the twelfth century B.C. Thrace was disrupted by invaders moving from Europe to Asia Minor, but by the mid-sixth century B.C. Thracian civilisation had recovered; political unity was achieved a century later under the Odrysae tribe and the Thracians now stood at the zenith of their creative achievement. Generally dismissed by ancient Greek writers as savages, the Thracians were in fact both artistically gifted and economically advanced; they began the minting of coins, for example, at much the same time as the Greeks.

The Thracians were weakened successively by Greek colonisation, King Darius's Persians who lingered thirty years in southern Thrace, Macedonian domination, and the arrival of the Celts. An independent Thracian Kingdom was re-established in the third century B.C., and this the Romans allowed to survive as a distinct but client state until the reign of Vespasian. The Thracian language, however, was still spoken in remote communities in the fifth century A.D., Thracian worship of the horse was passed on to later settlers, whilst the prevalence of 'mummers' in certain areas of south-western Bulgaria today is another legacy of the ancient Thracian civilisation.

I

Roman domination of Thrace and of Moesia, the lands between the Balkan mountains and the Danube, inevitably meant efficient government and economic development. A network of roads was established and Serdica, where Sofia now stands, grew as the crossing point of important trans-Balkan routes. Peace, prosperity and eventually Christianity came with Roman rule until that rule was undermined by internal and external pressures. With the division of the fourth century the Bulgarian lands became part of the eastern empire.

By the late fifth century the Bulgarian lands had begun to suffer from incursions by Slavs, many of whom became settlers, though as yet their colonies were confined to rural areas since the invaders could not or would not occupy the towns. In the seventh century came combined assaults by Slavs and Proto-Bulgarians. The latter were of Turkic origin but contained more than one ethnic component, the word *Bulgar* being an Old Turkic word meaning 'to mix'. The Proto-Bulgarians had originally come from the area between the Urals and the Volga, and had spent some time as pastoralists on the steppes to the north of the Caspian Sea. They arrived south of the Danube with a well-developed political system based upon their ruler, the Khan, and a formidable military reputation founded upon their cavalry. In the 630s a loose federation of Proto-Bulgarian tribes had been formed, and in 680 Khan Asparuh led one branch of this union across the Danube. In 681 the Emperor Constantine V Pogonatus was forced to sign a treaty with Asparuh by which the existence of a Bulgarian state was recognised for the first time; the capital of the new state was established at Pliska, near the present-day Shumen.

THE FIRST BULGARIAN EMPIRE, 681–1018

The power and extent of the new state grew rapidly. Bulgarian troops helped Byzantium fight off the Arabs in 717–18 and during the following century, with the collapse of the Avar Khagante, expanded westwards as far as the Tisza. The Byzantines were by now alarmed and attempted to check the rise of the Bulgarian state, undertaking a major campaign against it early in the ninth century. It was a foolhardy venture. In 811 Nicephorus became the first emperor for almost five hundred years to lose his life on the battlefield and his skull was made into a drinking goblet by the victorious Khan Krum.

As such practices might suggest the Bulgarian state was as yet still pagan, though many of the Slavs had retained the Christianity they had adopted before the Proto-Bulgarian invasion. In 864 Boris, who ruled from

852 to 889, agreed to the mass conversion of the Bulgarians. He did so partly to escape the military difficulties in which he found himself, but however opportunist the motives, the effects of this decision were profound and long-lasting. In the first place it greatly facilitated the amalgamation of the Slav and the Bulgarian inhabitants of the state. By the mid-ninth century all were known as 'Bulgarians' and a common, Slav-based language had emerged, but there remained important differences, the most important of which was religion. With the conversion that difference disappeared; the Slavs could more easily accept the state because it was now Christian, the Bulgarians had nothing to fear from the church because it was no longer purely Slav. After 864 the danger of Slav separatism disappeared.

Initially, as opponents of the move had feared, conversion weakened the Bulgarian state because the church tended to act as an agent of the Byzantine emperor, and was refused permission to appoint its own bishops or have its own patriarch. Boris therefore turned to Rome, asking if the pope would allow him to appoint bishops and nominate a patriarch; at the same time he sought guidance on a series of questions concerning the law and Christian *mores*, including that of whether sexual intercourse was permitted on Sundays. Despite a reassuring affirmative to the latter question the pope would not commit himself to allowing Bulgarian bishops, much less a patriarch, and therefore the Bulgarian church remained within the Eastern communion. It was not, however, to be completely dominated by the Byzantine patriarchate, and in 870 an autocephalous Bulgarian church was established. The new church was much influenced by hermitism, the most prominent practitioner of which was the founder of the great Rila monastery, Ivan Rilski (*inter* 876 and 880–947), whose pursuit of learning and sanctity in isolation from state and society established in the Bulgarian collective psyche a precedent and perhaps a reverence for this form of 'internal migration'.

Together with the adoption of Christianity came the equally important development of Slav literacy. A slavonic alphabet had been devised in the latter half of the ninth century by the slavophone monks, Cyril and Methodius. This made it possible for Bulgaria's rulers to adopt their own tongue rather than Greek as the language of the state. It also made possible the rapid development of Bulgarian culture, a process in which the church played a dominant role with one of its earliest leaders, Kliment Ohridski (*c.* 840–896), establishing a school of learning which spread far beyond the confines of theology. The development of Slav literacy which produced important temporal as well as secular works, for example the legal code

Zakon Sudnii Liudim, also prevented the absorption of the Bulgarians and the Slavs by the more advanced Greeks to the south or the Franks to the west.

The Bulgarian state was now equipped with its own language, its own branch of the Eastern church and a population which was rapidly overcoming ethnic diversity. It was on this consolidation of state, church and population that was founded the power of Simeon, later known as Simeon the Great, chosen as prince in 893. Simeon had been educated in Byzantium, and because he had originally intended to become head of the Bulgarian church he had gathered around himself a glittering collection of artists and men of letters which included the Monk Hrabr, John the Exarch and Konstantin of Preslav; yet for most of his reign (893–927) Simeon was engaged with military affairs. In a series of campaigns he extended Bulgaria's boundaries to the Adriatic in the west and the Aegean in the south, and twice he led his armies to the walls of Constantinople itself before pressure elsewhere caused him to lift his siege. During Simeon's reign the head of the Bulgarian church was accorded the title of patriarch whilst Simeon himself was recognised as an equal by the Byzantine emperor and given the title of *Basileus* or tsar; alone with the Holy Roman Emperor did the Bulgarian ruler enjoy equality of status with the emperor in Constantinople.

After the death of Simeon Bulgarian fortunes declined, but they were restored in the final quarter of the tenth century. The centre of the state was now in the south-west, at Ohrid, but in 1014 the spirit of the first Bulgarian empire was broken when the Emperor Basil II, later known as 'the Bulgar-Slayer', captured 15,000 Bulgarian troops on the slopes of Belassitsa mountain. Ninety-nine in every hundred were blinded, the remainder being left with one eye so that they might guide their stricken comrades back to their impudent ruler. By 1018 Bulgaria was incorporated into the Byzantine empire.

The rapid decline after Simeon's rule had many causes. Attacks in the north by Magyars and Russians had meant the loss of the trans-Danubian provinces with their important reserves of manpower. Even more serious had been the failure of the Bulgarians to produce a navy, a task which demanded more in the way of technology and the coordination of separate productive processes than the first empire could achieve. Internally Bulgaria had not developed economically and still relied upon Byzantine currency, whilst social cohesion had been undermined first by the rise of a new aristocracy and secondly by the spread of the Bogomil heresy. The Bogomils, whose influence eventually extended into Italy and northern France, if not further afield, preached restraint and asceticism, but also argued that the state and all its activities were derived from the evil side of a dualistic universe, whilst the world of the soul and the spirit were a product of the 'good'; thus there was no sin in a lack of respect or a lack of commitment to the state. This encouragement towards 'internal migration' could on the one hand complement the withdrawal practised by Ivan Rilski *et al*, but on the other hand the widespread nature of the heresy – and it was well-established in the Bulgarian lands by 950 – could encourage the articulation of popular discontent, particularly because the movement was deeply entrenched in the lower clergy with whom the general population was in constant and often close contact. The feeling that the state was a manifestation of a universal evil could, if taken to extremes, lead to pacifism, and even if extremes were avoided a populace soaked in the Bogomil heresy could not be relied upon to respond enthusiastically to calls for the defence of the political establishment. The Bogomils also questioned the social structure in that they preached that man should live in communities where property was shared and individual ownership unknown; all men would be levelled by a common commitment to and participation in agricultural labour. These ideas were to reappear in a different context in the late nineteenth century. The emphasis upon and reverence for education were also to reappear in later centuries, again with important results.

Bogomilism tended to be absorbed more by Slav than by Greek communities, and it could therefore have been in part responsible for the fact that although the first Bulgarian empire fell to Byzantium its population was not to be assimilated into the Greek world. The Bulgarian state had derived much from the powerful Byzantine empire but it also owed much to the traditions of Preslav and Ohrid. It had founded its own church which, in turn, had been primarily responsible for the development of Slav language, literature and culture, and its people had seen the evolution of their own forms for the rejection of entrenched political power. The Bulgarians had established a form of national cultural consciousness. Though far from the nationalism of the nineteenth century, with its concepts of popular sovereignty and organised political movements, this sense of identity was strong enough to preserve the concept of Bulgaria as a distinct religious, cultural and, perhaps, political entity.

THE SECOND BULGARIAN EMPIRE, 1185–1393

At the end of the twelfth century this sense of a separate identity was still alive when the rising costs of defending the Byzantine empire forced its rulers to increase taxation. In 1185 the social tensions which this decision created or exacerbated produced a rebellion in which two brothers, Assen and Petŭr, succeeded in re-establishing a Bulgarian state based in its religious capital, Tŭrnovo. With the Byzantine empire having to deal with the third crusade, the reborn Bulgarian state soon dominated the area between the Balkans and the Danube. The second empire, however, was seldom free from debilitating internal strife, and political stability was not achieved until the reign of Tsar Kaloyan (1197–1207). By 1202 Kaloyan had concluded a much-needed peace with Byzantium and in the following year he was able to drive the Magyars out of the area they had occupied in north-west Bulgaria. In 1204, after long negotiations, Kaloyan came to an agreement with the pope by which the Bulgarians recognised the supreme authority of the bishop of Rome, though there was little papal interference in the internal affairs of the Bulgarian church. The agreement helped secure Kaloyan's western borders whilst he attacked the crusading knights who now ruled Constantinople, and by the time of his death he reigned over a huge empire stretching from the Adriatic to the Black Sea and from the Aegean to the Dnieper.

After Kaloyan's death political stability was never fully recovered. Tsar Ivan Assen II (1218–41) succeeded through skilful diplomacy and opportunist marital policies in restoring Bulgarian dominance in the Balkans. He was not, however, able to maintain the agreement with Rome, and in 1235 he restored the Bulgarian church to complete independence. Ivan Assen II helped build up in Tŭrnovo a capital which was also a great cultural centre: from it emerged, before the end of the century, wonderful illustrated manuscripts such as the Gospels of Tsar Alexander, now in the British Museum, and the frescoes begun in 1259 in the church at Boyana near Sofia, arguably Bulgaria's greatest artistic treasure.

As culture flourished the political situation deteriorated. After Ivan Assen II Bulgaria had to withstand the Tatar onslaught and by the end of the century the Bulgarians had been forced to accept Tatar suzerainty. Yet again resistance had been weakened by internal dissension. From 1257 to 1263 the empire had been racked by virtual civil war between opposing local magnates whose exactions, together with the cost of dealing with foreign incursions, so distressed the populace that it rose in rebellion and, with some help from interested nobles, installed as tsar a swineherd, Ivailo, under whom cohesion was restored for three short years. In the early fourteenth century the Tatar tutelage was thrown off, Bulgarian authority in Thrace re-established and a powerful ruler found in Mihail Shishman (1323–30), the former feudal lord of the Vidin area. Shishman's main task was now to contain a new threat, that of Serbia, but in doing so he lost his life in battle near Kiustendil. Under Tsar Ivan

Alexander (1331–71) a series of campaigns asserted Bulgarian interests against opponents old and new, and commerce flourished as the arrival of the Ottomans on the Aegean coast had pushed trade routes northwards so that they now passed through Bulgarian territory. However the cost of Ivan Alexander's almost constant warfare was high and fuelled popular discontent, as did the seepage of real power away from the capital to local magnates, a process which was to be repeated with similar results five hundred years later. The much weakened Bulgarian empire was in no position to resist the dual threat from Serbia on the one hand and the Ottoman army on the other. With the benefit of hindsight the latter clearly appears the more serious danger, but it did not necessarily seem so in the mid-fourteenth century, and rivalries between Christian states therefore eased the progress of the Ottoman armies. In 1362 they took Adrianople (Edirne), and two years later they had advanced up the Martisa valley as far as Plovdiv (Philippopolis). This gradual conquest continued with the fall of Sofia in 1385, and culminated in the decisive defeat of the Serbs at Kosovo in June 1389, which removed the only serious Christian barrier to Ottoman domination of the Balkans. In July 1393 the sultan's troops entered Tŭrnovo; its defence had been led by the patriarch, who, with his clergy, was packed off into exile or slavery. Three years later the Ottomans subdued the small principality of Vidin, and the last separate Bulgarian political entity in the Balkans disappeared. It was to be almost five hundred years before another appeared.

BULGARIA UNDER OTTOMAN RULE

Resistance by the Bulgarians and the repression which was its reward continued until the Ottomans had consolidated their hold upon the Balkans by the conquest of Constantinople in 1453. The apparatus of the old Bulgarian state was completely destroyed, its dominant nobility was deprived of its property and power, and the separate Bulgarian church was placed under the authority of the Greek patriarch. Many churches, especially in the towns, were closed, and monasteries were forbidden. The subsequent exodus of monks, novitiates, scribes and scholars deprived Bulgaria of its medieval equivalent of an intelligentsia. In such conditions there were inevitably some Bulgarians who accepted the religion of their new political masters, although most of the converts retained their Bulgarian language and customs; these *pomaks* – the word may be loosely translated as 'collaborators' – were to be found primarily in the Rhodope mountains.

Relaxation followed the fall of Constantinople. By 1460 the great monastery at Rila had reopened, and social stability was soon achieved, albeit at the cost of some discrimination against the Christians. In the towns this was one of a number of factors causing a diminution of Bulgarian influence. Another was perhaps an absolute decline in the Bulgarian urban population, though modern scholarship has treated this contention with increasing caution. What certainly helped to diminish Bulgarian influence was the cosmopolitan nature of the new order. The sultans recruited their administrators from amongst loyal subjects of any race or creed from Albania to Arabia, whilst trade within the huge polyglot empire fell under the domination of Jews, the Dubrovnik merchants, Greeks and Armenians. Also, it was in the towns that Greek influence in the church was at its strongest. This reinforced the cultural damage inflicted by the departure of the scribes and monks, because under the Ottoman *millet* system religion embraced education and other aspects of cultural life. It was also the case that some towns in which the Bulgarians had been predominant declined in importance because of the shifts in the economic and cultural centres of gravity which the conquest produced.

In the villages the impact of the conquest was much less profound. Here the new landlords, with their obligations to provide troops in proportion to the amount of land held, were little worse or better than their Bulgarian predecessors, whilst, initially at least, central authority in the Ottoman empire was much greater than in the Bulgarian, and therefore provided some check upon the excesses of the local landholding classes. Few Ottoman officials paid more than irregular and fleeting visits to the villages. Some small communities never saw them at all, especially if the village were one entrusted with special functions such as the guarding of passes or the provision of falcons or horses for the imperial household. In the villages too Greek influence in the church was less pervasive than in the towns. It was in the small, remote, and often self-sufficient rural communities that the sense of 'Bulgardom' survived. It was here that folk songs and epic poetry relating the deeds of heroes real and legendary were preserved; it was here that pre-conquest Bulgarian holidays and festivals survived, as did Bulgarian forms of family organisation; it was here, too, that Bulgarian as opposed to Greek Christian names were predominant; and in a number of villages, more especially those entrusted with special functions, local 'councils' (*obshtini*) survived, in which Bulgarians were entrusted with the regulation of their own affairs and the discharge of their obligations to the sultan.

If national identity was preserved in the villages this did not mean that anything resembling a nationalist movement or a national political consciousness existed. Bulgarian nationalist writers have argued that there was a national commitment amongst the *haiduks*, the groups of armed bandits who operated in the mountains and woods. The *haiduk* was assuredly an example of the local rejection of authority, and in later centuries armed bands of them both associated with foreign armies invading Ottoman Europe, and provided a model for organised nationalist rebels, but for the most part the *haiduks* were simply bandits robbing Christian and Muslim alike.

Whilst the Ottoman system functioned efficiently little was heard of the Bulgarians whose traditions were quietly preserved in their small, introspective communities. The gradual decline of the system precipitated equally gradual change in the condition of the Bulgarians. In the seventeenth century the Roman Catholic church, resurgent after the counter-Reformation, began to exercise some influence in Bulgaria, especially in its north-western areas. A number of Bulgarian Catholics began to write about their past, the most prominent being Peter Bogdan Bakshev, a Catholic bishop of Sofia, who wrote *Opisanie na bǔlgarsko Tsarstvo* (*A Description of the Bulgarian Empire*) in 1640 and in 1668 completed a twenty-chapter *Istoriya na Bǔlgariya* (*History of Bulgaria*). Another Bulgarian, Petǔr Parčević, rose high in the papal diplomatic service, and was eventually sent upon the Sisyphean task of mediating between the Poles and the Ukrainians. Parčević and others could make Bulgaria and the Bulgarian lands known in the West, but their efforts were directed more to expanding the influence of the Catholic church than to ending the political domination of the sultans. There were, however, a series of revolts in the seventeenth century, all of them coinciding with external complications for the Ottoman empire. The most serious one, in 1688, focused upon Chiprovets, the centre of Catholic influence in north-west Bulgaria. The defeat of the revolt and the subsequent measures against the Catholics and their organisations ended the Catholic revival in Bulgaria.

THE NATIONAL REVIVAL

The decline in Ottoman strength continued apace during the eighteenth century. The cultural activities of the Catholic church were not given up, but they were now much weaker and of less eventual significance than the stirring of literary revival in the Russo-Slavic school. Here the most important development was the beginning of a movement away from the archaic, stylised Old Church Slavonic, or medieval Bulgarian, and towards a literary language more related to, though still a considerable distance from, the vernacular. The new movement focused on the southern Slavs in general, rather than on the individual peoples we recognise today, but it produced such important works as Hristofar Zhefarović's *Stematografia*, which was published in Vienna in 1741 and which related the histories of the Serbian and Bulgarian empires. At the same time there was also a tendency for education to move out of the monastic cells into the secular world, though as yet this was little felt in most Bulgarian communities.

By the end of the century two figures of enormous if not immediate influence had concentrated their attention upon the Bulgarians alone rather than the southern Slavs in general. Paiisi Hilendarski, a monk in the Hilendar monastery on Mount Athos, had written a history of the Bulgarian empires, in a lively mixture of Old Church Slavonic and more contemporary Bulgarian. The author not only rejoiced in the past but also enjoined his fellow countrymen not to forget or to be ashamed of that past, to cultivate their language, and 'to know your nation and language and study in your own tongue'. Some sixty manuscript copies of Paiisi's history are known to have been made before the work was printed in Budapest in 1845. Paiisi was not the only scholar to write in such terms, but his work was distinguished by its lively style and outstanding clarity. An admirer of Paiisi, Sofronii Vrachanski, carried on his mentor's cause, writing in a much more modern language than that of Paiisi, and also helping to promote new, secular ideas through his translations of Greek myths and through his *Zhitie i Stradanie greshnago Sofronii* (*Life and Tribulations of the sinner Sofroni*), a work which bore the imprint of the European Enlightenment.

Bulgaria was experiencing the 'pre-renaissance' or the beginning of a cultural revival which was to flower in the first half of the nineteenth century. The reasons for the early revival are numerous. Ottoman power had declined drastically, alarming the local communities by removing the protection of a neutral central authority, whilst some emigration and the frequent wars in which the empire was involved weakened the demographic power of the Turks who were increasingly called upon to provide the manpower for the sultan's forces. Epidemic diseases also tended to strike more fiercely at Turks than Bulgarians, for the former lived more in the towns and the other compact settlements of the marshy river valleys; and for reasons which are far from clear, Bulgarian birth rates seem to have been higher than those of the Turks. There were also economic causes for the increasing vitality of Bulgarian culture. On the land the *chiflikchii* (estate holders) of Macedonia, if not necessarily their peasants, benefited from central Europe's increasing demand for cotton, whilst in the towns Bulgarians were to an increasing degree entering into the various *esnafs* or guilds, more especially those for the manufacture of *aba* (coarse cloth) and *gaitan* (decorative braid), and for the working of wood and metals. It was also in the second half of the eighteenth century that a number of important Bulgarian merchant houses were founded. The rise of the economic power of the urban Bulgarian was a powerful stimulus to the cultural revival which was gradually spreading out from the monasteries, and Bulgarians in town and country were linked more productively than at any time since the end of the second empire. Amongst the most important Bulgarian urban communities was that in Constantinople.

The early progress made towards a greater awareness of their national culture was vitiated by the collapse of Ottoman central power at the end of the eighteenth century, a period known in Bulgarian as the *kŭrdjaliistvo*. During this 30–40-year period of anarchy the Balkans saw a repeat of the sins of the second Bulgarian empire, as local freebooters established their power in various parts of the peninsula; their tyranny and feuding, along with insecurity and savage taxation, led to a massive exodus from the towns, a number of which were destroyed. Many Bulgarians fled to the hills, whilst others emigrated north of the Danube to Romania and southern Russia, to form exile communities which were later to be of great importance in the nation's cultural and political development.

For some Bulgarians, including Sofronii Vrachanski, the Russo-Turkish war of 1806–12 offered hope of political change, but such hopes were illusory and political order was not fully re-established in the Bulgarian lands until the 1820s. In that decade both the sultan and his enemies contributed forcefully and unwittingly to the Bulgarian national revival. In 1826 the Ottoman empire underwent its first serious dose of internal reform, as a result of which the old Janissary corps was replaced by a regular army. Much of the cloth and the food, especially mutton, consumed by that army was supplied by Bulgarians, whose economic fortunes improved dramatically from the mid-1820s. Further improvement came when the Ottoman government lifted the ban on the export of wheat in the 1840s, by which time economic advance in the Bulgarian communities could be seen in the new houses, churches, schools, market places and clock towers which they had recently built. In the 1830s major changes in the social structure of the empire complemented the reforms of the previous decade, and intimated that change had become officially permissible and had therefore ceased to be the monopoly of the revolutionary. There were in fact very few of these in the Bulgarian lands, although some Bulgarians had taken part in the Serbian and Greek struggles which had also done much to transform the atmosphere of the Balkans in the 1820s: by 1830 the Serbs had secured some measure of autonomy, and the Greeks, with the help of a number of European powers, had won their independence. These new political entities could provide both a model for and a threat to future Bulgarian national development.

For some time, however, there was no sign that Bulgarians might wish to go to the extremes to which the Serbs and Greeks had resorted. From the 1830s to the 1860s, at least, the Bulgarian national revival was to remain primarily a cultural phenomenon.

It was in the 1830s that the Bulgarians first began their largely unconscious obedience to Paiisi's injunction to 'study in your own tongue'. In 1835 Vasil Aprilov founded a Bell-Lancaster school in Gabrovo with a monk, Neofit Rilski, as its teacher; it was the first school to teach in Bulgarian. The example was followed in other towns throughout the Bulgarian lands, and in 1840 the first school for girls was opened in Pleven. By the middle of the 1840s the educational movement was considerably helped by the return to Bulgaria of the first generation of young men who had been abroad for their schooling, some of whom were fired with a missionary zeal to educate their fellow Bulgarians. The returning graduates were also needed to man the secondary schools which were founded in the 1840s – particularly in Koprivshtitsa, Kalofer and other towns along the foothills of the Balkan mountains, where economic prosperity based upon textiles, sheep-rearing and other trades financed schools, teachers' salaries and scholarships abroad. It was frequently the guilds and local councils of these towns which administered such funds. As educational provision was given free to all Bulgarians a form of national unity was found in the pursuit of learning; by the 1870s there were two thousand schools in Bulgaria providing free education, together with a commercial school in Svishtov, pedagogic institutes in Shtip and Prilep, and theological schools in Samokov and at the Petropavlovski monastery near Lyaskovets.

The expansion of the educational system would have been impossible without a supply of practical grammars. The first attempt to produce such a grammar had been made in the 1820s when Petŭr Beron published his *Riben Bukvar* (*Fish ABC*), so called because of the fish motif on its back cover. Neofit Rilski was among the others who produced textbooks, but it was not until 1844 and the publication of Ivan Bogorov's grammar that a single textbook found wide popular currency, though this did not mean that the Bulgarians had yet agreed upon a standard literary form for their language. This sensitive issue was not settled until the 1870s.

The introduction of printing and book-publishing were also prerequisites for the successful development of the educational movement and of wider public literacy. Between 1806 and 1830 only seventeen original Bulgarian books had appeared, but 264 were published between 1830 and 1854, by which date printing had completely superseded manuscript copying. There was also a great expansion in the less substantial forms of publication. The first Bulgarian periodical, *Liuboslovie* (*Love of Words*) was published in Smyrna (Ismir) in 1844, but its stilted style condemned it to an early death; the first journal with any claim to longevity was Bogorov's *Tsarigradski Vestnik* (*Constantinople Gazette*), which appeared from 1848 to 1861. Between 1844 and 1878 no fewer than 90 Bulgarian periodicals or newspapers were published, but only 33 lasted more than a year and only ten survived for more than five years. Of the 90, 56 were the work of Bulgarian communities outside the Ottoman empire, the majority in Romania, an indication of the importance and power of the émigrés in the Bulgarian national movement. Of those journals and newpapers printed in the Ottoman empire, three-quarters appeared in Constantinople, a just reflection of the influence of the Bulgarian community in the imperial capital.

The cultural revival was not confined to education and journalism. The 1840s saw the first attempt to write modern Bulgarian poetry, with Dobri Chintulov producing early works which were pointers to a talent which was to dazzle his contemporaries in two to three decades' time. By the 1870s he was joined by other important writers such as Rakovski and Hristo Botev, both of whom were prominent in the political struggle for national independence. Bulgarian art in the 1840s began to break from the lifeless formalism which had previously characterised it. Religious paintings were enlivened by new colours and by the introduction of folk motifs, whilst secular art at last established itself, finding in Zahari Zograf a painter of genius. Wood-carving, a Bulgarian speciality, was also enhanced by the introduction of folk motifs. Architecture benefited from the prosperity of the Bulgarian towns and from the money which the guilds placed at the disposal of schools, monasteries and other institutions. Nor was music left out of the general quickening of artistic life. An identifiable form of Bulgarian church singing had emerged by the end of the eighteenth century, and by the 1840s the first Bulgarian musical ensembles had been formed. The traditions of church singing continued to develop, and at the end of the nineteenth century the cantor at the Bulgarian church in Resen in south-west Macedonia could draw large congregations; decades later the opera houses of the world were filled with admirers of his son, Boris Christoff. As Bulgarian culture became more self-aware and self-confident a small number of urban Bulgarians began to assert their newly-found sophistication by adopting Western, or as they would have said, 'European', habits in dress, furniture and other aspects of everyday life.

The expansion of Bulgarian culture would have been impossible without the *chitalishte*. The word's literal translation, 'reading room', is an inadequate description of the facilities provided in these institutions, the first of which was established in 1856 at Svishtov. In addition to small libraries the *chitalishte* could stage lectures, meetings, plays, musical performances, debates and other social events. They were particularly useful in widening the cultural horizons and educational experience of the older Bulgarians who had not been able to benefit from the schools founded in the 1830s and thereafter. The great Bulgarian poet Ivan Vazov later referred to the *chitalishte* as an informal national ministry of culture.

In its wisdom the Ottoman empire had not regarded ethnic differences as being of fundamental significance; its citizens were categorised according to religion. Thus Bulgarians and Greeks found themselves within the Orthodox *millet*, and as Bulgarians asserted their cultural identity they therefore clashed first not with the Ottoman state but with the Greek church. This clash did not take place immediately. Most of the early enlighteners in Bulgaria remained faithful to the Greek patriarchate and tended to regard education in Bulgarian as an addition to rather than an alternative to Greek schooling. The two were not yet mutually exclusive – indeed the Greek archbishop of Tŭrnovo had encouraged Aprilov's and Neofit Rilski's efforts in Gabrovo – whilst in most towns the guilds did not split into separate Greek and Bulgarian organisations until the 1850s. When it did appear the division between Greek and Bulgarian was prompted both by Bulgarian aspirations and by Greek propagation of the *Megali Idea*, the 'grand design' for the unification of all Greeks in one state, a design made less fantastic by the reconciliation in 1850 between the patriarchate in Constantinople and the Greek government in Athens.

Increasing consciousness of their cultural identity had, however, led Bulgarians to question Greek domination of the Orthodox church, at least within its Bulgarian congregations. The last vestiges of a specifically Bulgarian church had disappeared in 1767 when the revived Ohrid archbishopric had been reabsorbed into the patriarchate, after which there was an increasing tendency for Greek-speaking bishops to be appointed to Bulgarian sees and even for Greek-speaking priests to be assigned to purely Bulgarian parishes; to have to say confession through an interpreter could excite forceful emotions. The pocket as well as the conscience were affected by the increasing Hellenisation of the church, for the practice of selling ecclesiastical offices spread down from the highest to the lowest levels, with one dignitary recouping his expenses from those he appointed below him. Inevitably it was the peasant, Greek as well as Bulgarian, who paid, and by the beginning of the 1820s some Bulgarian communities were complaining that they paid more in church dues than in taxes to the state.

In the 1820s there were protests, albeit ineffective, against the venality of the episcopacy in Vratsa and Skopje (Üsküb), and in 1841 rebels in the Nish area, whose main grievances were social rather than cultural or political, demanded *inter alia* that they be given bishops who at least could understand their language. By the late 1840s there had been protests against their bishops by the Orthodox flocks in Russe (Ruschük), Ohrid, Seres, Lovech, Sofia, Samokov, Vidin, Tŭrnovo, Lyaskovets, Svishtov, Vratsa, Tryavna and Plovdiv, and by now the complaint was not against Greek bishops who were corrupt but against bishops who were Greek.

In general the patriarchate paid little heed to Bulgarian complaints, and because of this Bulgarian communities began to demand the right to administer their own churches and appoint their own clergy. In 1848 they achieved their first major success when the Porte agreed to the foundation of a Bulgarian church in the Fanar district of Constantinople. The church, St Stephen's, was to be built on land donated by a wealthy Bulgarian in the Ottoman civil service, and was to be financed and administered by a council elected by the local Bulgarian community; and though it was still to be subordinate to the patriarch in matters of dogma and ecclesiastical jurisdiction, the church was nevertheless the first officially recognised Bulgarian institution to appear during the national revival. The present church, built in the 1890s, can still be seen by those intrepid enough to brave the slums of the present-day Fanar.

The foundation of the Bulgarian church placed Constantinople very firmly at the head of the Bulgarian cultural movement and set a precedent other communities were anxious to follow, a petition from the Bulgarian colony in Bucharest in 1851 declaring presciently that 'Without a national church there is no salvation.' The desire for such a church was sharpened by the success of the Protestants in securing their own *millet* in 1850 – the Armenian Catholics had also done so in 1830 – but the Protestants' success had been achieved largely through British diplomatic support and illustrated the need for a sponsor amongst the great powers if progress were to be made.

Since they had weaned themselves from Greek cultural domination many Bulgarians had tended to assume that affinities of language and religion would make Russia their natural patron. In the 1850s, however, Russia's international standing received a serious setback with her defeat in the Crimean war, and in any case the Russian foreign ministry was not at all anxious to promote a division within the Orthodox church inside the Ottoman empire; Russia's already tenuous right to intervene on behalf of the Ottoman Christians referred to Orthodox Christians, not to members of a Greek or a Bulgarian faith. There were two possible solutions for the Bulgarians. The first was to reactivate the links with Rome which had proved useful in past difficulties. The Uniate church would require only that the Bulgarians acknowledge the pope as head of the church, in return for which they would enjoy complete liturgical and administrative autonomy, and, in all probability, diplomatic support from Austria. From 1851 to 1861 the Uniate answer was championed by the influential Constantinople activist, Dragan Tsankov, and even after 1861 uniatism was a powerful factor in the Bulgarian ecclesiastical equation.

The second answer for the Bulgarians was to follow the Italian precept of *fara da sè*. This course was adopted by bishop Ilarion Makariopolski, who, when officiating in St Stephen's on Easter Sunday 1860, virtually declared the Bulgarian church independent of the patriarchate. The gesture was widely welcomed by Bulgarians throughout the Balkans, and during the following decade many dioceses in Bulgaria, Macedonia and Thrace declared for the Bulgarian church. The problem now was to secure recognition from the Ottoman authorities. This was fiercely resisted by the patriarchate, whilst the Russians were anxious to secure a compromise which would prevent a rupture in Orthodox unity. The Porte did little, content to see two of its subject races at each others' throats. In the late 1860s, however, the Ottoman authorities became convinced of the need for a settlement. A number of armed Bulgarian bands had entered Ottoman territory, and although they were soon dealt with their very existence marked an unwelcome change in Bulgarian tactics. More importantly, the Balkans were not immune from the general instability affecting Europe between Bismarck's wars of 1866 and 1870. In Serbia Prince Michael Obrenović campaigned for a Balkan alliance, which alarmed both Bulgarians and Turks with its implications of Serbian expansionism as expounded two decades previously in Garašanin's *Načertanie*, the Serbian equivalent of the Greek *Megali Idea*. Even more alarming for the Porte was the Cretan rebellion of 1866, which showed that Greek expansionism might become a reality. From 1866, therefore, the Ottomans encouraged the series of meetings and councils which attempted to put an end to the Greek–Bulgarian dispute. By the end of the decade Russia had also come to favour a settlement, because its relations with Athens had deteriorated and because it feared failure to find a solution could only benefit the Uniate movement.

In February 1870 the sultan at last issued a *firman*, or declaration of intent, to recognise the Bulgarian church as a separate religious community headed by an exarch, an ecclesiastical rank between archbishop and patriarch. Of the seventy-four Orthodox dioceses twenty-five were to be included in the exarchate and eight were to be divided, the others remaining within the patriarchate. The Bulgarian dioceses were in the main confined to the area to the north of the Balkan mountains. Although there were provisions for the transfer of a diocese to the exarchate if two-thirds of its Orthodox inhabitants expressed a wish for such a change, the Bulgarians were naturally disappointed that this first modern attempt to define the limits of their race had allotted them so meagre a territory. The patriarchate refused to be reconciled to the new church, which it excommunicated in 1872 for the heresy of phylitism, or maintaining that ecclesiastical jurisdiction is determined ethnically rather than territorially.

The creation of a separate church was the crowning achievement of the Bulgarian cultural revival. Once established, the exarchate became the leading force in Bulgarian life, representing Bulgarian interests at the Porte, defending orthodoxy against uniatism, especially in Macedonia, and sponsoring Bulgarian churches and schools in the mixed dioceses.

By 1870 the modern Bulgarian nation had been born. Its progenitors were on the one side the intelligentsia, represented by the early enlighteners and by the activists in the cultural revival, the educational movement and the church campaign, and on the other the peasantry, who for the most part responded warmly to the prospect of their own church and even to the notion that their enclosed and introspective world would be enhanced by the education and enlightenment of their children and perhaps themselves. But it is a truism of modern history to observe that the birth of a nation and the creation of a nation–state may be different processes.

THE POLITICAL STRUGGLE AND THE SETTLEMENT OF 1878

The cultural and ecclesiastical struggles of the Bulgarians involved a much greater proportion of the population than the political campaigns of the 1860s and 1870s. The church movement had not been without its divisions and the more radical elements, generally referred to as the 'young' faction and found in the émigré rather than in the native Bulgarian communities, advocated more adventurous policies, but even they did not call for the forcible destruction of Ottoman political authority.

Bulgarians had taken part in the Russo-Turkish wars of 1806–12 and 1828–9 and in the Greek war of independence, but these efforts had no lasting effects. There were a number of outbursts against Ottoman rule in the 1830s, including the so-called Velchova rising of May 1835 in Tŭrnovo and the risings of 1841 in Nish and of 1850–1 in the Vidin area, but these were little more than the traditional outbursts born of social distress, and lacked both defined political objectives and armed organisation. The first organised armed group of Bulgarians was the small Bulgarian legion formed in Belgrade in 1862 by Georgi Rakovski. Rakovski was the first ideologue of an armed Bulgarian campaign for an independent political existence. His ideas, published in his own journal, *Dunavski Lebed* (*Danubian Swan*), called for armed bands, or *cheti*, to cross into Bulgaria and establish themselves in the Balkan mountains whence they would operate with the objective of provoking a full-scale uprising; the ultimate goal was a federal Balkan republic, from which, however, the Greeks would be excluded. Experience did not offer much encouragement. The Bulgarian legion, after having joined in the fighting against the Turkish garrison in Belgrade in 1862, was forcibly disbanded by the Serbs amidst fierce mutual recriminations, and when, in the late 1860s, a number of bands did cross from Serbia into Bulgaria, they were soon rounded up and defeated, though their very existence did, as has been seen, help to move the Porte towards recognition of the exarchate. A second Bulgarian legion founded in Belgrade in 1867 was no more successful than the first.

Rakovski died in 1867, but the Bulgarian Secret Central Committee (BSCC), founded in Bucharest in the previous year, continued working for a national uprising, the leadership now being taken by Liuben Karavelov and Vasil Levski. Karavelov also wished to create a federal Balkan republic via a general uprising, but he placed less emphasis on the role of *cheti*; as one who had close links to the later Russian Narodniks Karavelov argued that it should be a small group of 'apostles' who should prepare the people for their historic task. Levski both agreed on the importance of such apostles and acted as one, and in 1868–9 he was in Bulgaria establishing the first revolutionary committees inside the country. In 1872, however, he fell into the hands of the Ottoman police, and in February 1873 was hanged in Sofia. He was to become a national hero, and the nineteenth century has few figures more deserving of such a distinction.

The death of Levski was a bitter blow to the Bulgarian revolutionary cause. Whilst he had been active in Bulgaria itself Karavelov in 1870 had established a Bulgarian Revolutionary Central Committee (BRCC) in Bucharest. The BRCC had included Hristo Botev, a romantic poet with socialist inclinations. The Paris Commune reinforced Botev's socialist enthusiasm to such a degree that he and Karavelov found it difficult to continue working together, and the death of Levski ended any effort at further cooperation. The BRCC was, however, reconstructed at Giurgevo in 1875, this time without Botev but with another prominent activist, Georgi Benkovski, who had soon divided Bulgaria into four revolutionary districts with headquarters at Tŭrnovo, Vratsa, Sliven and Plovdiv. By this time the Balkans were becoming increasingly destabilised following the Bosnian revolt of 1875. In 1876 Serbia went to war with Turkey and a number of Bulgarian units were formed to fight with the Serbs. The BRCC was also determined to take advantage of the upheaval to provoke a rising inside Bulgaria. In April 1876 representatives from some fifty-eight local revolutionary committees met at Oborishte in the woods between Panagiurishte and Koprivshtitsa. After three days of discussion a simultaneous rising in all four revolutionary districts was decided upon. The original date had been in May but in Koprivshtitsa fighting broke out prematurely. The April rising had begun.

The rising itself was a failure, but it provoked the fearsome massacres at Batak and elsewhere which massively increased Bulgarian national consciousness and outraged opinion in Europe, not least that of Gladstone. The Bulgarian question had passed from the hands of the Bulgarians themselves to those of the European statesmen. They produced a scheme of reforms which was designed to prevent further outbreaks of Muslim fanaticism, but when the sultan refused to allow European inspection of these reforms the tsar declared war.

The events of the Russo-Turkish war of 1877–8 and the Berlin conference are too well known to need more than a brief description here. The Russians, after the siege of Pleven, and the epic struggle for the Shipka pass in which the Bulgarian militia played a valiant part, eventually drove the Ottoman army back to the very outskirts of Constantinople. There they dictated the treaty of San Stefano which created a large Bulgaria stretching from the Danube to the Aegean and from the Vardar and Morava valleys to the Black Sea. This alarmed the British and the Austrians, who feared the new state might be nothing more than a massive wedge of Russian influence in the Balkans. After a few months of tension the Russians gave way and at Berlin San Stefano Bulgaria was dismantled. The treaty of Berlin confined Bulgaria proper to the area between the Danube and the Balkan mountains; the area south of these mountains was to be formed into an autonomous Ottoman province, Eastern Rumelia; and Macedonia was to be returned to the sultan with vague promises that its administration would be reformed. The treaty of Berlin also stipulated that the new Bulgaria was to have a prince who was to acknowledge the suzerainty of the sultan and was not to be a member of any of the major European dynasties. The prince was to be elected by the Bulgarians and approved by the powers. The Bulgarians were also to elect an assembly of notables who were to meet in Tŭrnovo, where, in addition to nominating a prince, they were to devise a constitution which must guarantee freedom of worship and the absence of religious discrimination. The Bulgarian principality was to be allowed a militia, but in Rumelia the maintenance of internal order was to be entrusted to a local gendarmerie; should this fail the sultan had the right to reintroduce Ottoman troops to restore order and tranquillity. The governor-general of Eastern Rumelia was to be nominated by the great powers and was to serve for five years: the extent of his authority was to be defined by a European commission which was also to decide the composition and competence of the Rumelian assembly. Both Bulgaria and Eastern Rumelia were to observe the international obligations entered into by the Ottoman government with regard to tariffs, the Ottoman Public Debt, railway construction, and the capitulations, the agreements guaranteeing subjects of the European powers the right to be tried in consular courts and exemption from certain Ottoman laws.

The division of San Stefano Bulgaria caused deep resentment and the restrictions upon the full sovereignty of the principality were on occasions to prove irksome, but with the signature of the treaty of Berlin on 13 July 1878 the modern Bulgarian state had been born. Understandably it is the date of San Stefano rather than of Berlin which the Bulgarians have chosen to celebrate as the anniversary of their liberation.

2

From liberation to the end of the First World War

THE REIGN OF ALEXANDER BATTENBERG, 1878–86

Immediately after the end of the war the government of Bulgaria and Rumelia was entrusted to a Russian provisional administration whose most enduring decision was to accept Sofia as the principality's capital; the city, or town as it was in 1878, afforded easy contact with Macedonia. The permanent system of government for the new principality was defined by the assembly of notables, or constituent assembly, which, in accordance with the treaty of Berlin, convened in Tŭrnovo in February 1879. Of its some 230 delegates all but sixteen were Bulgarian, eighty-nine of whom were elected, the remainder attending as members of the provisional administration or as representatives either of religious institutions or of Bulgarian communities from outside the borders of the Berlin principality; only twelve came from the small villages which were the quintessence of the Bulgarian way of life.

The first preoccupation of the assembly was whether or not to accept the Berlin settlement. There had been a desperate attempt to resist the treaty in the Kresna and Razlog areas of Macedonia but in practical terms there was no alternative to acceptance, although this stark reality could be recognised at Tŭrnovo only after two weeks of intensely emotional debate. When the question of the constitution was tackled in March two distinct groups emerged. The Conservatives, believing the mass of the peasantry to be as yet unready for political responsibility, argued for a paternalist system in which a second chamber and a restricted franchise would entrust power to the minority of Bulgarians enjoying wealth and further education. Their opponents, who soon formed the Liberal Party, were besotted with popular sovereignty. Bulgaria was, they argued, socially homogeneous. Its national spirit, they said, resided within its intelligentsia and the peasant masses to whom should be entrusted ultimate power. The Liberals were arguing for the continuance of the peasant–intelligentsia alliance which had emerged during the national

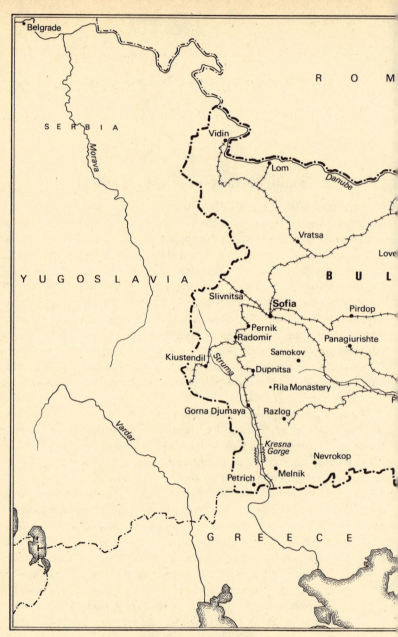

Map 2 Contemporary Bulgaria

revival, and as their views enjoyed overwhelming support the constitution which emerged from Tŭrnovo in 1879 was amongst the most democratic in Europe. The national parliament, or Sŭbranie, was to have only one chamber, elected by universal male suffrage, and was to meet every October after the harvest had been taken in; the prince was to have the right to appoint ministers and to prorogue the parliament, but the intervals between sessions were strictly regulated and executive power was to be exercised jointly with the council of ministers or cabinet, which was to be accountable to parliament. Constitutional amendments, territorial changes, and the nomination of a prince or of regents, would have to be sanctioned by a grand national Sŭbranie, an elected body twice as large as an ordinary assembly.

The Tŭrnovo constitution guaranteed individual rights but also insisted upon universal primary education and conscription. Orthodoxy was declared the official religion which all but the first prince must confess, but although the synod was to have its headquarters in Sofia the exarchate was to remain in Constantinople where it would be in a better position to promote the Bulgarian cultural cause in Macedonia. Finally the constituent assembly decided to offer the Bulgarian throne to the twenty-two year-old German, Prince Alexander of Battenberg, who had fought with the Russian army in 1877–8 but who was also acceptable to the other great powers, including Britain.

Alexander of Battenberg arrived in Bulgaria in July 1879. His political instincts were to favour the Conservatives, from whose ranks he formed his first government. It could not command the confidence of the extremely pro-Liberal assembly elected in September 1879 or of that returned early in 1880, the first having been dissolved by the prince. This was the beginning of a search for political stability which was to last for four years.

Alexander's preference was for a change of the constitution, but this the Russians, fearing internal unrest in Bulgaria, forbade, and the prince was therefore forced to accept a Liberal cabinet with Dragan Tsankov, the former champion of uniatism and now an inveterate Russophile, as chairman of the council of ministers or minister president. The Tsankov government concentrated upon the building of a state apparatus: it regulated the administration of justice, introduced a new coinage, the *lev* (lion), and took measures against the Muslim brigands, who much to the embarrassment of the new regime, were continuing the *haiduk* tradition in vigorous fashion. But despite Tsankov's concentration upon the building of a state apparatus, the tensions between the prince and his Liberal ministers could not be contained. Alexander used for his title a Bulgarian word which the Liberals would not accept, he had dissolved the Sofia municipal council, and he had embarrassed the Liberals by indulging in secret talks on union with the Rumelians. For their part the Liberals had alarmed Alexander with a proposal to create a militia which could rival the army, over which the prince had command, whilst Tsankov had also angered the bishops by cutting episcopal salaries and by attempting to democratise the organisation of the church. This manoeuvre had not pleased the Russians, who were also growing concerned at 'nihilist' activity in Bulgaria. They resented the fact that the Liberals would neither allow foreign investment in a new bank established in Bulgaria nor approve a Russian plan to build a railway from the Danube to Sofia. The Russians did not therefore object when Alexander dismissed Tsankov and appointed Petko Karavelov, brother of Liuben, as minister president. Karavelov was as intransigent as Tsankov in his attitude to the prince, but the minister president's position was undermined by the assassination of Tsar Alexander II on 1/13 March 1881.

The new tsar, Alexander III, being more reactionary than his predecessor, was better disposed to suggestions for changes in the Bulgarian constitution. On 27 April/9 May Battenberg therefore dismissed the Karavelov government and announced that a grand national Sŭbranie would meet in Svishtov to consider alterations to the constitution. He had acted, he insisted, not in defiance but in defence of the Tŭrnovo system, his aim being to secure stability before present excesses degenerated into anarchy. The Liberals acquiesced because they believed both that they would win the elections and that the assembly would be allowed a full and open debate. Both assumptions proved false. In May Alexander published his proposals for constitutional change which were very much in tune with the songs sung by the Conservatives during the constituent assembly; Liberal spirits were further depressed when, after some weeks of silence, the Russians announced that they approved of the proposals. In June and July Liberal morale sagged even further when their expectations of an open election were brutally confounded. During the voting Russian officers were posted in the polling booths 'to aid illiterates' and 'to prevent fraud' whilst outside the polling stations thugs were on hand to concentrate electors' minds. Only two constituencies returned Liberal delegates to the Svishtov grand national assembly which approved Alexander's plans in less than an hour. It had been a smooth and efficient coup but the representative system had been dealt a debilitating blow.

The new system approved by the Svishtov grand national assembly included a state council, a much reduced Sŭbranie, an indirect franchise and the restriction of civil liberties, but it did not furnish the stability which its architects were seeking. The Liberals were much weakened and many of their leaders went into exile in Rumelia, though Tsankov stayed in the principality hoping to soften the new regime from within. The Conservatives now had a political structure of their own design but they could not secure popular approval for it. It seemed that whilst Alexander could not work with the Liberals the politically conscious sections of the nation would not tolerate rule by the Conservatives. In the spring of 1882 Alexander therefore reconstructed his government with the major portfolios going to the Russian generals Sobolev and Kaulbars, the first named of whom became minister president and minister of the interior, whilst Kaulbars took command of the ministry of war.

The importation of the Russian generals did not improve the situation. Sobolev and Kaulbars objected to Alexander's plans to strengthen princely authority over the army with its largely Russian officer corps, and they were soon at odds with their Conservative colleagues over a series of issues, the most important of which was the railway question. Sobolev and Kaulbars continued Russian pressure for the construction of a line from the Danube to Sofia or across the Balkans to the Maritsa valley, for this would be of enormous strategic value to Russia in any future Balkan conflict. The Bulgarians could not afford to build such a line. They were obliged by the treaty of Berlin to complete that section of the Vienna to Constantinople trunk line which crossed Bulgarian territory, and the construction of this line, already delayed for financial reasons, would absorb all available capital. When the Bulgarian authorities agreed in April 1883 to construct their section of their trunk route the breaking point had been reached in relations between Alexander and the generals. The breach also precipitated a realignment of political forces in the principality. Sobolev and Kaulbars sought help from the Liberals, but even Tsankov had now become concerned at the overbearing and insensitive methods to which the generals had resorted. He in turn sought cooperation with the Conservatives, and though the more radical section of his party had doubts about this tactic it was the one which proved victorious in the extremely confused politicking of the summer of 1883.

The substance of the Tsankov–Conservative accord, to which the prince was a party, was that in return for the restoration of the Tŭrnovo constitution and a guarantee that in future the constitution would be amended only by constitutional means, the Liberals would sanction the convention on the Vienna–Constantinople railway. The generals, who were prepared to grant the former, could never accept the latter, and, outmanoeuvred, they left Bulgaria in September 1883. Tsankov then became minister president at the head of a coalition cabinet.

In December 1883 this cabinet first introduced a bill for constitutional reform which would have resurrected much of the hated 1881 system, and then used dubious methods to force the bill through the assembly, with Karavelov condemning the proceedings as 'a second coup'. The bill was never in fact put into effect, but because they believed it had given them all they wanted the Conservatives resigned from the government and retired to the political sidelines. This sharpened tensions already apparent in the Liberal ranks. The new government of moderate Liberals under Tsankov's leadership was criticised by those on the left of the party for having allowed the December bill to pass through the Sŭbranie, and early in 1884 this criticism was sharpened by attacks on the government's announcement that it was to purchase the Russe–Varna railway. Purchase of this largely British-owned line was another obligation laid upon the principality by the treaty of Berlin, but Karavelov and his associates insisted that the price of forty million francs was exorbitant. The elections of May/June 1884 became a contest between the two Liberal factions, in which the Karavelists were successful. Karavelov became minister president and immediately repealed the hated December 1883 act. He also formalised the Liberal split and by the end of the century had established a separate Democratic Party.

The constitutional problem which had dominated Bulgarian political life since the Tŭrnovo assembly now receded into the background. This allowed other issues to be settled. In 1883 Alexander concluded a twelve-point agreement with the Russians on the role of Russian officers in the Bulgarian army, and in December 1884 Karavelov's government ended all dispute over the railway question by legislating that all lines in Bulgaria would be nationalised and operated by BDZh, the Bulgarian state railways, and future railway construction was to follow a national strategy outlined in the act. The bank was also put into public ownership as the Bulgarian National Bank, the BNB.

Preoccupation with the constitutional question had confined the other great issue discussed at Tŭrnovo, that of national unity, to the background, but it rapidly rose to prominence once the constitutional problem seemed to have been settled. Karavelov won much popular sympathy by blocking any plans Alexander might have had for the return to Serbia of the Bregovo district, a small strip of territory belonging to the Obrenović family which at that point occupied the Serbian throne. More importantly, in late 1884 and 1885 there were signs of greater cohesion amongst the many Macedonian refugees, whose intrigues and excesses were soon to be amongst the most pervasive and least attractive features of Bulgarian political life. In 1885 two *cheti*, one of them armed with weapons seized from a Bulgarian arsenal with the obvious complicity of its guards, crossed into Macedonia. Though they were soon dispersed by Ottoman troops, they greatly worried Karavelov, for he knew that any destabilisation of the Balkans would be most unwelcome to the Russians, who at that time were preoccupied with central Asia. Karavelov, like the Liberals from whom he sprang, believed that Bulgaria should pursue a foreign policy designed to meet Russia's wishes, and to prevent any further embarrassment he therefore removed a number of known Macedonian activists from border areas.

Whilst Karavelov had been dealing with the Macedonians in Bulgaria, nationalist agitation was growing rapidly in Eastern Rumelia. The constitution of the province, devised by a European commission, included a regional assembly of elected and appointed members and a standing committee to be chosen from the assembly by a system of proportional representation. This was a device to ensure representation of the non-Bulgarian minority races, principally the Greeks and Turks, but this the Bulgarians frustrated by the application of higher mathematics, one of their leaders having a doctorate in the subject. Once Bulgarian domination was assured in this sector of the political system it was accepted in others, all six provincial prefects and thirty-one of the thirty-six elected members of the regional assembly being Bulgarian.

The Bulgarians who dominated Rumelia did all they could to stress similarities and strengthen ties between southern Bulgaria and the principality to the north. The literary alphabet, the school system, and military training and organisation were all copied from the Bulgarian example, and whenever possible the Bulgarian flag and national anthem were used. Union with the north, however, was as yet impossible, not only because the powers would not allow it but also because the Rumelians were not anxious to join Bulgaria whilst its political life was so tempestuous. Until the arrival of the Liberal exiles in 1881 Rumelian politics was dominated by small, conservative oligarchies whose orderly affairs contrasted sharply with the principality which in two years had seen the dissolution of seven cabinets and two Sŭbranies.

The return of constitutional stability in the north removed the internal, Bulgarian barrier to union. The alienation of the Russians by Bulgarian policies over the army, the railways, the humiliation of Sobolev and Kaulbars, and the poor relations between the prince and Tsar Alexander III – all made it possible that those powers which had previously vetoed union because they feared an extension of Russian influence would now think differently. Early in 1885 a Bulgarian Secret Central Revolutionary Committee was established. This pursued the aim of liberating all the

Bulgarian lands by a mass rising, but the defeat of the Macedonian bands in the spring and Karavelov's stern reaction to them showed that the maximalist path was blocked. The more limited aim of union between Rumelia and Bulgaria was more practical, and in the summer the committee adjusted its policy. Macedonia and Thrace were temporarily put aside and the organisation became the Committee for Union. At the same time the notion of a mass uprising was replaced by that of a coup carried out by the local militia. This would be quick, and speed was an essential part of the operation, for, it was calculated, if the union could be rapidly consolidated no European power would intervene to undo so popular an act.

The date set for the coup was 16/28 September, after the harvest had been collected. Premature action, however, led to the declaration of union in Plovdiv on 6/18 September. There was no doubting the popularity amongst all Bulgarians of this almost bloodless coup, but the union created severe problems with Russia. Prince Alexander had been warned of the plot and had had contacts with its organisers, but he had dismissed it as just another vague conspiracy, and in August had blithely assured the Russian foreign minister that there was no need to fear dramatic developments. In September the tsar was enraged at such apparent duplicity. Karavelov for his part was indecisive, fearing on the one hand to reject a popular nationalist gain and on the other to anger the Russians. A much more resolute line was adopted by Stefan Stambolov, the president of the Sŭbranie. He warned the prince that denial of the union would be more dangerous than acceptance of it and that therefore his choice was clear: he should go to Plovdiv or return to Germany for ever. Alexander accepted this stern logic and departed for Plovdiv. At the same time he ordered his troops south to the Turkish–Rumelian border.

Alexander's first objective was to secure international approval for the coup. He made conciliatory gestures towards the sultan and telegraphed to the tsar requesting his blessing. It was not given; on the contrary, the prince was chided for his adventurism and as a punishment for his foolhardiness all Russian officers were withdrawn from the Bulgarian army. The Bulgarians were stunned, and their worries were intensified by the attitude of the Balkan states. Both Greece and Serbia had denounced the union and were demanding compensation, whilst Turkish attitudes were not yet clear. In fact the sultan had no wish for a confrontation and the Greeks were dissuaded from one by the powers, but no-one could restrain Prince Milan of Serbia, who declared war on Bulgaria on 1/13 November. The Bulgarians' cause seemed hopeless. Their army had no officers above the rank of captain, and most of it was concentrated on the

Ottoman frontier at the other end of the country without a complete railway line to transport it to the north-west; nor was there any organised commissariat. Bulgarian soldiers and Rumelian militiamen had therefore to make their way north-westwards on foot and horseback, and had to rely upon the local inhabitants for food and supplies. That the army traversed the country in time to confront the Serbs at Slivnitsa was an extraordinary achievement which makes yet more remarkable the brilliant victory it won there between 5/17 and 7/19 November. Slivnitsa would have been the Serbs' gateway to Sofia, but now they were in headlong flight towards their own capital, and a Bulgarian entry into Belgrade was prevented only by Austrian diplomatic intervention.

The battle had secured the union. It had also greatly enhanced the reputation of Bulgaria, whose previous constitutional difficulties had tended to confirm many in their belief that small, relatively backward nations were not ready for the responsibilities of self-government. That argument would be heard no more where Bulgaria was concerned. In the long run, however, there was also a danger that Bulgaria would become too confident of its ability to tackle its Balkan neighbours; hubris was to give way to nemesis in 1913.

Though they had secured a great military victory the Bulgarians had little reason to celebrate the diplomatic settlement which followed the war. The treaty of Bucharest, signed in April 1886, did not even recognise the union – instead it agreed that for the next five years the prince of Bulgaria would also be governor-general of Rumelia; the Russians' insistence upon the omission of Alexander's name was an ominous indication that they did not wish him to remain in Sofia.

The imperfect nature of the union did much to undermine Prince Alexander's political authority, and his opponents were encouraged by Russia's policy of 'union without Battenberg', that is of insisting that there could be no recognition of the union whilst Battenberg remained prince of Bulgaria. The prince's opponents now included even the moderate Tsankovists, who, like most Karavelists, held to the old Liberal notion that Bulgarian foreign policy should be tailored to suit Russia's requirements. Others outside the ranks of the Liberal and Democratic Parties were concerned that so little had been gained from the war and that the union would so alarm other states that they would be much more vigilant in guarding against Bulgarian designs in Macedonia. The Rumelians too were far from content with the results of the union. Their sensitivities had been offended by the high-handed conduct of many politicians and administrators from Sofia, a city which the Rumelians were quick to point out was both less sophisticated and, as yet, smaller than Plovdiv. Not for the last time in Bulgarian history strong centralisation was to produce political problems. These complaints were aired in the Sŭbranie elected in May 1886, but the major issue in this most unruly session was not that of the union but that of the Russe–Varna railway, for which Karavelov was now willing to pay a sum much greater than the forty million francs which two years before he had condemned as exorbitant.

The disorderly scenes which the railway question provoked in the assembly were accompanied by violent public meetings throughout the country. The chief target of public anger was the prince, who was now losing support in the most important state institution, the army. This was in part his own doing, for the promotions he had posted after the war had caused considerable discontent, and he had always been somewhat distant from those officers who had been trained in Russia, many of whom were now in senior posts. In earlier years the prince had tried unsuccessfully to fashion his new army after the German rather than the Russian model, and it was the senior ranks of the largely Russian-trained officer corps which spawned the conspiracy which was to depose Alexander Battenberg on the night of 8–9/20–21 August 1886.

The putsch had been well-organised and well-executed, but the conspirators had thought little beyond the deposition itself and had not even secured the support of provincial garrisons; and they had misread the public mood. Despite the general atmosphere of discontent the removal of the prince was far from popular and the energetic Stambolov had soon organised an effective opposition. Within days Sofia was surrounded by troops loyal to Battenberg, who returned to Bulgaria on 17/29 August. He then telegraphed to the tsar that he would not remain in the country without Russia's support. Alexander III had been presented with an extraordinary opportunity: the chance to be rid of Battenberg without any danger of international complications. He seized it readily and informed the prince that Russian support would not be forthcoming. Alexander Battenberg had sacrificed himself and he stayed in Bulgaria only long enough to appoint a three-man regency consisting of Stambolov, Mutkurov, the minister of war, and Karavelov. On 26 August/7 September Battenberg left Bulgaria for the last time.

THE STAMBOLOVSHTINA, 1886–94*

The departure of Alexander Battenberg meant that the political stability which Bulgarian politicians had been seeking since 1879 was further away than ever. The regency appointed a government under Vasil

* In Bulgarian the suffix *shtina* added to a personal pronoun is the equivalent of the Russian *shchina* and denotes the events, ideas, policies and general atmosphere associated with that person.

Radoslavov, which joined with the executive in pressing for the rapid convocation of a grand national assembly. The objective was to nominate a prince whose appointment would betoken a return to normality. In this they were opposed by the Russians, led by the tsar's special commissioner in Bulgaria, Nikolai Kaulbars, a brother of the former minister of war. Kaulbars refused to recognise the legality of any grand assembly called by a regency whose appointment he regarded as unconstitutional. He also demanded the release of those arrested after the August putsch, an end to the state of siege, and the cancelling of the elections for the grand national assembly. Stambolov conceded the first two points but remained firm in his determination to call a grand national assembly, the elections for which duly took place in September. Despite his denunciation of the elections Kaulbars entered into the campaign vigorously though to little effect, for his heavy-handed interventions earned him the nickname 'general Sofiasco'. Kaulbars could take some satisfaction from the fact that the grand national assembly did not succeed in nominating a new prince; the majority would have been for Alexander Battenberg had that been possible. The convocation of the assembly did however have one direct result, for it brought to a head the Russo-Bulgarian tension which had been growing rapidly since August, and on 8/20 November Kaulbars and his staff left the country, citing a supposed insult to a Russian consular official in Plovdiv as their justification. Normal relations were not to be restored for almost a decade.

The departure of the Russians deepened the political crisis in Bulgaria. A prince was needed to restore order and tranquillity; order and tranquillity were essential if a prince were to be attracted to Bulgaria. Stambolov had no alternative but to impose order by force.

He had already shown his readiness to do this when a disorganised conspiracy was uncovered in three provincial garrisons, and when Nabo-kov, a ludicrous Russian adventurer, for the second time in two years charged into southern Bulgaria determined to raise a rebellion. On both occasions the population showed no inclination to join a revolt, and Nabokov, as had happened at the end of his first escapade, avoided punishment only because he was a Russian subject and could claim the protection of the capitulations. In March 1887 there was a far more serious threat to Stambolov. Dissident officers seized the garrison in Silistra and those in Russe and Varna soon declared for the rebels. The conspirators were known to have supporters in the country's largest garrison, Shumen, and Stambolov therefore acted swiftly and brutally to contain the danger. Eight leaders of the plot were put before firing squads, and in some disaffected regiments one man in twenty, chosen by lot, was shot by his comrades.

Whilst Stambolov was keeping tight control in Bulgaria a three-man delegation appointed by the grand national assembly was touring the European capitals in search of a new prince. It was not an easy task, and when eventually it was learned that Prince Ferdinand of Saxe-Coburg-Gotha might accept an invitation further months of negotiations were needed before he would come to a decision, his chief concern being the attitude of Russia. Stambolov did much to force the prince to a decision, and once it had been made the regent hastily arranged for the election of the requisite grand national assembly in July. The throne was then officially offered to Ferdinand, who arrived in the country on 14/26 August 1887. He was to remain for thirty-one years.

The early days of his reign gave no indication that Ferdinand's tenure of office would be so prolonged. His arrival had not, as was hoped, brought order and tranquillity, because the Russians and therefore all the other powers refused to recognise him as the legitimate prince. That being so, his pro-Russian opponents felt they were justified in using almost any means to remove him and his sponsor, Stambolov. Ferdinand was to remain in this anomalous state until 1896, and was to retain Stambolov as minister president until 1894.

After the arrival of Ferdinand Stambolov's first priority was still to preserve order, because now he had to prove that Bulgaria's prince would be allowed to rule effectively; order would be the *de facto* proof of Ferdinand's legitimacy, and from legitimacy should come recognition. The threat to order could still come from external forces, as a third and final incursion by Nabokov showed at the end of 1887; this time the Bulgarian forces made sure that Nabokov was killed in the field. A more serious threat was posed by the pro-Russian faction now under the leadership of Tsankov who had gone into exile first in Constantinople, and then in March 1889 in Belgrade where the pro-Austrian Milan had been replaced by a Russophile regency. Inside Bulgaria itself pro-Russian sentiment was strong amongst the clergy, who had been offended by the new prince's overt display of his catholicism when he first arrived. Even more dangerous were signs that the army was dividing into pro- and anti-Ferdinand factions. In May 1888 the regime suffered another setback with the completion of a railway from Nish to Salonika. The line would make the spread of Serbian influence in Macedonia easier.

Some consolation was found in loan and tariff agreements with Britain. The money from Britain did no more than provide funds for the purchase of the Russe–Varna railway, but it was followed by more helpful loans from Germany and Austria, and the tariff agreement was the first occasion on which Bulgaria was able to break through the restrictive bonds which the treaty of Berlin had imposed in this area. But these successes brought real consolidation of Ferdinand's position no nearer.

In internal affairs the turning-point was to come in 1890. During the previous year a major conspiracy had developed around Major Panitsa, a mercurial Macedonian who had been active in the national movement before 1885. As a dedicated Battenbergist Panitsa could not accept Ferdinand, and he also came to believe, despite his friendship with Battenberg, that the only hope for the liberation of Macedonia lay in Russia. The object of his conspiracy was therefore to remove Ferdinand and to re-establish close relations with Russia. Panitsa was far too flamboyant a character to make a good conspirator, and the police were soon aware of the plot and of its intention to strike at the prince at a court ball on 21 January/2 February 1890. The leaders were arrested on the night before the ball and were shown no mercy, Panitsa himself eventually being tied to a tree and shot by a firing squad made up of Macedonians from his own regiment. The trial and condemnation of the leaders did little to improve Stambolov's peace of mind, however, for the investigations which preceded them revealed a conspiracy much more wide-ranging than the government and the prince had realised. All discontented elements were involved, and through Panitsa were linked with Bulgaria's chief opponents abroad. It was, as Stambolov knew, the most serious of all the threats to his authority.

Much of the support given to Panitsa arose from dissatisfaction with the decline of Bulgaria's influence in Macedonia. The rise of Greek and Serbian propaganda in that area, and the Porte's favouring of the patriarchate at the expense of the exarchate, in part a result of the union of 1885, had meant that the prospects for the Bulgarian cause were bleak. In Bulgaria itself Stambolov would tolerate no manifestation of agitation over Macedonia, because he feared Russia might use this as an excuse for diplomatic action – or worse – against Bulgaria, and because he was also convinced that with so few friends in the Balkans the principality could not afford to alienate the sultan. Yet Macedonia could be made a factor of prime significance. If Stambolov were to persuade the Ottoman authorities to grant concessions to the Bulgarians in the area this would deprive any future conspirators of the mortar with which Panitsa had bonded the separate elements of his plot. Furthermore, given the nature of the Ottoman *millet* system concessions to the Bulgarians could only mean concessions to the exarchate which was the institutional representation of the Bulgarians in the empire. To secure concessions for the exarchate would also serve to reconcile the church to the new regime in Sofia. The exarch himself was unlikely to offer any opposition for he was by now desperate for concessions. The breach in relations with the Sofia government had deprived him of funds; and in Macedonia itself the Porte's antipathy towards the Bulgarian cause had meant that a number of dioceses which had voted to join the exarchate were still attached to the patriarch, with the result that exarchist priests could not be ordained locally. A number of communities had been left without priests to baptise their children, marry their young folk or bury their dead. Some of these communities had turned to the Uniates in despair.

Stambolov exploited this situation with great skill. He used the Panitsa plot to persuade the Turks that Ferdinand was in danger, and that if the prince were removed a successor regime would be forced to make uncomfortable demands in Macedonia. If, on the other hand, relatively minor concessions were given, Ferdinand's hand would be strengthened and the Ottoman empire would thereby be made more secure. To make doubly sure of his position Stambolov bolstered his requests with threats that if they were not granted Bulgaria would declare full independence; this might plunge the Balkans into turmoil, and the Porte therefore gave way. In June/July 1890 the exarchate was promised the dioceses of Ohrid, Skopje and Bitolya, three of the most important sees in Macedonia. The exarch was also given the right to establish relations with the Bulgarian communities in the Adrianople vilayet and to publish a newspaper in Constantinople.

These concessions were a triumph for Stambolov. The church was won over immediately, and in elections held later in the year he secured a massive victory, and one not solely due to the use of government 'influence' at the polls. Even enemies such as Tsankov now recognised that the regime had established itself, and their criticism was henceforth directed not at its existence but at its methods of governing. The regime was still not free from acts of individual terrorism: in 1891 the minister of finance was gunned down in mistake for Stambolov, and the prince received numerous threats to his life. To make him yet more secure it was decided that the prince must marry. Ferdinand was still vulnerable because if he were to be removed the way would be open for the nomination of a prince acceptable to the Russians; if, however, Ferdinand had an heir this would not be the case. The search therefore began for a wife. The choice fell upon Princess Marie-Louise of Bourbon Palma, but her family was devoutly Catholic and insisted as a condition of the marriage that any children must be brought up as Roman Catholics. This contravened article

38 of the constitution. Stambolov was not one to be discouraged by something so pliable as constitutional law and in February 1893 a grand national assembly was elected to enact the desired change, but this was achieved at the cost of a renewed breach with the Bulgarian episcopate, and in particular with its leading Russophile, Kliment of Tǔrnovo. Stambolov had gambled on the chance that popular approval of the wedding would be greater than disapproval of the change in the constitution, and in this he was proved right. Even more popular than the marriage was the birth nine months later of a son, who was christened Boris in commemoration of the medieval tsar who had converted the Bulgarians to Christianity and asserted Bulgarian power by attacks aimed at mighty Constantinople itself.

Despite the popularity of the marriage and the birth of Boris, Stambolov's power was now in decline. The country was beginning to see signs of peasant dissatisfaction which would become much more serious at the end of the decade, but social unrest was a phenomenon which Stambolov and his ministers found difficult to comprehend and to which they could find no other riposte than a brutish repression which naturally aggravated rather than soothed the pain. Further hostility was aroused by a pointless decree insisting that all Christian children must receive their primary education in Bulgarian, a ruling which greatly offended the country's Greeks. A much more serious enemy was the large Macedonian community. The Macedonians had suffered more than most groups from Stambolov's strong-arm methods, and it was these rather than the concessions to the exarchate in 1890 which they remembered. Equally dangerous to the minister president was the decline in his influence over the army after 1891, when ill health caused the resignation of his brother-in-law, Mutkurov, from the ministry of war. In 1894 Ferdinand appointed to this vital post Petrov, who was already chief of the general staff. Petrov enjoyed more control over the army than any of his predecessors in either post but because he was a sycophant real power resided with the prince. Ferdinand had insured himself against a repetition of 1886.

In the summer of 1893 a number of dissident Liberals, southern Unionists and some Conservatives, led by Stoilov, the former secretary to the recently deceased Alexander Battenberg, joined forces to publish a new opposition newspaper, *Svobodno Slovo* (*Free Speech*). The group enjoyed considerable popular support, for many considered that the justification for the tough policies Stambolov was still employing no longer existed; order no longer needed to be imposed by force.

This was the basic weakness in Stambolov's position: he had became an anachronism. His function had been to find, to install and to consolidate a new prince, all of which he had done. All that remained was to secure international recognition, and by 1894 it was obvious that this was beyond his grasp. Ferdinand, who had no love for Stambolov and who had a keen political intelligence, was fully aware of this fact and of the intense unpopularity of his minister president; like his young imperial colleague in Berlin he too could drop his pilot with safety. This he did in May 1894 after unseemly accusations that Stambolov had had an affair with the wife of a ministerial colleague. A year later Stambolov was brutally murdered by Macedonians seeking revenge for the treatment he had meted out to one of the kinsmen. Contemporary suspicions that Ferdinand was implicated in the murder, however, are generally discounted by modern scholars.

THE ESTABLISHMENT OF PRINCE FERDINAND'S PERSONAL REGIME, 1894–1900

Stoilov succeeded Stambolov as minister president. The new administration was drawn mainly from the Conservatives and its first political priority was to secure recognition for Ferdinand. This was to come in February 1896. It was made possible partly by a series of gestures on the part of the Stoilov government, including an amnesty for political offenders which allowed Tsankov to return to Bulgaria and Karavelov to be released from the prison cell to which he had been consigned since the Silistra rising of 1887. The amnesty did not apply, however, to army officers who had fled after the conspiracies of 1886 and 1887; Stoilov also made it plain that the Bulgarians were not prepared to have Russian officers in the army, would not allow the Russian navy use of Burgas or Varna, and would not contemplate any change of prince. More important than Bulgarian attitudes, however, were external factors. The death of Alexander III on 20 October/1 November 1894 removed an inveterate foe of the prince and gave Ferdinand an excuse to send condolences to Nicholas II in the name of the Bulgarian people. Equally important was growing anxiety, generated by the Armenian massacres, that the Ottoman empire was about to collapse. Both the Russians and the Bulgarians knew that if this did happen they would need each other's cooperation to defend their interests.

It was some time before this recognition of common interests could be translated into an agreement. The Russians still regarded Ferdinand's election as illegal and they were angry at what they believed was Bulgarian connivance at the activity of Macedonian insurgent bands in the spring of 1895. Nevertheless, a delegation from the Sŭbranie was allowed to visit Russia in the summer to lay a cross on the grave of Alexander III. From this visit and from other sources it became clear that the chief demand the Russians would make in return for the recognition of Ferdinand was that Prince Boris be received into the Orthodox faith. Throughout the autumn of 1895 Ferdinand faced a decision which, as Stoilov insisted, had to be his alone. Advocates of conversion were quick to point out that the king of Romania had allowed his son to enter the Orthodox church, but as a Protestant he did not have the pope to contend with, nor did he have to face a phalanx of implacably Catholic relations. The prince was genuinely and deeply troubled by this dilemma, but in the end political considerations prevailed. Ferdinand knew that conversion and reconciliation with Russia would increase both internal stability and Bulgaria's chances of significant gains should the Ottoman empire be partitioned. On 22 January/3 February 1896 Ferdinand announced that Boris would receive an Orthodox baptism on 2/14 February and that the tsar had agreed to stand as godfather. On 19 February/2 March 1896, the anniversary of San Stefano, the sultan recognised Ferdinand as prince of Bulgaria and governor-general of Eastern Rumelia. The great powers followed suit within the next few days.

Reconciliation with the liberating power marked the final achievement of political stability within the Bulgarian principality. Since 1879 the state had achieved much. Union with Rumelia had been brought about and defended in the war with Serbia, whilst Macedonia had been neither forgotten nor allowed to pull the government into rash adventures. A start had been made in the construction of a modern economic infrastructure with the completion of the Bulgarian section of the Vienna to Constantinople line in 1888 and the construction in the early 1890s of a line linking the port of Burgas to Yambol, though the major expansion of the economy was to come in subsequent years.

Politics had in fact dominated the nation's public life. The contest for constitutional supremacy had initially been won by the legislature. The Liberals enjoyed more popular support than the Conservatives and had also established a party machine which could dominate both electoral and Sŭbranie politics. This was done by the standard practices of intimidation and persuasion, by dominating the electoral bureaux which conducted the polls, by using parliamentary rights to vet individual constituency elections, and by removing known anti-Liberals from government posts, which were then offered to supporters; the Conservatives, when they had the opportunity, did precisely the same. All governments could also rely on the 'government dowry', a handful of largely Muslim or Jewish constituencies which always returned pro-government deputies. The prince had attempted to break Liberal domination by revising the constitution in 1881, but his revisions had not been sufficiently radical, nor had he taken full advantage of the powers which the 1881 system offered to the executive; popular opinion and ministerial muscle wrecked Battenberg's attempts to rule without the Liberals. He also discovered that Russian friendship could be as burdensome as Liberal opposition. By 1884 Prince Alexander had no choice but to allow Karavelov the dominant role in internal affairs. At its moment of victory, however, the power of the legislature began to weaken as divisions within the Liberal Party widened into the split of 1884. It was the first of a number of such fissures, the next coming in 1886 when Tsankov's and Karavelov's dedication to a pro-Russian foreign policy, the events of 1885–6 notwithstanding, led Stambolov to establish his National Liberal Party. In 1886 the intervention of the army meant that a new factor had entered into politics and constitutional supremacy could not be guaranteed without control of this new factor. In general it was easier for the executive than for the legislature to establish this control.

In the period between the departure of Alexander and Russia's recognition of Ferdinand in 1896, the power of the executive increased enormously, particular in the years when Stambolov dominated affairs either as regent or in the first years of Ferdinand's reign. Control over the army was maintained, albeit with fierce methods, and the disciplining of the electorate was brought to a fine if unsavoury art. General elections were now held not to discover the popular mood and therefore determine the complexion of a government, but to confirm in power ministers already chosen by the executive.

Political trafficking in public office, *partisanstvo* as it was known in Bulgaria, was a powerful weapon at the disposal of the executive. This ugly disease, to which a pre-industrialised society with a developed educational system is prone, was well-established in Bulgaria by the 1890s, when the supply of educated persons had for the first time outstripped the number of lucrative public offices available to them. The unemployed bureaucrats gave support to opposition groups, in return for which they were rewarded with jobs when those groups were given power and had purged the political appointees of the previous administration; Stoilov's government, for example, removed twenty-one of the twenty-four regional prefects, five hundred mayors and heads of villages and seventy out of eighty-four rural magistrates and police inspectors. The executive's power was also increased by further fragmentation amongst the political parties. The Liberal split of 1884 had been over constitutional issues, but in later years there were divisions over attitudes towards Russia, a division which also affected the Conservatives. The southern Bulgarians, at least until the late 1890s, also constituted separate factions within existing parties. The greater the number of parties and the weaker their internal discipline, the easier it was for the executive to play off one group against the others. A further weakening of the parties derived from the absence of real policy differences between them. The settlement of the constitutional debate in favour of the executive, the lack, as yet, of serious social divisions, and the command assumed by the prince over foreign affairs, meant that there was very little over which the parties could fight other than the spoils of office. Parties therefore became little more than hunting packs in pursuit of patronage, and they were held together by little more than affiliation to a particular leader.

The power which the prince came to exercise over those leaders was founded both upon patronage and upon an extensive secret archive in which their peccadilloes were copiously recorded. Stambolov and then Ferdinand had also been careful to secure control over the ministry of war, and Ferdinand dominated the ministry of foreign affairs because of his extensive knowledge of and family connections with the royal courts of Europe. Should the prince need to remove a ministry all he had to do was to order one or both of these dependent ministers to resign. He would then reconstruct the government according to his own desires. This was the basis of the 'personal rule' which Ferdinand had established by the turn of the century.

YEARS OF CRISIS, 1900–3

The recognition of Ferdinand left Stoilov to concentrate upon his efforts to modernise Bulgaria, but modernisation was not to be a process exempt from political difficulties.

After the union of 1885 the railways in what was formerly Eastern Rumelia had remained in the ownership and under the control of the concern that had built them, the Oriental Railway Company (ORC). This originally Austrian company owned almost all the lines in European Turkey. Unlike the BDZh, the ORC did not align its carriage charges with those of the Serbian and Austrian railways. Its tariff for grain was twice as high as that on other sections of the trunk route, and this placed an unfair burden on exporters in southern Bulgaria at a time when world grain prices were falling drastically. The ORC's policies were at times irrational, and, more seriously, discriminatory. The company owned the concession to levy harbour dues at Dedeagach (Alexandropolis), and therefore did what it could to funnel traffic to that port rather than to

Burgas, where it had no concession. The policies of the ORC had long been resented but the Rumelian government had not dared to tackle an institution which had powerful support in Europe, the chief shareholder in the company by the 1890s being the Deutsche Bank of Berlin. From 1887 to 1896 an administration with an unrecognised prince was in a similarly weak position, especially as the railways of European Turkey were coming to be regarded in Germany as part of the projected Berlin to Baghdad route. Yet after 1896 something had to be done about the company. Stoilov's attempts to encourage Bulgarian industry included preferential charges on state railways for essential imports and for finished products, yet these preferential charges were not levied by the ORC, and thus the would-be industrialists of southern Bulgaria were disadvantaged compared with those in the north. Southern complaints were loudly voiced in the Sŭbranie, and as Stoilov's majority in the assembly depended on the votes of southern deputies, action had to be taken.

Stoilov had three options. He could nationalise the ORC, purchase its operating rights, or build an alternative line. The first option was too dangerous diplomatically, and the second was impossible because the Deutsche Bank, its gaze fixed upon Baghdad, would not sell; therefore Stoilov reluctantly agreed in August 1896 that the so-called parallel railway should be built, to by-pass the ORC tracks.

It was a disastrous decision and one which could not be implemented. The government was already hard-pressed for funds and was therefore forced to seek a loan on the European money market, but when one was secured it was to be allocated, Stoilov told the Sŭbranie in December 1898, to the rescheduling of existing loans, to the purchase of ORC running rights and equipment in southern Bulgaria, and to a number of new lines. At no point did he mention the parallel railway despite the money already spent on it. Public reaction was greater than on any other issue except Macedonia, with hundreds of protest meetings throughout the country, and the Sŭbranie galleries full to overflowing on both days of the intense debate. The government insisted that at the end of the debate it had a majority, but from the debate and from petitions submitted to the Sŭbranie it was known that a number of government deputies had defected to the opposition. So shaky had Stoilov's hold become that he submitted his resignation. It was all to no avail because German diplomatic pressure induced the sultan to torpedo the loan project by refusing to sanction the sale of the ORC in Rumelia. The Stoilov government had been wrecked by external factors over which neither it nor the prince had any control.

There was worse to come. In March 1899 the succeeding administration had to accept an agreement with the ORC by which the Sofia government promised not to build any railway which might compete with the company's lines, and to allow the ORC to take over the Yambol to Burgas line, a clear contravention of the 1884 railway act. The only crumb of comfort was the company's agreement to impose the preferential charges for Bulgarian industrialists. Following this a loan was granted in Vienna to replace that lost with the collapse of the 1898 project. By October 1899 yet another foreign loan had been taken out, this time in Paris. It marked the beginning of over ten years of French domination of foreign lending to Bulgaria. It was also the first occasion on which creditors insisted that certain revenues be earmarked for the service of the loan, the revenues in question being those from the *banderolle*, a tax upon processed tobacco. Financial security could be had only at the cost of sacrificing some national sovereignty.

The loan, for twenty-six million francs, was no more than a stop-gap, but before the government borrowed again from abroad it sought extra sources of internal revenue. The treaty of Berlin forbade further increases in customs dues; taxation of nascent manufacturing industries was impracticable, and extension of the professional tax politically dangerous because it would anger the bureaucracy. There remained the land. Part of Stoilov's modernisation programme had been to replace the tithe with a land tax in 1894 – a reform which was also prompted by the continuing decline in world grain prices, for the government did not wish to rely for its revenue on the sale of a commodity whose value was constantly depreciating. By the end of the decade grain prices were at last moving upwards, and once again there was profit in its sale. On 29 October/10 November 1899 it was announced that for the years 1900 to 1904 the land tax would be suspended and replaced by a tithe in kind. The government had stepped in to seize much of the grain just at the point when rising prices for that grain had at last given the peasant producer hope of a better return on his crop. The north-east of the country, where there was great concentration upon grain production, was hardest hit, and it was here that the unrest which the tithe announcement had precipitated was at its fiercest.

Rural Bulgaria had long been heading for the crisis into which the November announcement plunged it. There had been a series of poor harvests with phylloxera and rinderpest as additional afflictions. Equally serious was the problem of indebtedness. After the liberation large tracts of land had become available for purchase as Muslims left Bulgaria for the Ottoman empire; with no banks to provide loans purchasers of land and of the implements to work it had to rely for credit upon the private money-lender. High interest rates and declining returns from the land had forced many peasants to borrow to pay off their original loans, and by the end of the 1890s hundreds of villages were in the grip of the usurer. In addition to increasing indebtedness the peasant had also to face a tax burden which almost doubled in the years from 1887 to 1897. The peasant felt he was taxed far more heavily than the townsman, who also enjoyed much better provision of education, health, postal and other facilities. The peasant had thus come to harbour a deepening resentment against the towns. This resentment was increased by the realisation that many intelligent and educated peasants were not returning to the villages as teachers or agrarian advisors but were remaining in the towns to enjoy lucrative posts in the bureaucracy. *Partisanstvo* was destroying the old alliance between peasant and intellectual, and the national tradition of rural Bulgaria was in revolt against its perversion by the nation–state.

Even before the announcement concerning the tithe a number of agrarian associations had been formed in the north-east, with a leading part in this movement being taken by the trio of Yanko Zabunov, the editor of *Zemedelska Zashtita* (*Agrarian Defence*), Tsanko Bakalov, who used the pseudonym 'Tserkovski' and who now penned a powerful pamphlet, *An Appeal to the Peasants of Bulgaria*, and Dimitŭr Dragiev, who published an equally influential tract, *Must the Peasants Pay the Tithe?* At the end of December the agrarian movement called a congress at Pleven in which was born the Bulgarian Agrarian Union, whose object was to 'to raise the intellectual and moral standing of the peasant and to improve all branches of agriculture'. For the moment the union refused to act in any way as a political party or a contender for government. It was a pressure group, and an increasingly popular one. Yet its very existence and its vehement opposition to the tithe, the principal reason for its popularity, had massive political implications, and within a few months Stoilov admitted that it was the true representative of peasant interests and the strongest political force in the land. Its opposition to the tithe also led to confrontation with the government, although the union did it all it could to keep to the legal path, not least because it knew that the authorities would use the slightest illegality as justification for swift and severe repressive action. Such action was in any case taken, and in the spring of 1900 there were fatalities when troops clashed with protestors in Trŭstenik and in Daran Kulak in the Dobrudja. Such incidents only intensified the agitation which swept northern Bulgaria throughout the summer. The second congress of the union in Sofia in December showed the movement to be a national one, and one in which the teachers and priests were taking a significant part; the national alliance of peasant and intelligentsia was being reborn.

The strength of the peasant reaction to the tithe destroyed the credibility of the government, which therefore resigned in December 1900. The elections held in February 1901 were relatively free of government interference as the return of twenty-three supporters of the Agrarian movement and eight socialists testified. The traditional Sŭbranie parties were represented in more or less equal measure, and a coalition cabinet was formed of the Progressive Liberals (Tsankovists), under Stoyan Danev, and the Democrats, who were still led by Karavelov. The latter became minister president whilst Danev became minister for foreign affairs. It was one of the few occasions in modern Bulgarian history when the formation of a new administration was the consequence rather than the cause of a general election.

The new government abolished the tithe, the returns on which had in any case been disappointing. That eased the political atmosphere but it did nothing to improve the nation's finances. Karavelov had little alternative but to go in search of another loan. In Paris the Banque de Paris et des Pays Bas, Paribas, was prepared to lend one hundred and fifty million francs but it required as surety the revenues from both the *banderolle* and the *mururie*, a tax on raw tobacco. It also required the introduction of a government monopoly over the manufacture and sale of tobacco, and that Paribas be consulted whenever major changes in Bulgaria's financial position were under consideration. By the middle of 1901 Bulgaria's finances were in such desperate straits that Karavelov had to accept these harsh terms, but he found it impossible to persuade the Sŭbranie to do likewise, and in December the assembly rejected the loan. Karavelov resigned, handing the premiership to Danev in January 1902. In March 1902 Danev went to St Petersburg in search of better terms. He did not find them. The loan which he negotiated with Paribas and Russian bankers, and which the Sŭbranie accepted in July, contained not only the objectionable terms offered to Karavelov but also new conditions concerning Macedonia. These represented a bitter blow to the Bulgarian interests in the Macedonian question, a question which since the mid-1890s had vied with finance and social unrest for the attention of Bulgaria's politically-minded public.

From 1894 to 1896, with the Ottoman empire seemingly on the point of collapse and with Stoilov still needing to consolidate popular support for his government, the minister president had released and encouraged the Macedonian activists whom Stambolov had clapped in gaol. In December 1894 a number of them came together to form the Supreme Macedonian Committee, which rapidly became a major lobby within Bulgarian politics. In response to its urging, Stoilov both pressed the Porte for reforms and connived at the crossing into Macedonia of the *cheti*, one of which, under the leadership of Boris Sarafov, occupied the town of Melnik for two days. In 1896 diplomatic action in Constantinople secured promises that reforms would be introduced throughout the Ottoman empire, but nothing came of these promises which had been given only because of the pressure created by events in Armenia and Crete.

In the following year the situation changed completely when the Ottoman army thrashed the Greeks in Thessaly; the sick man seemed to be recovering his health. Reassured that the Near East was not about to dissolve into anarchy Russia turned its attention to the Pacific, and came to an agreement with Austria–Hungary that the Balkans should be put 'on ice'. Without the backing of one of these two powers no Balkan state could hope for significant advancement of its claims upon Turkey-in-Europe, and as Bulgaria's relations with Catholic Vienna had been poor since the conversion of Boris St Petersburg alone could offer help. Without hope of support from the great powers Stoilov was forced back on to the Stambolovist tack of seeking concessions from the Porte, but he was too weak at home to be able to apply the corollary of seeking concessions: rigid control of the Macedonian extremists.

This became even more difficult in 1897. After the Turco-Greek war the Porte began to favour the Hellenist cause in Macedonia, as Greece, now the weakest of the potential successor states, would be less of a threat than Bulgaria or Serbia. Even more serious was the appearance of an indigenous Macedonian movement outwith the control of the government in Sofia: IMRO, the Internal Macedonian Revolutionary Organisation, had appeared on the scene. IMRO, though not known by this name until 1906, had been founded in 1893, and its objective was an autonomous Macedonia which could then become an integral part of a Balkan federation; IMRO would have no truck with the Supreme Committee's notion that autonomy should be but the prelude to absorption into Bulgaria, as had been the case with Rumelia. There were also differences in strategy. IMRO recognised the close cultural affinities between Bulgarians and Macedonian Slavs but had no appetite for inclusion in Ferdinand's state. It wanted instead to prepare for a mass rising in Macedonia, and therefore resented the incursion of the *cheti*, which were controlled from Sofia and whose presence sharpened Turkish vigilance and thus made it more difficult to prepare the populace for revolution. Furthermore, IMRO suspected that Ferdinand was trying to exploit the Macedonian question for his own political objectives. If Macedonia were to fight, argued IMRO, it should be when it suited the Macedonian people rather than the Bulgarian government and its puppet, the Supreme Committee. In 1898 IMRO decided to use 'entrism' to seize control of the Supreme Committee, and by 1900 it had successfully infiltrated the Sofia organisation, which was now led by Sarafov, an IMRO supporter. Ferdinand's ministers, beset with their financial and social problems, had now lost control of the Macedonian movement.

The real danger of this development was that it was generally assumed that Ferdinand was in charge of the Macedonian insurgents, and he and his government were therefore held responsible for whatever happened in that troubled land. Were serious disorders to break out Bulgaria would be blamed, and this could impair its effort to find loans and might even persuade the Russians to put all their Balkan eggs into the Serbian basket. In an effort to soften pressure from St Petersburg the Bulgarian government in April 1901 first forbade membership of Macedonian organisations to serving officers and then arrested Sarafov; though he was soon acquitted by a court there had been time for the government to re-establish its control over the Supreme Committee. These concessions, it was hoped, would mollify European and, especially, Russian opinion; meanwhile Supremacist bands were allowed to cross into Macedonia with a consequent increase in tension, not least because of the rivalry between the two insurgent organisations.

When Danev went to St Petersburg to negotiate the loan agreement in March 1902 the Bulgarians paid dearly for Ferdinand's duplicity. The Russians insisted not only that effective measures be taken to end the activities of the *comitadji** but also that the Bulgarians accept the nomination of Firmilian, a Serbian priest, to the vital post of administrator of the Skopje diocese. There were a number of other items in the 1902 agreement, including a military alliance which never came into effect, but the appointment of Firmilian, which the Bulgarians had been resisting since 1897, was a devastating blow to Bulgarian interests in northern Macedonia. A further Russian condition for the loan was that measures be taken to contain the Macedonians in the principality, and Danev therefore banned the sale of weapons, dismissed a number of officers known to be involved in the Macedonian movement, expelled some activists from Bulgaria and seized arms and ammunition held by private citizens.

The terms which Danev had been forced to sign in St Petersburg were a humiliation and destroyed his political credibility at home. But it was not yet time for his departure, as Ferdinand had one more task for his discredited minister president to perform. On 25 September/8 October 1902 the Bulgarians celebrated the twenty-fifth anniversary of the battle

---

* A Turkish work meaning literally 'committee men', but it came to mean members of the *cheti*.

of the Shipka pass, and it was in this highly charged atmosphere that the Supreme Committee chose to launch a substantial raid into Macedonia with the objective of bringing about a popular rising centred upon the town of Gorna Djumaya (Blagoevgrad) in the Struma valley. The local inhabitants showed little inclination to join the *comitadji* but the Turks took their inevitable reprisals upon them.

The Gorna Djumaya 'rising' did have some impact outside the Struma valley. In St Petersburg and Vienna it was seen as an indication of the febrile state of Macedonia, and Russian and Austro-Hungarian diplomatists began serious consideration of how they might stabilise the region. Before that was to be settled the Russian foreign minister, Count Lamsdorff, hurried to Belgrade and Sofia to read a diplomatic riot act. There must, he insisted in quite unequivocal terms, be an immediate end to all connections between the governments and armies of the two Balkan states and the insurrectionists who wished to destroy Ottoman rule in Macedonia. The Serbs agreed immediately and after that the Bulgarians dared not be the only ones to defy the tsar and his foreign minister. In February Danev ordered the dissolution of the Macedonian organisations in Bulgaria and the arrest of leading activists. After a three-day debate the Sŭbranie agreed. Shortly thereafter the Russians and Austrians announced details of a reform scheme for the Macedonian vilayets.

Danev's position had long been almost untenable and now he had procured the loan and severed links with the *comitadji* there was little more for him to do. After a series of unseemly scandals and disputes with the prince he resigned and was replaced by a government under the leadership of the non-party figure, general Petrov, with the tough Stambolovist party leader, Petkov, as his minister of the interior and the dominant personality in the government.

FROM THE ILINDEN–PREOBRAZHENSKO RISING TO THE DECLARATION OF INDEPENDENCE, 1903–8

The dissolution of the Macedonian committees in Bulgaria had little impact on Macedonia itself. Here IMRO faced serious difficulties. It had been alarmed by the events in Gorna Djumaya and feared that the Supremacist tactic of incursion could be repeated yet again, for IMRO leaders were far from convinced that its official disbandment meant the end of the Supreme Committee's existence. In January 1903 IMRO's central committee decided to stage its own rising in the coming summer, even though in ideal conditions they would have wished for longer to prepare for this mass revolt. IMRO's decision had been hastened by a fear that it might lose control of events in Macedonia if it did not act soon, a fear which was confirmed in the early months of 1903. The Austro-Russian reform scheme posed the danger that if it succeeded the Macedonian people as a whole might no longer feel provocation enough to rise; diplomacy might deprive IMRO of the revolutionary situation it needed. Also in April 1903, a series of anarchist outrages in and around Salonika showed that there were forces within Macedonia which, like the Supremacists, could precipitate Ottoman repression or intervention by the powers, both of which could make action by IMRO very difficult if not impossible.

The IMRO rising began on 2/15 August, St Elijah's day, or in Slavonic, *Ilinden*. A few days later, on the feast of the transfiguration, *Preobrazhenie*, there was a revolt in the Adrianople vilayet. Independent administrations were established at Krushevo in Macedonia and Strandja in Thrace, but despite the careful organisation of the rising and the generally enthusiastic response of the populace the revolt was doomed. In May IMRO had lost its most talented leader, Gotse Delchev, in a chance encounter with Turkish troops, but even had he lived the revolt could not have succeeded without external assistance. The Petrov–Petkov government refused to send its troops. To do so would alarm the other Balkan states and anger Austria–Hungary and Russia beyond measure, and after the defeat which the Greeks had suffered in 1897 the Bulgarians would not wish to be the only state to go to war with the Ottoman empire. By the end of October the revolt had been snuffed out. Within Macedonia itself large numbers of exarchist priests and school-teachers were arrested and deported to Asia Minor; the Turks knew the potential of the peasant–intelligentisia alliance. Exarchist villages were destroyed, their animals seized and their crops burnt. Many of their inhabitants went wearily into exile in Bulgaria or the New World whilst those who stayed could in many cases only find food and shelter from Hellenist or Serbian organisations.

In international terms the Ilinden–Preobrazhensko rising produced the most important of the reform schemes devised by European diplomacy, when the Austrian and Russian foreign ministers agreed at Mürzsteg to bolster their previous project by introducing European supervisors who would work in Macedonia itself. Unfortunately the Mürzsteg scheme also contained the provision that Ottoman administrative boundaries should be redrawn so as to produce the greatest possible degree of ethnic homogeneity within each unit; this merely made the Greeks, Bulgarians and Serbians more determined to establish cultural dominance in as wide an area as possible, and thereby sharpened the struggle between the protagonists of the three potential successor states.

After the failure of the Ilinden–Preobrazhensko rising the Bulgarian or exarchist element in Macedonia was gravely weakened, and the Petrov–Petkov administration sought to remedy this by agreement with Constantinople, a solution to which the Stambolovists who formed the majority of the cabinet could easily give their approval. Serious negotiations were possible only after the passions of the late summer of 1903 had cooled, but by March 1904 an agreement had been signed by which the Porte promised to implement the Mürzsteg reforms, and also to grant an amnesty to all detained exarchist priests and teachers with the exception of those who had been guilty of acts of sabotage. There were also undertakings from Constantinople that funds would be made available to help the resettlement of refugees and that restrictions upon the movement of Bulgarian goods introduced in 1903 would be removed. For their part the Bulgarians promised to make much greater efforts to prevent the *comitadji* passing into Macedonia and Thrace. The agreement contained further provisions for extradition, for the regulation of posts and telegraphs and for the setting up of Bulgarian commercial agencies in the more important Macedonian towns.

The Petrov–Petkov government also sought an accommodation with Serbia. In March and April 1904 there was a series of military agreements by which the two states approved the Mürzsteg programme, condemned fighting between Bulgarian and Serbian sympathisers in Macedonia, promised joint action to contain any outside interference in that region, and pledged military aid should the other party be attacked. In the summer of 1905 the military treaties were complemented by commercial agreements which, it was hoped, would lead to a customs union between the two states, but the likelihood of real cooperation between Belgrade and Sofia was slim as long as the Macedonian question remained unsolved.

And remain unsolved it did. In 1904 and 1905 Serbian and Bulgarian bands had clashed in the Kumanovo area, and in 1906 there were fierce encounters between them around Skopje. By 1907 the Serbs were extending their influence as far south as Resen, an area which before 1903 the exarchists had regarded as their own. Clashes between exarchists and Hellenists were even more serious. The first Greek bands had appeared in central Macedonia in 1904, having benefited considerably from a new society formed in Athens with secret government backing; the Bulgarians bitterly resented the fact that the Greek government could now pursue the policy which the Bulgarians had followed until Lamsdorff's decisive intervention.

In Bulgaria itself the Macedonian question declined as an issue in internal politics. The Stambolovist government was less indulgent than its immediate predecessors, which dampened Supremacist fires, but it also had less reason to discipline the other Macedonian organisation. After 1903 IMRO could exercise relatively little influence in the principality and its power in Macedonia itself waned; in 1903 its organisation had been torn apart, its finances devastated and its membership depleted, and efforts to repair these losses by force caused some resentment in the exhausted exarchist communities. After the defeat of 1903 a demoralised IMRO was less united both upon tactics and upon its ultimate objective, whilst its disputes with the other Macedonian organisations became ever more ferocious and more frequent, and a series of spectacular killings in Sofia in 1906 and 1907 foreshadowed the evil influence inter-Macedonian strife was to exercise in Bulgaria in later years. Such public displays of disunion did not help the Macedonian cause in Bulgaria and by 1907 Macedonian journals were losing their readership and the Macedonian organisations seemed to be dissolving; in that year only three NCOs and thirty men deserted from the army to join the *cheti*, a tiny proportion of the number doing so a few years previously.

The Petrov–Petkov administration, as will be seen, had other problems to consider in 1907, but it could not disavow an interest in Macedonia. Instead it insisted that the re-acquisition of the lost territories of San Stefano was a sacred national objective and as such could not be left to disorganised and unreliable adventurers. So important a task could be safely entrusted only to the national army, which would be successful only if it were backed by all the resources of a modern state. The strategy advocated by the government was therefore to bide its time until the diplomatic situation had changed and removed the Austro-Russian veto on change in the Balkans, and to use this waiting period to modernise the state and to provide it with an army equal to the demands which would one day be made of it.

This professed faith in the future could not, however, disguise the fact that in the recent past the Bulgarian cause in Macedonia had suffered devastating blows. The appointment of Firmilian had established Serbian influence in the heart of northern Macedonia and the failure of the Ilinden–Preobrazhensko rising had gravely weakened the exarchist organisation in Macedonia and Thrace.

URBAN UNREST, 1903–8

Between 1903 and 1908 Bulgaria experienced its first taste of serious urban unrest. At the height of the Ilinden rising the Bulgarian minister of the interior had spoken of having to choose between war in support of the rising or revolution at home. Although there had been some unrest over the government's failure to help the rising this had been contained with ease. In 1905 and 1906 anger at Hellenist activities in Macedonia was used as justification for a series of attacks upon Greek churches and monasteries, with a particularly serious incident in Anhialo (Pomorie) in the summer of 1906. The 1906 disorders had begun with protests against the arrival in Bulgaria of Neophytus, the newly appointed bishop of the patriarchist see of Varna, and within a few weeks the whole country, with the exception of the capital, had seen violence against Greek property or, in some cases, against the Greeks themselves. The magnitude of the disorders forced Petrov from office. He was replaced by Petkov, the Stambolovist party leader.

The anti-Greek riots had been preceded by other disturbances. The political atmosphere had been sharpened in 1905 by attacks upon government ministers for their corruption and upon Ferdinand for his long absences from the country. The febrile state of public feeling was in part a reaction to events in Russia. Sympathy with the Russian war effort in Japan had been clearly evinced amongst the whole Bulgarian nation in 1904 but in 1905 the urban poor and sections of the intelligentsia showed an equally clear solidarity with those in Russia who were protesting against the tsarist regime. What was more, there were signs that many Bulgarians not only wished to sympathise with but also to emulate Russia's revolutionaries. In January 1905 political activity amongst students was forbidden and demonstrations against this ruling led to the closure of the university from April until the opening of the next academic year in the autumn. There was also an increase in industrial unrest early in 1905, with strikes amongst compositors at the state printing plant in Sofia, textile workers in Sliven and miners at the state-owned mines in Pernik.

These strikes had little real effect, but proved to be symptoms of a discontent which was to reach its peak in the first major confrontation between the state and organised labour. Agitation for higher wages and better working conditions had begun in 1906 amongst lower ranking members of the non-political civil service, and the government had reacted with typical Stambolovist severity. Demonstrators were heavily fined and would-be strikers threatened with loss of pension rights. The railwaymen, who as employees of a state concern were civil servants, refused to be intimidated and at the end of the year withdrew their labour. The government mobilised all railwaymen of military age and used the army's railway battalions to maintain a rudimentary if erratic service. Industrial and political dissatisfactions fused four days after the beginning of the railway strike, when Ferdinand opened the newly-constructed National

Theatre. On arriving at the building he was jeered and his entourage pelted with snowballs and lumps of ice by a crowd of strikers and students. It was an ugly incident which produced a savage reaction. The university was closed for six months and its entire academic staff dismissed.

There could be no such swift and draconian solution to the railway strike. Ferdinand, distraught at the attack upon him at the theatre and more so at the death of his mother, was ready for a compromise, and in this he was supported by the nation's merchants and traders. The railwaymen too were ready for a settlement. They had been without wages for a month and were disheartened by the death of one of their leaders. In February they went back to work in return for a slight increase in wages and a promise of no victimisation.

This was not quite the end of the violence which flashed across the Bulgarian political stage in 1906–7, for on 27 February/11 March Petkov was murdered in an act of personal revenge. Petkov had lost an arm in the struggle for liberation; he had two sons, one of whom was to die at the hand of Macedonian terrorists in 1924 and the other of whom was to hang on a Communist gibbet. Petkov's successor as minister president in 1907 was Gudev, who remained in office for almost a year and was remembered for little else than the assiduity and expertise with which he amassed an immense personal fortune at the public expense.

In January 1908 Ferdinand appointed as minister president Malinov, who had become leader of the Democratic Party on Karavelov's death in 1903. Malinov introduced a series of minor reforms which included the reinstatement of the dismissed academics, the relaxation of the tough press laws enacted by the Stambolovists, and the introduction of proportional representation in local elections and for parliamentary constituencies in the Tŭrnovo and Plovdiv provinces. In 1912 a successor government extended this to the entire country.

Malinov's major achievement, however, was to bring about Bulgaria's declaration of complete independence. The vassal status which the treaty of Berlin had enforced upon the country had initially been a severe disadvantage in matters such as tariffs and the use of the capitulations by foreign citizens, but by the 1900s these disadvantages had to a large extent been overcome or were simply ignored. The resurgence of Ottoman self-confidence which followed the Young Turk revolt of 1908 reawoke Bulgarian disquiet, for the new government in Constantinople began to talk of reasserting Ottoman authority in all territories of which the sultan was technically the ruler. These included Bosnia and Hercegovina, occupied by the Austrians since 1878, and also Rumelia. Bulgaria's first discomfiture came when her representative in Constantinople was treated as an equal not of the other foreign representatives but of the chief officials of the Ottoman vilayets. This incident was quickly played down, but a more serious one followed within days when a strike, based in Constantinople, paralysed the ORC network. The Bulgarians were furious that at a moment of such tension in the Balkans half their rail network should be put out of action by a strike in a foreign country. They were more alarmed when Ottoman officers appeared on the frontier intending to pass into southern Bulgaria to negotiate with the strikers. To end any possibility that Ottoman sovereignty in southern Bulgaria might be asserted in this way, Bulgaria on 6/19 September nationalised the ORC tracks on Bulgarian territory. It was a bold step and one which Ferdinand had been characteristically reluctant to take, but having gainsaid the treaty of Berlin on this issue there was little sense in stopping there and not declaring full national independence, the more so as Austria's blessing for such a move had been received. On 22 September/5 October full Bulgarian independence was proclaimed and Ferdinand assumed the title of king. The following day Austria–Hungary annexed Bosnia and Hercegovina.

Bulgaria's act provoked considerable international condemnation and was not universally popular within the country. The Macedonian lobby disliked the fact that full independence had been declared before the reunion of their homeland with the rest of Bulgaria, and Ferdinand's critics objected because they believed his change of title had associated the monarchy with what should have been a purely national victory. Foreign doubts were settled by Russian diplomacy which managed to contrive a series of financial settlements which saved Ottoman face and left the Bulgarians with the substance of their gains. At home, however, criticism of Ferdinand intensified, with Stoilov's Nationalist Party, now under the leadership of Geshov, prominent in these attacks upon the 'personal regime'.

Criticism of Ferdinand was most pronounced at the grand national assembly which met in Tŭrnovo in the summer of 1911, shortly after Malinov had left office. The assembly had a secure majority in favour of the new government under Geshov, but it also included fifty oppositionists, most of them Agrarians. Their leader, Stamboliiski, mounted a flamboyant demonstration against Ferdinand during the latter's opening address, but given the solid government majority there was never any doubt that the assembly would agree that Ferdinand's title should now be 'King of the Bulgarians', a wording which did something to appease the Macedonian lobby. Of the other constitutional amendments agreed at Tŭrnovo the most important was that which stated that the king and the council of ministers were to be free to negotiate treaties with foreign states, and need only inform the Sŭbranie of their content if the interests of the state allowed. Given the dominance over his ministers in matters of foreign policy the king now had a virtual free hand in committing the country to foreign agreements.

The Tŭrnovo grand national assembly had shown that even a cabinet dominated by a party virulent in its criticism of the personal regime would be seduced into conformity by the spoils of office. It had also made possible the secret diplomacy which was to prove fateful in the next half decade, and it had also pointed to the growing strength of the Agrarian movement.

THE DEVELOPMENT OF AGRARIANISM AND SOCIALISM BEFORE THE FIRST WORLD WAR

In the election of 1908 Stamboliiski's followers had polled over 100,000 votes or eleven per cent of the total votes cast, and had won twenty-three seats; the next largest non-government party, Radoslavov's National Liberals, had five seats and 46,000 votes. The Agrarians had the potential to become a major political force in the country, but their evolution since the crisis of 1900 had been uneven. For the first two years of its existence the Agrarian movement had been preoccupied with the problem of how far it should commit itself to participation in party-political affairs. The fact that sixteen of the twenty-three Agrarian supporters elected in 1901 were immediately suborned into joining existing Sŭbranie parties was used by the opponents of participation to show the futility of such action; the advocates of participation argued that a political programme was essential to avoid such disasters. The latter faction won, and in October 1901 the third congress of the union decided to enter fully into electoral politics and to appeal to the entire nation rather than just to the peasantry; the title of the organisation was accordingly altered to the Bulgarian Agrarian National Union (BANU). Following this change Agrarian fortunes declined. Harvests improved, peasant living standards rose, and from 1903 the Stambolovist regime frustrated all opposition activities whether of the old or the new parties.

The revival of BANU as reflected in the 1908 election was not simply the result of the lifting of Stambolovist restrictions. The 1907 harvest had been poor but peasant opinion had also been mobilised by the spread of the cooperative movement which broke the power of the usurer and with which BANU was closely associated. Agrarians had also been helped by reforms in the party's structure, by the impact of rural unrest in Russia and more so in Romania in 1907, but most of all by the rise of Alexandŭr Stamboliiski.

In 1906 Stamboliiski had been appointed editor of the party paper, *Zemedelsko Zname* (*Agrarian Banner*), which he used to fire the movement with his own enthusiasm and ideas. His basic objective was justice and equality for all. The latter goal meant the elimination of excess so that no-one should have too much and no-one be left with too little property, a premise which led to the advocacy of the confiscation of land from those who had too much and its redistribution to those in need; land would be taken both from individual owners and institutional owners such as the church. Stamboliiski believed that there were two aspects to human nature, an individual and a communal, the former requiring private ownership of property and the latter developing as social and economic relationships became more complex. This contradicted the Marxist notion that economic development brings about a simplification of social relationships, and Stamboliiski also rejected the Marxist doctrine of class. He divided society not into antagonistic classes but into 'estates' whose members shared common economic occupations but might have different social backgrounds, so that a small peasant farmer would be a member of the same estate as the large landowner. Stamboliiski defined the estates as the agrarian, the artisanal, the wage-labouring, the entrepreneurial, the commercial and the bureaucratic. Of these the most important was the first, because the varied life of the peasant provided man with the greatest degree of self-fulfilment. By contrast, urban life, and the industry and division of labour associated with it, frustrated man's quest for self-fulfilment by forcing him to concentrate on a limited number of activities. For this reason Stamboliiski held towns in contempt. More so did he despise the contemporary form of the state, all the appurtenances of which he saw as needless impositions upon the peasant and the artisan; and especial contempt was reserved for the state's non-productive institutions such as the bureaucracy, the legal profession, the church – at least the higher ranks of the clergy – the monarchy and the army. Stamboliiski did not openly advocate republicanism, as that would have exposed the movement to needless persecution, but he did attack the army, arguing that its reduction or abolition would prove Bulgaria's good intent in foreign affairs and make it easier to move towards the Balkan peasant federation which was the ultimate objective of Agrarian foreign policy.

Although BANU never gained more than fifteen per cent of the vote in any election before the First World War, it enjoyed wide support amongst the independent proprietors who formed the vast majority of Bulgaria's rural population. Agrarianism understandably made less of an impact in the towns, where the urban poor were turning to socialism. In 1885 a Macedonian, Dimitŭr Blagoev, who had links with Russian Marxists, began publishing *Sŭvremeneni Pokazatel* (*Modern Indicator*), in which social-ist ideas were expounded, and within a few years Engels had been translated into Bulgarian by Christian Rakovski. In 1891 a number of socialist activists met at Buzludja in the Stara Planina and founded the Bulgarian Revolutionary Social Democratic Party, which in 1893 adopted a programme modelled upon that of the German party's Erfurt programme. In 1894 the BRSDP won four seats at the general election and in 1897 this was increased to six; of the eight members elected in 1901 five were disqualified before they could take their seats in the Sŭbranie.

Bulgaria's workforce, including those in the numerous small workshops, was not large, and even by 1910 numbered no more than 160,000. But in the early years of this century its age profile revealed a high proportion of young people who in the immediate future would be marrying and bringing up families. They would feel the increase in the urban cost of living, which rose from 67.22 *leva* per month for a family of two adults and two children in 1901 to 86.47 *leva* in 1907; at the latter date the average industrial wage was 49.56 *leva* per month. In addition to meagre wages many workers had to endure appalling working and living condi-tions. There were frequent protests against such conditions. The first strike had been recorded in 1893 amongst the textile workers in Sliven, but this and many stoppages which followed achieved little for as yet trade union organisation, except amongst the teachers, was weak. Most unions were still only local rather than national bodies, they were primarily trade rather than industrial organisations – there was, for example, no metal-workers union, though there were unions for smelters, cutters, etc. – and they were having to fight for such basic rights as that to collective rather than individual wage agreements. Above all, however, the unions were weakened by the divisions within the socialist movement which led to the split of 1903.

The Bulgarian socialists had never been firmly united. In 1893 an 'economist' wing had seceded to form a separate body, and although a reconciliation was effected in 1894 new divisions soon appeared. On the right, Yanko Sakŭzov, the editor of *Obshto Delo* (*Common Cause*), was prepared to cooperate with left-wing Sŭbranie parties such as the Demo-crats. He was also prepared to tolerate private property on a small scale, and wished to see trade unions open to all irrespective of political affiliation. Opposed to the 'Broads' were Blagoev and the 'Narrows', who held to pure Marxist doctrines no matter how inappropriate they were to Bulgaria in the first decade of the century. In *Novo Vreme* (*New Age*) Blagoev rejected all cooperation with the bourgeois parties, however radical, called for the confiscation of all private property, even that of the small peasant proprietor who did not hire labour, and demanded the total subjugation of the trade unions to the political needs of the party. By 1903 doctrinal differences and clashes of personality could no longer be contained and the party split. The trade union movement did likewise, some unions aligning with the Broads in the Free Trade Union Federation, others declaring for the Narrow-dominated General Workers' Trade Union Federation.

After 1903 there were numerous attempts, both by Bulgarians and by the world socialist movement, to mend the debilitating divisions, but all failed. In fact the tendency was for the socialist movement to follow the fissiparous example of Bulgaria's bourgeois parties. Yet despite these disabilities, by the eve of the Balkan wars Bulgaria's socialist movement was the strongest in the Balkans.

FROM THE DECLARATION OF INDEPENDENCE TO THE FIRST BALKAN WAR, 1908–12

The immediate origins of the Balkan wars were to be found in the Young Turk revolution of 1908. The new regime, rather than being the stabilising factor for which many had hoped, was to plunge the peninsula into renewed and radical turmoil; the Young Turks proved yet again that those who hoped that attempted modernisation would bring stabilisation were hopelessly deluded. The attempts by the new government to impose taxation and the other horrors of modern rule upon Albania bred the spirit of rebellion in a previously loyal people. This unexpected development raised the danger of great power intervention, for Austria had treaty rights in and Italy had pretensions to Albania, and the danger was much heightened when the Italians declared war on the Ottoman empire, whose possessions in Tripoli they had decided to seize. The direct involvement of the great powers in Ottoman Europe would close the door to expansion by the Balkan states, who now had to seek means to safeguard their interests. Russia, whose objective after the annexation of Bosnia was to prevent Habsburg penetration into the Balkans, argued that this could best be achieved through a Serbo-Bulgarian alliance.

Little progress in this direction could be made, however, whilst Malinov was in office, for he was as suspicious of the Serbs as they were of him. The situation changed with his replacement by Geshov in March 1911. Ferdinand's detestation of the new minister president was extraordinary even within this monarch's capacious reservoir of hatred. He clearly had pressing reasons for making such an appointment. As Geshov's party was so bitter in its opposition to Ferdinand's domestic politics the explanation could only lie in foreign affairs; as Geshov's first demand in this sector was for cooperation with Russia it was widely assumed that Bulgaria would now seek the alliance with Serbia for which St Petersburg was pressing.

This assumption was false. Geshov was coming under considerable pressure at home to take action to alleviate the sufferings of the Macedonian Slavs, but his first instinct was not to turn to Belgrade, particularly as the nomination of Serbian bishops for the sees of Veles and Dibra had enraged Bulgarian public opinion. Instead Geshov first approached Constantinople asking for the implementation of reforms in Macedonia and for the much-coveted and never-to-be-achieved rail link between Sofia and Kumanovo. Only when these efforts had proved unproductive did Geshov begin to make soundings in Belgrade. These were not encouraging, for the Serbs favoured a partition of Macedonia whilst the Bulgarians stuck to the demand for autonomy, hoping still that Macedonia would follow the Rumelian example. Geshov was eventually forced into a more accommodating frame of mind by rumours of a Russo-Turkish *rapprochement* and of Turkish troop concentrations in Thrace, but even when the Bulgarians had conceded the principle of partition there remained the problem of defining the two states' spheres of interest. This could be achieved only by delineating a 'contested zone' in central Macedonia and agreeing that if later discussions revealed that no agreement on the division of the zone could be found then both parties would ask for arbitration by the tsar. This compromise cleared the way for the signature in February 1912 of a Serbo-Bulgarian treaty, which, together with its secret military annexes, formed the first link in a chain of bilateral agreements which constituted the Balkan league. By May continuing unrest in Macedonia had led to the conclusion of an accord between Bulgaria and Greece, and so anxious were the contracting parties to reach an agreement that they did not even attempt to define their goals in Macedonia. An arrangement between Greece and Serbia and verbal agreements with Montenegro completed the league.

Whilst the diplomats drew up their treaties public opinion in Bulgaria became ever more bellicose. In addition to the continuing cycle of violence in Macedonia, opinion was excited by developments affecting the exarchate. Until 1908 all exarchist sees were technically in Ottoman territory, but following the declaration of independence this ceased to be so, and the Porte refused to allow one of its officials, the exarch, to take instructions from the synod of the Bulgarian church which met in Sofia, now the capital of an indisputably foreign state. A second synod was therefore established in Constantinople. Inevitably the two squabbled, and the

Russians welcomed these disputes as yet another argument for confining the exarchate to Bulgarian territory and ending the schism in the Orthodox church within the Ottoman empire. Such a development would spell disaster for the Bulgarians, whose major vehicle of influence in Macedonia remained the Bulgarian church. The Stambolovists and other opposition parties lost no opportunity to raise this problem in meetings and newspaper polemics, and in August a special but inconclusive conference of clerical and lay representatives met to discuss the issue. In the same month a bomb attack in the Macedonian village of Kochane led to serious proposals from Vienna for massive decentralisation of the Macedonian administration. This would match concessions recently awarded to the rebellious Albanians who had toppled the Young Turk cabinet; but such concessions, if sponsored by the great powers, would rule out intervention by the Balkan states, for the great powers would not allow their reform scheme to be ruined by intervention on the part of the smaller states. On the other hand, if the Balkan states did not act soon there was also a danger that the initiative would be taken by the extremists: fear of independent action by the *comitadji* had been one reason why Geshov had signed the alliance with Serbia, and this fear was equally powerfully felt in the summer of 1912 as the Balkan states moved rapidly towards war.

On 24 August/5 September Sofia witnessed a massive pro-war meeting, which Ferdinand and his cabinet used as their justification two days later for deciding upon war. Some weeks were absorbed in negotiations with the Serbs, who were anxious to settle details of what was to happen if Austria–Hungary attempted punitive action against the allies; meanwhile, to prevent the great powers stepping in either to enforce reforms in Macedonia or to contain the exuberance of the Balkan governments, the Montenegrins declared war on the Ottoman empire on 17/30 September. On 4/17 October Serbia, Greece and Bulgaria joined the conflict.

YEARS OF WAR, 1912–18

The Bulgarian army consisted of 592,000 men with the addition of some 15,000 volunteers in the Macedonia–Adrianople militia. The army's main task was to engage the large Ottoman forces in eastern Thrace, although two divisions were sent to the Struma valley to assist the Serbs and to try and reach Salonika before the Greeks. In Thrace the Bulgarians were successful beyond even their own imaginings. In a series of battles culminating in those at Lule Burgas and Bunar Hissar from 14/27 October to 20 October/2 November, the Turks were routed and driven back to their huge defensive complex, the Tchatalja lines, some forty kilometres from

Constantinople. Meanwhile the Rila division had stormed down the Struma valley only to arrive at Salonika a day behind the Greeks. The Turks were now ready to conclude an armistice, but the Bulgarians were divided as to whether to accept the offer or to try and capture Constantinople. The king, eagerly anticipating a triumphal entry into the city, was reported to have bought clothes and carriages appropriate to such a grand occasion, whilst Geshov looked forward to the bargaining power which he knew temporary occupation of Constantinople would give him at the peace conference. The military were less sanguine. They knew the strength of the Tchatalja lines and they were worried by signs of fatigue in an army which had accomplished so much in so short a time; but most worrying of all was the rising incidence of cholera amongst the troops. The civilians, however, prevailed, and an assault upon the Tchatalja lines began on 4/17 November. It failed, and on 20 November/3 December it was the Bulgarians' turn to request an armistice. This was agreed, and representatives of the belligerents made their way to St James's Palace in London to settle the terms of a peace treaty, having been told by the great powers than an independent Albania must emerge from this redrawing of the Balkan map. The creation of this new state was to bring hideous difficulties, but initially the major problem facing the conference was the inability of Bulgaria and Turkey to agree upon the fate of Adrianople, one of the few forts left in Ottoman hands. On 21 January/3 February 1913 fighting began again. The Serbs sent a number of troops and guns to help the Bulgarians, who also used aerial bombardment, the first European experience of this new form of barbarism. On 13/26 March Adrianople surrendered and on 1/14 April a second armistice was signed. Fighting was now confined to the siege of Scutari (Shkoder) in the west of the peninsula.

The Bulgarians were not concerned with the Scutari problem, which was to bring the great powers of Europe close to war, but Sofia was anxious about Romanian attitudes. The Romanians had followed the advice of the great powers and remained neutral, but were now demanding extra territory both as a reward for their good behaviour and as compensation for the expansion of their neighbours. That compensation could be found only at the expense of Bulgaria, and eventually Geshov was forced to agree to a rectification of the frontier along a line from Silistra to Balchik. This loss of territory in the north-east made the Bulgarians all the more determined to retain that part of Macedonia assigned to them in the Serbo-Bulgarian treaty of 1912, and to secure as great a share as possible of the contested zone. Meanwhile in Thrace and those parts of Macedonia already under Bulgarian occupation the Bulgarian local government system was introduced, prefects were nominated to the newly-formed provinces, a census was held and land reforms were introduced.

The St James's conference ended with the signing of the treaty of London on 17/30 May 1913, but the peace it brought was fragile and transitory. The treaty required the allies to divide amongst themselves the territories between Albania in the west and a line from Enos on the Aegean to Midia on the Black Sea. It was an impossible task. Bulgarian claims to the area were based upon the treaty of 1912 with Serbia, and on the principle of 'proportionality', by which the allies' rewards would be in direct proportion to the magnitude of their military effort and sacrifice. The Serbs and the Greeks disagreed. The Serbs demanded revision of the 1912 treaty because their expected expansion to the west had been thwarted by the creation of Albania. Both the Serbs and the Greeks countered the notion of proportionality with that of balance, arguing that the division of Turkey-in-Europe must be so contrived as to prevent any one Balkan state becoming over-powerful. Prospects for a peaceful settlement of these disputes were not improved by ugly recriminations on the amount and effectiveness of the military support given by one ally to another. By the end of May the Greeks and Serbs had signed a secret agreement to divide Macedonia west of the Vardar and to allow the fate of the areas east of that river to be determined by the principle of effective occupation. Geshov suggested Russian arbitration but the Serbs refused, insisting that direct negotiations in which the Greeks should take part must be tried first. They were, and they failed utterly. Geshov resigned in despair and was succeeded by Danev. Geshov's decision was determined not only by his inability to agree with Pašić, the Serbian premier, but also because Ferdinand, without full consultation with the minister president, had joined the ever-growing faction demanding a military solution to the present difficulties. The war faction included most Macedonians, all opposition parties except the Agrarians and socialists, and – most importantly – the general staff. The latter's concern was for the morale of the troops, who had expected demobilisation to follow the signing of the treaty of London; they were now becoming fretful in their inactive state, the more so as summer and its attendant work in the fields approached. There had already been a number of serious cases of unrest amongst the troops. The decisive point came when the Russian foreign minister, Sazonov, summoned both Bulgarian and Serbian minister presidents to St Petersburg; at the same time the high command was insisting that if the army were not sent into action within ten days it must be demobilised, which would leave Bulgaria defenceless. Even Danev, a leading Russophile, was now for war, because he knew that Russia would insist on impossible concessions to Serbia. His reply to Sazonov contained so many conditions that it amounted to an ultimatum. Sazonov was furious, but he was less in control of events than he had ever been. On 16/29 June general Savov ordered his troops forward. Danev now lost his nerve and rescinded the order, only to have his instructions over-ruled by the king. For daring to obey the minister president general Savov was removed from his command; Ferdinand's personal regime had no place for senior officers who obeyed anyone but the king. Initially the army, almost all of which was concentrated on the western front, was successful, but within two weeks the Romanians had mobilised and moved across the Danube. There was nothing to prevent them entering Sofia, whilst in the south the Turks had crossed the denuded frontier and by the middle of July were again in Adrianople. Even in the west the early momentum was lost. Danev appealed to Russia but in the light of recent Bulgarian conduct even he knew it was hopeless. On 4/17 July he resigned to make way for a cabinet of various Liberal factions under the minister presidency of Vasil Radoslavov.

Radoslavov concluded an armistice as rapidly as he could and on 28 July/10 August signed the humiliating treaty of Bucharest. On 30 September/13 October the treaty of Constantinople ended the war with Turkey. The great gains of the first Balkan war had been lost, and despite all her sacrifices Bulgaria received only Pirin Macedonia to a point mid-way down the Struma valley, the Kǔrdjali district, and a part of Thrace which included the coastline around Dedeagach.

Some had hoped that the war would force the Greeks and Serbs to the negotiating table, but most had looked to Slivnitsa and Lule Burgas and assumed that in a new war of conquest the Bulgarian army would be more than a match for its erstwhile allies. The least sanguine had taken comfort in the belief that if things went awry Russia would not allow the complete humiliation of the state it had done so much to create. This was an illusion: Bulgaria had shattered the Balkan league, Russia's best defence against supposed Austro-Hungarian expansionism; Bulgaria had refused to cooperate in Russian attempts to win Romania away from the triple alliance; and St Petersburg could not dismiss the possibility that were it to achieve its full objectives Bulgaria would become too powerful for Russia's comfort. Serbian designs, on the other hand, were focused upon the western Balkans and could never conflict with long-term Russian goals, besides which Serbia would always be more reliable than Bulgaria as a partner against Austria-Hungary.

The second Balkan war, which had cost more lives than the campaign against the Ottoman empire resulted in the second partition of Bulgaria, and one far more damaging than that agreed at Berlin in 1878. The new rulers of *Bulgaria irredenta* were not the politically weak and culturally indulgent Ottomans but aggressive, nationalistic states which would not allow any equivalent of the *millet* system in which different cultures could flourish; there was no place for the exarchate in Serbian or Greek Macedonia, where dejected exarchists talked once more of uniatism. In 1913 the exarch himself went to Sofia, where he remained until his death two years later. The treaty of Bucharest created a revanchist mentality amongst Bulgarians, and not without cause, for those in the territories now alienated who showed any sign of affiliation with Bulgaria or Bulgarian culture were dealt with harshly. This naturally complicated relations with Bulgaria's immediate neighbours and exposed the Greek communities in Bulgaria itself to increased hostility. Economically the results of the war were disastrous, though the major damage was done by the loss of the Dobrudja in the second war. Railway and harbour construction in northern Bulgaria since 1878 had been based on the grain trade through Varna, much of which depended upon the Dobrudja, where the country's few commercial and modernised farms were to be found. In 1913 Varna was deprived of its hinterland and left within a few miles of an undefended frontier. Whilst Bulgaria lost its most productive and profitable agricultural region the areas it acquired were backward and undeveloped. To reap any gain from these lands a new infrastructure would have to be created based upon a harbour to be built at Porto Lagos, Dedeagach being useless because the railway to it wound in and out of Ottoman territory.

The disaster of the second Balkan war temporarily shook Ferdinand's personal regime. In November 1913 Radoslavov had to go to the country to secure a reliable Sŭbranie, but the elections took place not only against the background of embitterment caused by the war but also under the system of proportional representation. The government parties returned only ninety-seven deputies to the opposition groups' 109, in which were included forty-seven BANU supporters and thirty-seven socialists. Rado-slavov attempted to win over the Agrarians, but having failed went to the country again in April 1914. This time he allowed the new territories in Thrace and Pirin Macedonia to take part, although they had not been formally accepted by a grand national assembly and most of their Muslim inhabitants were not yet Bulgarian citizens. The Muslims were also subjected to great pressure from government propagandists whilst oppo-sition supporters were not allowed to campaign in the new lands. The trick worked and the new Sŭbranie gave the government a workable majority; political cynicism had triumphed even over proportional representation.

After the election Radoslavov's first preoccupation was to find a loan to finance the recent wars and the development of the new territories. The traditional opposition parties accepted the need for a loan, not least because they knew that if they did not Radoslavov would call another election in which the non-established radical parties might make such advances as to bring in an Agrarian or even an Agrarian–socialist administration. There remained the question of where the loan should be raised, a question which in the summer of 1914 was inevitably linked to that of Bulgaria's alignment in the conflict between the great powers. The issue was decided by the French, who stated that if they lent money they would expect in return a government in Sofia well-disposed to the entente. That again could mean a general election for Radoslavov, and his party were traditionally pro-Austrian and pro-German. The loan was therefore raised in Germany in July 1914. The Sŭbranie debate on the agreement produced scenes of extraordinary disorder, with Radoslavov at one point waving a revolver above his head, and although government supporters insisted that the show of hands had revealed a majority in their favour this was accepted by none of their opponents and few of the neutral observers present.

The terms of the agreement were to many as unwelcome as the manner of its enactment. The loan was to be for five hundred million gold *leva* at five per cent for fifty years. It was to be guaranteed by those revenues from import dues, from the government monopoly on the sale of cigarette papers, and from the returns from the *mururie*, the *banderolle* and the stamp duty not earmarked for the service of existing debts. Bulgaria was obliged to purchase military supplies from Austria, to grant the contract for building the railway to Porto Lagos to a German consortium, and to allow a German company a large share in the management of the state mines at Pernik and Bobov Dol. The first instalment of the loan was to be paid at the end of September unless European war broke out in the interim, the Germans understandably wishing to exclude the possibility of their money being spent to finance campaigns against them.

Some opponents of the loan argued that its conclusion breached the 'strict and loyal' neutrality which the government had declared at the outbreak of the European war. At the same time the government itself had also declared a state of emergency, which increased its powers to control the press, the Sŭbranie and public meetings. After the exertions of 1912 and 1913 the government did not have to face pressure from any strongly pro-war lobby within the country, but Bulgaria could not escape pressures from both sides in the great conflict being waged in Europe. Bulgaria's army was still a sizeable force, and Bulgaria occupied a strategic position in the Balkans, commanding the supply routes to the entente's Serbian ally and to the Ottoman empire, which joined the central powers in October. Ferdinand and Radoslavov wished to keep out of the war for as long as possible but in the meantime they sounded both camps. The central powers offered Bulgaria those parts of Macedonia to which it had an 'historic and ethnic' claim, and, if it joined the war, any additional areas in Macedonia which its armies might occupy. The entente was prepared to allow Bulgaria to take Thrace up to the Enos–Midia line, but Bulgarian gains in Macedonia would be dependent upon what the Serbs were prepared to concede. Ferdinand and Radoslavov were attracted by neither offer, not least because there was as yet no indication of which side might win. Military developments were to play a decisive role in determining Bulgarian allegiance.

Early in 1915 it seemed that the military balance was swinging in favour of the entente. The Russians captured Przemyśl in March, and in the same month French and Commonwealth forces had established a bridgehead in Gallipoli, from which they seemed set to threaten Constantinople and open the supply lines to the Russians; and in May Italy joined the war on the entente side. Malinov and his Democratic Party, and Genadiev, the Stambolovist leader, intensified their efforts to make Bulgaria follow the Italian example, in response to which the government tightened its political control, having already introduced in March 1915 the public welfare bill which provided for government control of large sectors of the economy. The clouds of war were gathering once more on Bulgaria's horizon.

Before any decision was made further soundings were taken in the entente capitals. Thrace up to the Enos–Midia line was again on offer, and so too was an extended zone in Macedonia which would give Bulgaria possession of Bitolya, Ohrid, Drama, Seres and Kavalla, but only at the end of hostilities and only if adequate compensation were given to Serbia in Bosnia and to Greece in Asia Minor. Financial assistance was also promised, as was help in negotiations with Romania over the Dobrudja. This offer touched upon all three areas in which Bulgaria had claims, Thrace, Macedonia and the Dobrudja, but it was too vague. Ferdinand asked for clarification.

Whilst they had been negotiating with the entente the Bulgarians had naturally maintained contact with the central powers. By the summer of 1915 the latter had far more to offer and seemed in a much stronger military position. A massive assault upon Serbia was being prepared, the French and Commonwealth troops were pinned to their lethal Gallipoli beaches and the mighty Russian army was driven out of Lemberg,

Warsaw, Vilna and Kovno; not even Petrograd seemed safe. Furthermore, German diplomatic pressure in Constantinople induced the Turks to allow the Bulgarians a small portion of Thrace, including complete control of the railway to Dedeagach.

These were terms which the entente could never match. In the second half of August and early September final details of Bulgaria's accession to the central powers were settled whilst Austrian and German troops massed along the Austro-Hungarian/Serbian front. On 8/21 September the Bulgarian army was mobilised and 'strict and loyal' altered to 'armed neutrality'. Ten days later Russia demanded an end to Bulgaria's warlike measures; instead, on 28 September/11 October Bulgarian troops joined the attack on Serbia, and three days later Russia declared war on Bulgaria. Britain and France did likewise within a few days.

The entente's position in Bulgaria had always been weak. The Bulgarians assumed, rightly, that the entente powers had promised Constantinople to Russia in the event of final victory, and there was reason to question whether that was in the best interests of Bulgaria. Also, the entente focused its diplomatic efforts upon winning the support of opposition figures, when a more thorough analysis of recent Bulgarian politics, even after the second Balkan war, would have revealed that in such matters the real decision-maker was the king; western efforts to buy up the entire 1915 grain harvest through des Closières, a former official of Paribas, had been inept and smelt too strongly of bribery even for Bulgarian politics. Above all, however, the entente was limited by its obligations to Serbia, which would not concede an inch of Macedonia to the Bulgarians, a refusal strengthened after the entry of Italy into the war had made Serbian expansion to the west and north more difficult.

Bulgaria's joining the conflict was expected to bring the war to an end within a few months, but even this did not make it popular. The opposition parties – which in August 1914 had declared themselves to be 'resolute partisans of peace' – formed a United Bloc which only the Narrows refused to join. The block's leaders declared against entry into the war and demanded a full discussion of the issue in the Sŭbranie as well as an interview with the king. The latter was granted on 4/17 September, but it ended with a furious confrontation between Ferdinand and Stamboliiski. When he published details of the meeting Stamboliiski was clapped in gaol for *lèse majesté*. The full Sŭbranie debate demanded by the Bloc did not take place, Radoslavov preferring to consult only pro-government deputies in an irregular meeting in the Sŭbranie building. Once the decision to fight had been taken, however, the opposition reluctantly accepted it, and when the Sŭbranie finally met in December all parties except the Narrows voted for war credits.

By the time the Sŭbranie had voted for war credits the Bulgarian army had occupied most of Macedonia; the Germans then refused permission for an attack on Greece which might unite the Greeks in support of the entente. This view was relaxed in 1916 when Bulgarian and German troops moved as far as Fort Rupel, after which an attack upon Bulgarian positions later in the year allowed further forward movement in which Drama, Seres and Kavalla were taken. Towards the end of 1916 the Bulgarians suffered their first serious setback in Macedonia, when, after a huge battle for Mount Kaimakchalan, the Serbs repossessed Bitolya. Meanwhile in the north Romania had entered the war on the side of the entente. The Bulgarian Third Army, with Turkish assistance, thereupon moved into the southern Dobrudja, and later in the summer crossed the Danube into Romania proper, after which the military situation remained little changed until the final collapse of 1918.

The most extreme expression of Bulgarian war aims was for the retention of all territory occupied by Bulgarian troops, but few advocated such a policy. On the other hand few disputed that Bulgaria had just claims upon Macedonia, Thrace, the Dobrudja and the Morava valley, though moderates such as Geshov were prepared to admit that Bulgaria should only take areas which were indubitably Bulgarian. For the first year and a half of Bulgaria's war these minor differences caused little concern to Radoslavov and Ferdinand, who had little to fear in the way of internal political opposition. They and their German allies remained confident that military victories and official propaganda had weakened popular attachment to Russia, and there was no resistance in Easter 1916 when Bulgaria switched to the Gregorian calendar; in the 1890s an attempt to do this by the modernising Stoilov had been wrecked by Russophile, clerical opposition.

Opposition to Radoslavov's cabinet in 1916 came not from its traditional political opponents but from the army. In 1915 mobilisation and military advance had absorbed the energies of senior officers who by 1916 had a little more time to observe and reflect. They disliked much of what they saw, particularly in the occupied territories where newly-introduced civilian officials were accused, usually justly, of massive incompetence. In August the army attempted to seize control of the administration of all of occupied Macedonia. Radoslavov denounced this as the political machinations of the Democratic Party, many of whose supporters had moved into the higher ranks as a result of recent promotions.

It was much less easly to slough off military complaints over the problem of supplies to both civilian and military consumers. The economic powers assumed by the government in the public welfare bill of March 1915 had enabled it to control the price of and to ration any commodity for which demand outstripped supply, and by 1916 such items included even bread. Many factors contributed to the shortage of supplies, which eventually became chronic in 1918. Mobilisation in 1915 had partially disrupted the harvest and in that year too much grain had been requisitioned and handed over to the army. Competition between military and civilian authorities made matters worse, but great damage was also done by German and Austrian troops, by the allied food-purchasing agencies, which were greatly helped by German control of the railway and telephone systems, and by the willingness of many corrupt Bulgarian officials to cooperate in mulcting the nation of its food. After December 1915, when German and Austrian currency was made legal tender in Bulgaria, allied troops, who were far better-paid than their native comrades-in-arms, purchased quantities of food on both the legitimate and the black markets; furthermore, they abused their right to send limited amounts of food to their families at home, and on occasions stole supplies on a grand scale. Bulgarian hopes that the acquisition of the Dobrudja might increase the supply of grain were dashed, because the Germans requisitioned so much of it that in 1917 three-quarters of the region's rich soil lay unused for lack of seed.

In 1916 the administration of food and other supplies was reorganised and placed under the control of the Central Committee for Economic and Social Welfare, a civilian body dominated by members of the Sŭbranie. By the spring of 1917 there had been no improvement. On the contrary, conditions were worse and in the occupied territories they were fast becoming critical: in Ohrid deaths from starvation were reported whilst in the Morava valley there was widespread rebellion. The civilian committee admitted its failure, and in April 1917 was replaced by the Directorate for Economic and Social Welfare which was entirely under the control of the military.

Declining living conditions and the seemingly endless war produced political protest and civil unrest. In December there had been demonstrations to protest against the rejection by the entente powers of the German peace initiative, but it was events in Russia rather than on the battlefield which quickened Bulgaria's domestic political life. The fall of the tsar and the appointment of Miliukov, who had once taught in Sofia university, as foreign secretary in the provisional government raised hopes for peace; secret, but in all cases fruitless, approaches were made to the Russians in

Stockholm, Petrograd and Switzerland. Whilst these vain initiatives were being undertaken pro-Russian feelings were being revived in Bulgaria, and they soon led to public demands for a negotiated peace with the new rulers in Petrograd. The army too was affected, and by the summer of 1917 Bulgarian commanders, particularly on the northern front where Bulgarian faced Russian troops, were reporting the formation of councils or 'soviets' amongst their troops, five hundred of whom soon found themselves in gaol.

Radoslavov's constant reply to his critics was that in wartime some disaffection was inevitable but it was a price which had to be paid to achieve national unity. A serious dent in this argument was made in March 1917 when the Radical Democratic leader, Tsanov, declared in the Sŭbranie that Bulgarian occupation of parts of Romania was unjustifiable on ethnic grounds; this, he said, was not the legitimate pursuit of national unity but foreign conquest. At the same time Stamboliiski in his Sofia prison cell was urging complete withdrawal from the war, because he was convinced that the fall of tsardom would bring about the entry of the U.S.A. on the side of the entente and with it the end of any hope of victory for the central powers. Agrarian propaganda was responsible for much of the military unrest in 1917 and for the frequent calls for a peace without indemnities or annexations. Initially Radoslavov did not pay much attention to such talk, but he was alarmed when a motion in favour of such a peace passed the German Reichstag on 19 July. Had even the German parliament been converted to a solution which, if strictly applied, would reduce Bulgaria to its 1913 frontiers? An official visit by the kaiser to Sofia in October, the first by the head of a great power, was meant to reassure the Bulgarians on this point. The Sŭbranie, however, was not easily consoled, and the uproarious scenes which it witnessed in December were the first real signs of the collapse of Radoslavov's political authority and with it of Bulgaria's commitment to the war.

Radoslavov's eventual fall was occasioned by both internal and external factors. At home continued deterioration in the supply of essential goods intensified popular resentment; in December 1917 over 10,000 people responded eagerly at a public meeting when Blagoev called for an end to the war and to the political system which had allowed it. In January 1918 there were anti-war protests in Gabrovo and in the following months riots in Stanimaka and Samokov; in May a woman was killed in Sliven as a wave of unrest, the so-called 'women's revolt', swept through Bulgarian towns. By the summer anger turned to despair when it became obvious that Bulgaria was to receive little food from the Ukraine and that the forthcoming harvest at home was going to be a disaster.

In external affairs, Radoslavov's claim that despite discomfort at home he could secure full national unification was increasingly called into question. In January 1918 President Wilson published his fourteen points, which called, somewhat naively, for the settlement of frontiers along lines of nationality. Clearly no such boundaries existed in the Balkans, but from the Bulgarian opposition's point of view Wilson's solution was as good as any one based upon the principle of no indemnities or annexations. And as Bulgaria was not at war with the U.S.A. why should she not withdraw from the conflict and put her faith in a Wilsonian peace? Arguments of this nature undermined Radoslavov's position, but that position was finally destroyed by the treaty of Bucharest in May. Bulgaria had expected to be granted all of the Dobrudja, yet its northern half was to be put under joint Austro-German–Bulgarian administration; if Bulgaria could not secure the Dobrudja, the least contentious of its territorial claims, what hope was there, asked Radoslavov's critics, for Macedonia and Thrace? Even Radoslavov admitted that at Bucharest Bulgaria had been treated more as a defeated enemy than a victorious ally, and on 20 June he resigned.

His successor was Malinov, who attempted to bring Stamboliiski into the government, but the Agrarian leader would join the cabinet only if Bulgaria withdrew from the war, a condition which Ferdinand was as yet unwilling to accept. Stamboliiski therefore returned to his prison cell. In addition to promising to continue the war Malinov also offered the Bulgarian people honest government and a tougher line with their allies. The latter had some initial success and in July the northern Dobrudja was given to Bulgaria. Such gestures were by now irrelevant to a nation racked by shortages of food and other essentials. Efforts to alleviate the shortages, though well-intentioned, often aggravated the problem. Requisitioning had always been unpopular with the peasants because the requisitioning parties frequently seized goods such as soap or sugar which they were not meant to take but which they could sell profitably on the black market. Conditions were much worse for the urban dwellers who had less opportunity to grow food and therefore had little defence against inflation and the black marketeers. The official cost of living index, taken from a base of 100 in 1914 had risen to 200 by the end of 1916 and in July 1918 stood at 847; on the black market, frequently the only source of many goods, inflation was much steeper.

The sufferings of the villagers and the poor of the towns were witnessed by the soldiers who came home on furlough or on harvest leave, and this increased dissatisfaction in the ranks of an army which was itself desperately short of uniforms, boots and ammunition. Links with political activists in BANU and the socialist parties were strengthened and morale was thereby further impaired, whilst government propagandists sent to restore the fighting spirit were derided and frequently howled down. This demoralised army could not withstand the Franco-British assault which began at Dobro Pole on 15 September. Within thirty-six hours the Bulgarian front had been pierced and the army was in headlong retreat through the narrow Kresna gorge, where it suffered grievously from aerial attack. By 25 September the French and British had entered Bulgaria proper, military discipline had collapsed and the army was disintegrating. A crown council decided for an immediate armistice and the minister of finance, Liapchev, and the American consul in Sofia set out for Salonika, where a cease-fire was agreed on 29 September. Bulgaria, the last state to join the central powers bloc, had become the first to leave it.

SOCIAL AND ECONOMIC DEVELOPMENT, 1878–1918

Between 1878 and 1912 Bulgaria experienced relatively little change in its social structure, though it did see the beginnings of modern manufacturing and the emergence of a new and heavily centralised administrative machine.

The population increased from two and a half million in 1892 to three and a half million in 1910, and stood at over four and three-quarter million in 1920. This increase took place despite the emigration of a large number of Bulgaria's Turkish-speaking inhabitants. In 1881 they represented almost a quarter of the population of Bulgaria and Rumelia, yet by 1892 the proportion was 17.21 per cent and in 1910 11.63; in the same years the Bulgarian-speaking elements were 67.84 per cent, 75.67 per cent and 81.63 per cent of the total.

The principal cause of Turkish emigration was the unwillingness of the former dominant element to adapt to the *mores* of the new, Christian state. Its most important consequence was that large areas of land became available for purchase by Christians, and possibly as much as a quarter of the arable land in Bulgaria and Rumelia changed hands in the decade after 1878, usually with the assistance of the private money-lender. The purchasers of émigré property were peasant proprietors who could subsist on their land without having to employ extra-familial labour, and most of the very few large holdings which did exist were split into small lots and rented; the large, compact and capitalised agrarian enterprise existed only in the Dobrudja. Table 1 shows both the dominance of small properties and how little the pattern of land ownership changed in Bulgaria between 1878 and 1908.

Table 1 *Distribution of land by size of holdings, 1897 and 1908*

Size of holding in hectares	No. of holdings		Percentage of total holdings		Area of land in hectares		Percentage of total area	
	1897	1908	1897	1908	1897	1908	1897	1908
Below 2	363,646	424,898	45.48	45.52	265,653	321,568	6.68	6.95
2 to 10	334,384	386,725	41.82	41.43	1,681,119	1,954,854	42.27	42.26
10 to 30	92,509	111,632	11.57	11.96	1,409,890	1,689,371	35.44	36.52
Above 30	9,049	10,119	1.13	1.09	620,896	659,994	15.61	14.27
Total	799,588	933,374	100.00	100.00	3,977,558	4,625,787	100.00	100.00

Sources: Figures adapted from those given in, *inter alia*, G. T. Danailow, *Les effets de la Guerre en Bulgarie* (Paris, 1933), K. G. Popoff, *La Bulgarie Economique, 1879–1911* (Sofia, 1920) and Cpt. I. Atanasov, *Staticheski godishnik na knyazhestvo Bŭlgariya* (Sofia, 1897).

The predominance of the non-capitalised peasant proprietor had many causes. First and foremost was the continued availability of land, for when the supply of émigré land dried up state or communal properties could be taken over, and therefore, despite population increases, the supply of land could keep pace with demand. This being so, there was almost no reserve of landless labourers to work commercialised enterprises, and even during the crisis years at the turn of the century full-time agricultural labourers constituted no more than two per cent of the total population. In the years immediately after the liberation a shortage of draught animals, many of which had been taken by the armies or by departing Turks, also acted as a powerful impediment to the capitalisation of farming. The minimal levels of agricultural education and technology kept profitability low, as did an over-dependence on grain, whose value on the world market was in decline. For anyone with capital to invest, agriculture could not match the returns offered by commerce, industry and, until the first decade of the twentieth century, usury.

From the mid-1890s there were consistent efforts to improve agricultural productivity, and the annual tonnage of imported agricultural machinery rose from 199 tons for the years 1886–90 to 2,612 tons for 1906–11, yet even by 1910 no more than 18 per cent of holdings had metal ploughs. The main crop continued to be grain, mainly wheat, but immediately before the wars production of industrial crops began to increase, albeit from a very low base. Although industrial crops still accounted for only a tiny proportion of total acreage farmed, the Bulgarian peasant had shown a willingness to try new crops which was to be of great importance during the First World War and the depression years of the 1930s.

The Balkan wars had little direct effect on Bulgarian agriculture. The first war was fought between harvests and in neither war did much of the fighting take place on Bulgarian soil. The campaigns of the First World War also took place outside Bulgaria, but the length and intensity of that conflict inevitably affected agriculture. In 1915 the Bulgarian army mobilised 800,000 men and in 1918 there were no less than 857,000 with the colours; at 38.83 per cent of the total population Bulgaria's proportion of mobilised men was the highest of all the belligerents. Because a large part of the army operated in Macedonia, where there were few roads and fewer railways, draught animals and carts were also mobilised in large numbers. The effect on agriculture was predictable, and by 1917 29.2 per cent of useable land was left fallow compared to 17 per cent in 1912; yields fell accordingly, especially in grain. Whilst the staple grain crops declined the newer industrial crops increased. Bulgarian ports on the Aegean were blockaded, and the resulting import substitution encouraged greater production of commodities such as sugar-beet and rapeseed oil. The most startling change in Bulgarian agriculture during the First World War, however, was the increase in tobacco cultivation, which rose from 8,891 hectares producing 58,000 quarters in 1912 to 32,431 hectares producing 202,000 quarters in 1918. The acquisition of Pirin Macedonia and the influx of refugees from tobacco-growing areas after the second Balkan war helped to stimulate production, but much more important was the near monopoly which Bulgaria enjoyed in the central European tobacco market during the First World War.

Although relatively little change took place in the structure of Bulgarian agriculture between 1878 and 1918, some aspects of traditional rural life were under pressure from modernising forces. The old, extended-kin collective unit, the *zadruga*, declined, and traditional patterns of trans-humance fell victim to the railways, and, in the years 1878–85, to the levying of a sheep tax in both Bulgaria and Rumelia. The fairs at places such as Uzundjovo, once so important in Balkan mercantile life, atrophied and died, with the Plovdiv exhibition, first held in 1892, standing as a symbol of the new Bulgaria. And even if the three- or two-field system with its scattered strips still dominated the Bulgarian village, voices were being raised against it and in favour of the more profitable, consolidated holdings.

The disparity between rural and urban conditions which had sharpened social tensions at the end of the 1890s was an established phenomenon. What was new, however, was that the towns were not now Greek, Turkish or Armenian centres, as they had frequently been before the liberation. Even before Stamboliiski raised anti-urbanism into an ideology the peasant had seldom liked the town, but he could write it off as a 'non-Bulgarian' institution, just as radicals had dismissed the ecclesiastical hierarchy as a Greek imposition upon a democratic, Slav church. By the time of the agrarian crisis at the turn of the century the towns were predominantly Bulgarian. Government, itself a centralised, urban phenomenon, was also dominated by Bulgarians rather than by Greeks or Turks. If the Bulgarian peasant could say, as he frequently did around the turn of the century, *ot turkso po-losho* (things are worse than under the Turks), he was rejecting not the foreigner-dominated administration of a foreign and dominating empire, but his own nation–state.

The problems of the new nation–state derived in part from *partisanstvo* and the political debauching of the intelligentsia. Service of the nation in the national revival had become service in the nation–state's bureaucracy and political civil service. Those who had saved the nation by reviving its culture now sought to serve the nation–state by manning its apparatus, but in doing so they lost contact with those with whom they had originally cooperated and on behalf of whom they now pretended to act. Symbolic of the changing role of the educated elements in the 1880s were the difficulties experienced in finding teachers for the growing number of schools, and in later years only a minority of graduates from the country's various vocational training institutes went into the jobs for which they had been prepared. One of the great institutions of the national renaissance, education, had been forsaken for the flesh-pots of urban life and bureaucratic office. Stamboliiski's dislike of the towns had deep social roots.

One chance to recreate the old alliance between peasant and intelligentsia was offered by the growth of the cooperative movement, in which priests, teachers and agricultural advisers were prominent. The first credit cooperative had been formed at Mirkovo in the Pirdop district in 1890, but it was not until reform of the laws regarding limited liability, in 1902, and mortgage loans, in 1903, that real expansion was possible. In 1904 the number of cooperatives had risen to 68 and in 1911 had reached over 1,400, with at least 40,000 members, by far the largest number in any Balkan country. Most cooperatives were credit cooperatives based on the Reiffeisen system, but others were involved in production and distribution. The Bulgarian Agricultural Bank had played a vital role in financing credit cooperatives, and in 1911 it helped them establish their own Central Cooperative Bank. By bringing money-lending under control and forcing interest rates down towards six to eight per cent the cooperatives were an important, though not the only, cause of the stability of rural Bulgaria after 1901. In the inflation of the First World War peasant families were able to liquidate their debts, and with few goods to buy could accumulate some savings. The lodgement of those savings reflected peasant confidence in the cooperatives: the deposits of the BNB rose from 42,000,000 *leva* in 1914 to 85,000,000 in 1917, those of the Bulgarian Agricultural Bank from almost 9,000,000 *leva* to just over 14,000,000 *leva*, and those of the Central Cooperative Bank from 8,500,000 *leva* to almost 80,000,000 *leva*.

Between 1880 and 1910 the proportion of urban dwellers to the total population scarcely changed, rising from 18 per cent to 19 per cent between 1880 and 1910. In the same period their absolute number rose from 543,000 to 829,000, and the population of Sofia grew from 20,000 to 103,000. The latter's growth was exceptional, and reflected, first, the concentration of administrative posts in the capital – one in four of whose working population was classified as a bureaucrat, whereas for the country as a whole the ratio was one in twelve – and secondly, the fact that industry was attracted to the city, where, despite its distance from the ports, contracts could more easily be secured and influence exercised. Not all Bulgarian towns prospered after the liberation, and many traditional manufacturing settlements along the Balkan foothills suffered sharp and in some instances irreversible decline. The departure of the Turks in some cases deprived the workshops producing luxury goods of their chief customers, and elsewhere the adoption of modern or Western tastes in dress and furniture destroyed the home market. The textile producers suffered when the Ottoman army ceased to buy Bulgarian yarn; this blow was compounded by the import of cheap, factory-produced yarn forced upon the manufacturers because Muslim emigration and the acquisition of land or more attractive employment by local Christians had reduced the labour supply. This, and other factors, raised the money wages of those still employed in spinning, but their real wages were not increasing and imported yarn presented a visible and comprehensible explanation of their sufferings, and in 1883 demonstrators in a number of textile towns burnt foreign yarn and attacked its importers.

The disruption of established patterns of manufacturing and the social dislocation which it occasioned led a number of writers to argue for a state industrial policy. State involvement in the economic sector had been seen with the creation of the BDZh and the BNB, and there had also been attempts to protect home manufacturers by legislating that all state officials must wear uniforms made in Bulgaria, but as far as the promotion of home industry was concerned these were uncoordinated and haphazard responses to particular emergencies. The first systematic attempt to promote Bulgarian industrial expansion came in 1894 with Stoilov's encouragement of industry bill. The bill offered to any concern within defined sectors of manufacturing industry, and having at least 25,000 *leva* of capital and a minimum of twenty employees, a range of privileges which included free grants of land for factory construction, duty-free imports of machinery and of raw materials not produced in Bulgaria, tax exemptions, lower rates on the state railways for their finished goods, and preference in the granting of government contracts. In 1905 and 1909 subsequent encouragement of industry acts lowered the qualifications for and widened the compass of the scheme.

A corollary of the encouragement of industry bill was tariff reform aimed at protecting home manufacturers. This had been difficult in the immediate post-liberation period because of the restrictions imposed by the treaty of Berlin, but by the mid-1890s, once recognition had been secured, the powers were more relaxed in this matter. In 1896 the Stoilov cabinet raised the general tariff from 8 per cent to 14 per cent. There were many exceptions to this general rate, with machinery and sought-after raw materials incurring only low rates and luxuries being taxed more heavily. In 1906 the general rate was increased to 24.6 per cent, and thereafter tariff protection remained a standard feature of Bulgarian economic policy.

Together with the encouragement of industry and tariff protection went state promotion of the economic infrastructure. Construction of modern port facilities at Burgas and Varna began in 1894 and was completed in 1903 and 1906 respectively. Roads were improved and the telephone network extended, but the most important work in improving internal communications was seen in railway development. From 220 kilometres in 1880 the system expanded to 1,566 kilometres in 1900 and 2,109 kilometres in 1912, by which date much of the basic rail network as outlined by Karavelov in the 1884 railway act had been completed, though there was still no bridge across the Danube to join the Bulgarian with the Romanian system.

The promotion of manufacturing and trade was also encouraged by the relaxation of banking regulations in 1893 and the subsequent expansion of the banking system, by the creation of chambers of commerce in 1894, the codification of commercial law in 1897, the opening of a grain bourse in 1907, and by legislation on trade-marks in 1904 and 1910. Cartels were formed in a number of industries and trades but these seldom lasted long enough to have any real effect.

The strategy of promoting native industry achieved some success. The number of factories in state-encouraged industries rose from seventy-two with 3,027 workers in 1894 to 345 with 15,886 workers in 1911, and from 1904 to 1911 the value of industrial production trebled. Between 1896 and 1911 home-produced goods as a percentage of total consumption increased from 13 per cent to 57 per cent, but in 1911 almost 90 per cent of the goods manufactured in Bulgaria were food or other products closely related to agriculture; the production of machinery and other advanced manufacturing techniques had hardly progressed at all. Industry also remained too reliant upon imported raw materials and semi-manufactured goods, in many cases because local products were not of a high enough quality for use in manufacturing. There was, in sum, no real attempt to coordinate the agrarian and industrial sectors of the economy, a failing which was acutely felt during the First World War when the enemy blockade cut off supplies of raw materials and fuel. By the end of 1916 over half the state-encouraged enterprises had ceased production, and of all factories only three in five were still functioning, mostly on a part-time basis.

Bulgaria's external trade expanded steadily for most of the post-liberation period and by 1911 was valued at a total of 384,000,000 *leva*, some 60 per cent above the level for the first half of the 1890s. Food and drink provided 77.17 per cent of the exports in the years 1896–90 and 79.5 per cent in 1907–11, with the main markets being the Ottoman empire and France up to the mid-1890s, though by 1911 France had been replaced by Belgium because larger quantities of grain went to Antwerp before re-export to Britain and other parts of western Europe. In the mid-1890s Austria–Hungary and Britain were the main providers of Bulgaria's imports, predominantly manufactured and semi-manufactured goods, but by 1911 Germany had replaced Britain as the second most important source. During the First World War markets and sources of imports were confined to the central powers and neutrals such as Switzerland and Holland. The war witnessed a dramatic rise in tobacco as an export commodity. In 1909 it had provided 9.9 per cent of total export earnings; the figure was 70 per cent in 1917 when tobacco earnings were 40,000,000 *leva* greater than the total cost of imports. Wheat declined from 61.2 per cent of total export earnings in 1912 to 33.7 per cent in 1922.

The forty years following the liberation had seen the creation of a Bulgarian state. In addition to an army and a bureaucracy it had expanded education to the extent that in primary and secondary school provision Bulgaria was unrivalled in the Balkans, and in 1912 could mobilise an army whose literacy rate was 75 per cent compared to 70 per cent for Greece, 59 per cent for Romania and 50 per cent for Serbia. The Sofia Higher Institute or High School was established at the end of the 1880s and became the university in 1904.

The expansion of the governmental apparatus and the promotion of an economic infrastructure had raised state expenditure from around 20,000,000 *leva* in 1880 to 181,000,000 in 1911. Revenue could not keep pace with such an expansion and foreign loans were increasingly used to balance the national books. State and local authority borrowing rose by 70 per cent in the decade after 1900 with effective borrowing standing at 461,000,000 *leva* on the eve of the wars, although Bulgaria's per capita debt, 149.25 *leva*, was lower than any of its neighbours. The service of the debt accounted for about a fifth of state expenditure, much the same as the military and less than the amount spent on the economic infrastructure.

During the First World War the functions of the state expanded in Bulgaria as they did elsewhere. The various committees formed to regulate food and other supplies, however ineffective they may have been, acquired formidable powers. They could not only regulate prices, but by 1916 had become involved in production too, both in agriculture and in industry. The military-dominated Directorate for Economic and Social Welfare placed the entire textile industry under military control in 1916, and in the following year was responsible for 170 creameries, at least as many vegetable-drying plants, and a jam factory. It had also brought about a significant increase in leather production, and directed conscripted men and prisoners of war into work in the fields and in manufacturing industry. The Directorate also assumed some responsibility for housing, and in April 1918 froze urban rents at their pre-war levels. The country also derived long-term benefit from the hygiene and safety act of 1917, which established national and local health councils, which in turn brought about a number of improvements in sanitation and working conditions and did something to supplement the grossly under-staffed factory inspectorate set up in 1907.

Whilst the state apparatus was being built cultural activities continued, though they were no longer a major factor in the nation's political evolution, as they had been before 1878. For a decade after the liberation the national struggle was almost the only theme in Bulgarian literature, and for another decade after that it remained a predominant one. Amongst the major works in this area were Konstantin Velichkov's *V Tŭmnitsa* (*In Prison*), Zahari Stoyanov's three-volume epic *Zapiski po bŭlgarskite Vŭstanie* (*Notes on the Bulgarian Uprising*), and Pencho Slaveikov's poem, *Kŭrvava Pesen* (*Song of Blood*). Slaveikov, the son of the Liberal politician, Petko Slaveikov, is generally acknowledged to be Bulgaria's greatest poet, and is the only Bulgarian ever to have been recommended for a Nobel prize in literature (in 1912). Even his work, however, was overshadowed by that of Ivan Vazov, whose classic *Pod Igoto* (*Under the Yoke*) described in loving and graphic detail pre-liberation society and the revolution. *Pod Igoto* is the most translated of all Bulgarian works of literature, being available in the early 1980s in forty-nine languages. Vazov's talents were widely applied, his writings gracing Bulgarian prose, poetry and drama. By the 1890s post-liberation as well as pre-1878 Bulgaria was being subjected to literary examination. Vazov was again to the fore with his *Nova Zemya* (*New Land*), a sequel to *Pod Igoto* covering the years down to union with Rumelia in 1885, but Vazov seemed less at home with this subject than the earlier one and the most enduring work on Bulgaria after 1878 is to be seen in Aleko Konstantinov's stories about *Bai Ganiu* (*Gaffer Ganiu*), an uneducated and assertive but basically well-intentioned Bulgarian whose business plunges him into the sophisticated milieux of central and western Europe and North America, with predictably hilarious results. From the mid-1890s a more educated and less Bulgaro-centric school of writing appeared, associated with Krŭstiu Krŭstev, who edited the influential *Misŭl* (*Thought*) from 1892 to 1907. This new generation with its 'open gaze and clear brow' wanted to link Bulgarian literature more closely to that of the rest of Europe, and was more concerned with the individual than the collective either of nation or of class. Prominent members of this school of modernism and individualism were Stoyan Mihailovski, Petko Todorov, Petko Slaveikov, whose poetic genius could not be confined to writing of the national liberation struggle, and another author and poet of strong patriotic emotions, Peyo Yavorov. Symbolism also had its devotees in Bulgaria. Its chief advocate was Ivan Radoslavov, and from 1905–12 the journal *Nash Zhivot* (*Our Life*) printed poetry and prose from writers such as Kiril Hristov and Nikolai Rainov, whose works included *Bogomilski Legendi* (*Bogomil Legends*).

In addition to a flourishing and increasingly sophisticated native literature Bulgaria acquired the 'cultural infrastructure' of a modern state. The National Library was founded in 1879, and local copyright arrangements were made for it in the second half of the 1890s. Schools of fine art and music were opened, both of which became academies in the 1920s, and the Bulgarian Literary Society, founded in Braila, Romania, in 1869, moved to Sofia immediately after the liberation, becoming the Bulgarian Academy of Sciences in 1911. In 1880 the first professional theatre companies were established in Plovdiv and Sofia, but they did not enjoy the success that was to come to the *Sŭlzi i Smyah* (*Tears and Laughter*) company founded in 1892. It was from this company that the state-financed National Theatre Company was formed in the 1900s. The theatre was initially hampered by a lack of native stage directors and to some extent by a dearth of Bulgarian dramatists. Vazov was one of the first to step into the gap, and by the beginning of the First World War he was still the most performed playwright in the National Theatre; his nearest rival was Shakespeare, and in general the great European classics shared the stage with Vazov and other Bulgarian writers such as Yavorov, Petko Todorov and Anton Strashimirov. In fact, after 1915 Bulgarian drama never regained the heights to which these authors had taken it.

Perhaps it is not surprising that a nation with a strong tradition of introspection should not make a major impact upon world culture, but for the land of Orpheus music was somewhat slow in its development. The first opera by a local composer, Emmanuil Manolov, was performed in 1900, and in 1907 came the foundation of the Bulgarian Operatic Association, a private institution which was later to become the Bulgarian National Opera. Like its composers, Bulgaria's painters and sculptors achieved little renown outside their own borders, but artists such as Ivan Angelov, Ivan

Mrkvichka, the portraitist Tseno Todorov and the landscape painter Stefan Ivanov secured a justified local prominence.

Much had been achieved in the forty years since the liberation, and the measure of that achievement is that the state and the nation, despite the differences between them, were able to survive the impact of the First World War and the defeat with which it ended. But it was a close run thing.

3

Revolt, radical rule, repression and war, 1918–44

In an effort to staunch the flood of desertions and the collapse of military discipline which had followed defeat in the field, Ferdinand on 25 September released Stamboliiski from prison in the hope that the BANU leader might pacify the troops. On the following day Stamboliiski, together with fellow Agrarian Raiko Daskalov, the Broad socialist Yanko Sakŭzov, and general Savov set out for the rebel camp at Radomir. Stamboliiski seems to have been undecided as to whether he should join the revolt, but when he addressed the soldiers on 27 September he did try and persuade them to disperse. He failed. The following day they were again marching towards the capital and within hours Daskalov had put himself at their head. At the same time Stamboliiski, after appearing in the council of ministers to insist that he had had no part in the mutiny, was in hiding in Sofia intending to raise a revolt there to coincide with Daskalov's impending assault. That assault never materialised. Daskalov's army reached the outskirts of the city but was easily contained by a hastily assembled force of two German divisions and a Macedonian unit under the command of general Protogerov.

The Radomir rebellion had fizzled out partly because it was poorly led, but primarily because the major objective of the discontented troops – peace – had been achieved with the signing of the armistice in Salonika on 29 September. The willingness to engage in revolution was further weakened by the realisation that the allies would ruthlessly suppress any such action, and also by the welcome knowledge that they would insist upon the abdication of Ferdinand. On 3 October he left Bulgaria, and was succeeded by his son, Boris III.

The containment of the Radomir rebellion did not bring a restoration of stability. Food remained in short supply and the towns were fed mainly by wheat imported from the U.S.A. On the political front dissatisfaction with the old parties was increasing; the mandate of the Sŭbranie had expired and a coalition cabinet cobbled together in October 1918 could muster little respect. Only a general election could produce an administration which might pretend to legitimacy.

The elections were held in August 1919. The Agrarians, with eighty-five seats and 28.22 per cent of the total vote were the most successful party, but they failed to secure an absolute majority. Stamboliiski, who was asked to form a government when he returned from the peace 'negotiations' in France, immediately looked to the left for support. The Narrows, who had become the Bulgarian Communist Party (BCP) in May 1919, had been the second most successful party in the election, increasing their vote by 174 per cent compared to 1914, whereas the increase in the Agrarian vote had been 22 per cent, but the Communists refused to join with 'the Bulgarian Kerensky' and the petty-bourgeois Agrarians. The Social Democrats, as the Broads were now known, were equally unresponsive, though their attitude was determined less by an arrogance of doctrine than by an overt lust for power: they had learnt the lessons of Ferdinand's personal regime, and refused to join a government in which they did not control the ministries of war and the interior. Stamboliiski was forced therefore to turn to the right and on 6 October 1919 assembled a cabinet of five Agrarians, two Nationalists and Danev, leader of the Progressive Liberals.

The first act of the new administration was to arrest members of the Radoslavov cabinet and a number of prominent Macedonians, including Protogerov. A civilian rather than a soldier was appointed as minister of war in order to remove control of the army from the palace. Both these measures gratified Agrarian desires, but were also intended to signify to the allies that the *ancien régime* in Bulgaria had been discarded. Stamboliiski believed that once the allies had become convinced of this they would be prepared to consider relaxing the terms of the peace treaty, terms which he had accepted partly because he had no alternative and partly because he believed that, like the worst aspects of the treaty of Berlin, they could not remain in force for more than a few years.

The peace treaty with Bulgaria was signed at Neuilly-sur-Seine on 27 November 1919. Bulgaria was required to relinquish all territory occupied by her during the recent war, as well as a few areas on her western border with Yugoslavia. Thrace, too, was lost, though article 48 of the treaty offered a guarantee of economic access to the Aegean. The Bulgarian army was to be limited to 20,000 men and was to be a volunteer not a conscript force. Reparations were to be exacted. Yugoslavia, Romania and Greece were to receive deliveries of coal, livestock, railway equipment and other items, whilst a massive 2,250,000,000 gold francs were to be paid to the allies within thirty-seven years. The latter was an impossible burden, and, much in line with Stamboliiski's predictions, it was reduced in March 1923; 550,000,000 were to be repaid over sixty years and the remainder in a further thirty years. Between 1925 and 1929 41,000,000 gold francs were paid, a sum equal to the budget deficits of those years, before the obligation was again reduced and finally abandoned at the Lausanne conference of 1932. Territorial losses which totalled 5,500 square miles and involved the alienation of 90,000 Bulgarians were not great in comparison to the deprivations suffered by the other defeated states, and after Neuilly only about a million Bulgarians, or 16 per cent of the total, were left outside the boundaries of the nation–state, a figure which the Hungarians could envy. The treatment meted out to this 16 per cent, however, was sufficient to keep the flame of revisionism burning, and all Bulgarians felt deep resentment at the loss of the Aegean coastline and at the burden of reparation imposed upon them.

Immediately after the conclusion of the peace treaty Bulgaria faced an intense power struggle between its leftist factions. As the old regime crumbled, competition over who should inherit power intensified and finally came to a head in the great transport strike of 1919–20.

The background to this industrial unrest was that of deteriorating living conditions in the towns. Whereas the peasant who had survived the war found that he could now pay off his debts and that his living standard was certainly no worse than before the wars, the same could not be said of the urban worker or bureaucrat. The cost of living had risen by a factor of twelve since 1914, whereas wages had risen at only half that rate. The Communists fed richly on such material, and their image was enhanced by their anti-war propaganda, and, after November 1917, by their close relations with Russia. On 27 July 1919 they staged a massive and impressive demonstration on the streets of Sofia, which was intended to advertise their programme; the fierce repression of this demonstration arranged by the Social Democratic minister of the interior brought the Communists the added advantage of being able to castigate the Social Democrats as lackeys of the police. This useful ammunition helped the Communists to their spectacular success in the poll of August 1919, but they were also gaining strength at a formidable pace in the industrial sector, where their General Workers' Trade Union Federation had some 30,000 members, ten times the number supporting the Social Democratic unions.

The Communists were also helped by the fact that the Stamboliiski government could not fulfil the radical expectations which many had of it. Some substantial reforms had been enacted, including the eight-hour day for factory workers, but most urban radicals saw this only as a first step, and they became disenchanted when others did not follow. Stamboliiski himself had to return to France to complete the treaty negotiations, and he left his cabinet under the domination of Turlakov and Radolov, the least adventurous of his Agrarian colleagues. Nor could the Agrarians be certain of forcing through extreme measures without destroying the coalition government. At the same time there was always the fear that excessively radical policies might incur the displeasure of the allies, whose troops were to remain in Bulgaria for some months to come. Nevertheless, pressure for reform was rapidly building up. The workers of the towns were joined by civil servants and pensioners, whose income could not keep pace with the rising cost of living, and by former officers whose careers had been cut short by the reduction in the size of the army. The decline in their status and in their life-styles was more dramatic than that of any other group, and in November their representatives approached the Social Democratic trade union leaders with suggestions for a coup.

The trade unionists did not want conspiracy but they did not oppose direct action on the streets. A day of action was called for 24 December, and for the first time since 1903 both wings of the socialist movement were to take part. The government acted swiftly, banning public meetings and arresting a number of leading activists, but this did not prevent thousands of Sofiotes taking to the streets on the appointed day. A petition was presented but its demands were rejected, and two days later the railway and telegraphic workers struck and established a strike committee of three Social Democrats and one Communist. On 28 December a general strike was declared throughout the country.

This was a decisive test for the Stamboliiski regime, and its leader was not found lacking in resolution. He declared martial law and turned against the strikers all the forces he had at his disposal, including the army, the police, some allied troops, and the Orange Guard. This force, armed usually with clubs, had been recruited from BANU supporters in the early days of the regime, and was intended to counteract the semi-armed groups maintained by both the Social Democrats and the Communists. It was also intended to compensate for the reduction in and the changing nature of the army, for Stamboliiski feared that the new army would be both too small to be able to preserve internal order and too radical to wish to do so; a volunteer army would, said Stamboliiski, be raised primarily from the urban poor who would turn it into a socialist force. In addition to using open force the government also conscripted peasants trained in railway work during the war, deprived striking families of their ration cards, evicted some from their homes, and arrested their leaders, especially Communists.

Such pressure was unendurable, and on 5 January the general strike was abandoned, though the transport workers and the Pernik miners held out for another six weeks. The state had been too strong and the strikers' leaders had been far from united. The Social Democrats had joined less from conviction than from the fear that if they did not their standing amongst the working class would be even further eroded, whilst the Communists, many of them still closer in ideas to Kautsky and Plekhanov than to Lenin, were not prepared for a full scale revolution, and were frightened of provoking the government to yet greater measures of repression. Recent events in Hungary gave justification to such fears.

Stamboliiski, it seemed, had won the struggle for the inheritance of the old regime, and to sanctify his victory he dissolved the Sŭbranie and called a general election for 28 March 1920. It was in effect a contest between the Communists and the Agrarians. Despite, or perhaps because of the failure of the general strike, support for the Communists continued to grow, with membership of the party reaching over 36,600 in 1920, some 70 per cent higher than the previous year, whilst the party newspaper, *Rabotnicheski Vestnik* (*Workers' Gazette*), had a circulation more than double that of the next most popular daily. Not surprisingly, therefore, the Communist vote in 1920 increased by 52.96 per cent on the 1919 figures, represented 20.31 per cent of the total poll and brought the party fifty-one seats in the new Sŭbranie. The Agrarians did even better, not least because in December 1919 Stamboliiski had made voting compulsory in general elections and the entire peasantry had therefore been mobilised. BANU increased its poll by 92.06 per cent, garnered 38.82 per cent of the total vote and had 110 representatives in the new assembly. The Social Democrats meanwhile had lost a third of their supporters and had only seven deputies in the new Sŭbranie, whilst the remaining sixty-one seats were distributed amongst the established parties, twenty-three of them going to the Democrats. Despite BANU's impressive showing it was not enough to give Stamboliiski an absolute majority, and he therefore annulled the election of thirteen deputies on technical grounds. The seats, nine of which had been won by Communists, were not refilled. Stamboliiski thereby achieved an absolute majority of two in the assembly, but his use of intimidation at the polls and the disqualification of deputies afterwards showed that however much he might denounce the old parties he was not averse to borrowing their methods of operation. Such tactics inevitably dented the moral standing of his party.

The electoral victory of 1920 provided Stamboliiski with the majority he needed to drive through his programme of reforms, to prove that he was, in the words of James Bourchier, *The Times*' famous Balkan correspondent, 'the harbinger of a new era...the outcome of the transference of power from the political coteries of the towns, the office seekers and the parasites of the court, to the honest hard-working tillers of the soil, the bone and sinew of Bulgaria'.

It was only in 1918 that BANU adopted an official programme, the ultimate objective of which was to create an egalitarian society based upon private ownership of the means of production and the absence of the exploitation of one man's labour by another. The focus was primarily but not solely upon the peasantry. The party's, and especially Stamboliiski's vision, was of a society in which no peasant owned too much and none too little land, in which they lived in clean, modernised villages furnished with electricity, communications and recreational facilities and a developed educational system. Though private property was to remain the basic form of ownership – Stamboliiski had once described it as 'the motive force for work and progress' – individual proprietors were to help each other through the cooperative system, which was to provide credit, to store harvested crops, and to market produce. The cooperative idea was a fundamental aspect of Agrarian ideology, and was meant not only to provide material benefit, but, through that provision, to lead to the evolution of new forms of civic political morality and organisation. Stamboliiski's long-term vision saw a society in which all producers had voluntarily joined the cooperatives, and in which the latter had become so influential that they provided the basis for local government and administration. Cooperation was not only to provide a new form of local organisation, but could, it was felt, even lead to the merging of nation-states into a free association of peasant communities – a true peasant, or green, international.

Despite his parliamentary majority and widespread support, especially in the countryside, Stamboliiski did not have an entirely free hand. The payment of reparations forced the Agrarian regime into such unpopular measures as the requisitioning of the rare draught animals, which were desperately needed at home but which had to be handed over to the Serbs. The chaotic conditions bequeathed by the war were a further restraint upon Agrarian radical enthusiasm, not least in the social problems caused by the influx of nearly half a million refugees, all of whom had to be given shelter and food; an even greater embarrassment was the presence in Bulgaria of 36,000 veterans of Wrangel's defeated White Russian army. Nor could Stamboliiski entirely dismiss the political opposition in Bulgaria. He had not declared a one-party state, nor had he banned opposition parties or their newspapers; and the monarchy remained. The bourgeois parties maintained a steady stream of criticism and could always turn to the allies, or perhaps the king, if they felt themselves in real danger. The Communists, too, were far from being a *quantité négligeable*. In May 1920 they were accused of throwing a bomb into a crowd of school-children during the traditional St Cyril and St Methodius day parade, for which their party headquarters were burnt down, but this did not prevent them making an impressive showing in local government elections in October.

The Communists did not contest Agrarian action against what both parties saw as social parasites, such as the court, the legal profession, the merchants and the usurers. Civilian control had been established over all court appointments by the post-war coalition ministry, but it was not until the BANU government had been formed that action was taken against the lawyers, who had always been prominent in Agrarian demonology. Practising lawyers were denied the right to sit in the Sŭbranie, or on a local council, and they could not hold major public office. In addition to these limitations on their political activities lawyers were also excluded from the new lower courts which the Agrarians established. In these courts, some of which were to be concerned with nothing other than boundary disputes, peasants were to present their own cases and judges were to be elected by the local populace. The money-lender, by 1920, was a much less powerful figure in the Bulgarian countryside than he had been at the turn of the century, but to frustrate any reappearance of this particular parasite Stamboliiski's government insisted that the banks make funds available to the credit cooperatives on reasonable terms.

Like the money-lender, the merchant was an unwelcome middle-man who had no place in an ideal Agrarian world. In an effort to lessen the influence of the grain merchants and resurrect Bulgaria's devastated grain trade the post-war coalition government had established a government grain consortium. Backed by funds from the major banks, it was to set up grain 'centrals' to which peasants would be required to sell their surplus grain. This would then be stored until the optimum moment for its sale in the international market. Profits from these sales would in the main be shared between the primary producer and the consortium itself, with only a small proportion going to the banks. The consortium, however, was plagued by administrative difficulties and opposition from the bourgeois parties, who feared for the livelihood of the grain merchants, and more importantly from the allies, who were concerned that it might interfere with the freedom of trade. In September 1921 they intervened, forcing Stamboliiski to dissolve the consortium.

The major reforms introduced by the Stamboliiski regime were those concerning land redistribution and the compulsory labour service. Although Bulgaria had for long been a land of small peasant proprietors, there was, in the eyes of the Agrarians, still room for improvement in land distribution. In June 1920 they introduced a bill to establish a state land fund. The fund would consist of land confiscated from all owners, individual and institutional, who, according to the new bill, held more than was socially acceptable; the confiscated land would be redistributed amongst the landless and the dwarf-holders. The act allowed all holders four hectares of inalienable land, but for absentee landlords all land in excess of that maximum was to be confiscated. For those who actually worked their land the maximum socially acceptable holding was to be thirty hectares, with a more generous allowance for woodland and in mountainous areas or if the land were used to produce fruit and vegetables. If the family of the owner consisted of more than four persons it was to have five extra hectares for every member in excess of that number. Compensation was to be paid to the former owner in the form of treasury bonds and on a sliding scale which discriminated against the largest landowners. In an effort to prevent owners selling before the reform came into operation there were restrictions on land sales, but this did not prevent the more wealthy farmers, both before and after the reform came into effect, bribing officials and thus escaping the process of redistribution. The law for labour property of April 1921 closed many of these loopholes. It established a directorate of labour property in land which was to supervise the reforms, and the new act also widened the scope of the reform to include monastic lands not worked by monks. The second act further laid down that the dwarf-holders and landless peasants were to be allowed more generous terms for the purchase of land allotted to them. The Agrarian leaders had hoped that the land reforms would implement their treasured doctrine of 'labour property', that is, that the ownership of the means of production should be vested in those who worked them, and in the process it was hoped that some 230,000 hectares of land would be redistributed. When the Stamboliiski government fell in June 1923 only 82,000 hectares had changed hands; of this 60.44 per cent had come from private owners, 24.99 per cent from village councils, 10.22 per cent from the state, 2.96 per cent from monasteries, 1.26 per cent had been in dispute between communities, and the remaining 0.13 per cent had been forest land in state or village ownership. In 1926 only 1 per cent of land held had been acquired as a result of the reforms, whereas 15 per cent had been attained by direct purchase and 84 per cent by inheritance. After the fall of the Agrarian government some land was restored to former owners, but the general principle of a maximum for any individual was retained, although the allowance was greater than that of the 1920 and 1921 legislation.

The principle of a maximum holding was applied to urban as well as rural property. The post-war refugee invasion had placed severe strains upon the already hard-pressed housing resources of Bulgaria's towns, particularly Sofia. According to Agrarian legislation no family was to occupy more than two rooms and a kitchen, with an extra room for every two children over fourteen. Office space was also subject to restriction, and in the case of both domestic and office accommodation commissioners acting on behalf of the ministry of the interior had extensive powers to enforce the new and widely resented regulations. A second and more popular response to the housing shortage, and one much in conformity with Agrarian philosophy, was to encourage the building of new apartment blocks cooperatively financed and thereafter owned by their inhabitants. This reform survived the fall of the Stamboliiski regime and cooperative building continued throughout the inter-war period.

Perhaps the most startling of Stamboliiski's reforms was the compulsory labour service. Introduced in June 1920, it was another application of the cooperative idea, this time in the arena of communal work. The scheme required all males between the ages of twenty and forty to perform a total of eight months' labour and to be available for further work, if needed, until the age of fifty. Unmarried women between sixteen and thirty were to work for four months. The *trudovatsi*, those involved in labour service, were put to work building roads, railways, bridges, schools, etc., and a number of industrial enterprises were also founded on such labour, most of them producing uniforms and other goods for use by the service itself. The compulsory labour service was unpopular with the old parties and their supporters, the more so as the original act of 1920 prohibited the purchasing of exemptions. For the allies the institution was suspect because of its military appearance. Not only did the *trudovatsi* wear uniforms, but they were organised into units which bore military names, and the first director of the compulsory labour service was a general. The suspicion that this 'labour army' was being used to circumvent the peace treaty's restrictions upon the size of the army rapidly gained ground. Though this was probably misplaced, for the Orange Guard was much more an alternative military force than the labour army, the allies intervened once more, and in October 1921 the Stamboliiski government was forced to modify the scheme, one modification being to allow the purchase of exemptions.

The major reforms of the land redistribution and the compulsory labour service did not exhaust the Agrarians' reforming energies. A progressive income tax was introduced; dwarf-holders who benefited under the redistribution of property were frequently required to consolidate their existing strips into one compact plot before they were allowed to purchase extra land, and in 1921 there was legislation to encourage more commassation – again these reforms were continued by later administrations. The government was also anxious to encourage greater crop diversification and to promote the use of better strains of seed and cattle. At all times the cooperatives were favoured. Peasants were not required to join them but were encouraged to do so, and cooperatives were extended into as many areas of production and marketing as possible.

The Agrarians had always called for the expansion of education, especially in rural areas, and for more vocational schools. They therefore made secondary schooling compulsory and built 300 new elementary schools and over 800 pro-gymnasia. The vocational content of all teaching increased, especially in rural areas, whilst, at the same time, the government attempted to eliminate both the official jingoistic teaching and the unofficial Marxist indoctrination which had been the hallmarks of much Bulgarian schooling under the old regime. To cleanse the teaching profession the Agrarian minister of education, Omarchevski, first sacked all known Communists and then made teachers' jobs subject to confirmation by a plebiscite every four years. At a higher level the Agrarians added faculties of agronomy, veterinary science and medicine to Sofia university, and created new higher academies for forestry and commerce. Their record in education is amongst the greatest of the Agrarians' achievement.

Stamboliiski's foreign policy was every bit as radical and controversial as his domestic reforms. It had been assumed before 1918 that Bulgaria had to have the patronage of a great power if she were to be able to pursue her territorial objectives in the Balkans. Stamboliiski abandoned the notion of territorial expansion, which in the past had provided the justification for the standing army, the large military budgets, conscription, the officer caste, the monarchy and much else that he thought was wrong with pre-Agrarian Bulgaria. In abandoning the objective of territorial expansion Stamboliiski dispensed with the need for a great power patron. In this he was lucky, in that what was desired fortuitously coincided with what was possible, for after 1918 Bulgaria could not have found a great power patron even if she had sought one. Austria–Hungary no longer existed, the United States and Germany either could not or would not concern themselves with Balkan affairs, Italy – until the advent of Mussolini in 1922 – was too riven by internal strife to be accounted a great power, and Britain and France were not yet prepared to champion the interests of a defeated state. Russia, like Italy, was hardly in a position to act as a patron to anyone, and in any case cooperation between Sofia and Moscow was impossible whilst Russia's peasants suffered under War Communism and

Bulgaria's Communists were repressed by their peasant government. Only after Lenin had introduced his New Economic Policy and Stamboliiski had victoriously concluded his duel with the Bulgarian Communists could stable relations with Moscow be contemplated, and even then Stamboliiski was suspicious of the Communists' international aspirations and much preferred to find partners in the green international of fellow peasant leaders in Poland, Czechoslovakia, Croatia and Romania.

If Stamboliiski had abandoned the notion of territorial expansion, he did not neglect Bulgarian interests. In 1920 he embarked on a tour of Europe which took him to London, Paris, Brussels, Prague, Warsaw and Bucharest, after which Bulgaria became the first of the defeated states to be admitted to the League of Nations. Thereafter he pressed in that body for implementation of article 48 of the treaty of Neuilly concerning economic access to the Aegean, and for greater security for the Macedonians under the League's minority protection treaties.

Within the Balkan context the most important feature of Stamboliiski's foreign policy was his determination to establish friendly relations with the triune kingdom (Yugoslavia). This was in part because he knew that friendship with his western neighbour was essential if any progress were to be made towards a Balkan, and preferably a Balkan peasant federation. The difficulty was that Stamboliiski could only convince his critics of the wisdom of this policy if it secured some concessions for the hard-pressed pro-Bulgarian elements in Macedonia; Stamboliiski stood in relation to Belgrade in the same position which Stambolov had occupied *vis-à-vis* Constantinople. But in Stamboliiski's case he faced an internal Macedonian lobby which was both more embittered and more powerful. In Sofia Macedonian extremists were vociferous and numerous; by 1934 Macedonian and Thracian refugees, excluding their children born in Bulgaria, would account for 11 per cent of the capital's population. The Macedonian activists resorted to frequent acts of violence against their opponents within and without the Macedonian fraternity, and IMRO mounted numerous raids into Yugoslav territory, most of them being launched from the 'no-go area' which the organisation had established around Petrich where the Bulgarian, Greek and Yugoslav borders meet.

The Macedonian zealots bitterly opposed any improvement in relations with Belgrade. Belgrade refused to contemplate better relations with Bulgaria until measures had been taken against the Macedonians. Stamboliiski had to choose therefore between, on the one hand, indulging the Macedonians and forsaking better relations with Yugoslavia, or, on the other, winning Yugoslav approval by cracking down on the Macedonians. He chose the latter, and in May 1921 sent to Belgrade his minister of the interior, Alexandŭr Dimitrov, who assured the Yugoslavs that the Bulgarian government did not support the terrorists and would take energetic steps to contain them. He was as good as his word. Having been made minister of war on his return to Sofia, he purged the army and the frontier police of their leading IMRO sympathisers and set up a federalist movement whose object was to compete with and infiltrate IMRO. (In October he was murdered.)

Yugoslav attitudes were further softened by the advent of Mussolini, which presaged the more vigorous assertion of Italian claims on the Adriatic coast. In November 1922 Stamboliiski was at last received in the Yugoslav capital, where he denounced the Macedonian extremists, declaring them responsible for all Bulgaria's misfortunes, including the second Balkan war. In March 1923 came the Nish convention by which Yugoslavia and Bulgaria agreed to cooperate in the containment of the extremists, and in the following month in Bulgaria all terrorist organisations were declared illegal, their publications suspended, and their leaders arrested and confined to camps in the east of the country. A special force was also set up to combat IMRO in the Petrich district.

THE FALL OF STAMBOLIISKI AND THE SEPTEMBER REVOLT, 1923

The *rapprochement* with Yugoslavia and the explicit rejection of expansionism were naturally unpopular in Macedonian and chauvinist circles, but they were only two of a number of aspects of Agrarian rule which excited discontent. From the very beginning of the Agrarian government there had been complaints of corruption on a gargantuan scale. Stamboliiski argued that his party had not had time to train a leadership cadre sufficiently large to fill all the administrative posts which the spoils system made vacant in 1919, and the established parties were not willing to cooperate by seconding trained officials to help the new regime. Untrained and careerist elements therefore had to be recruited into the administration.

The urban workers found little to convince them of the virtues of Agrarian rule. The Communists derided the land reform as a fraud and wrote off the compulsory labour service as a return to feudalism. Whilst urban living costs increased – inflation had reduced the *leva* to a seventh of its 1919 value by the end of Agrarian rule in 1923 – Stamboliiski had not, it was argued, done anything to prevent the exploitation of factory workers, to limit speculation, or to impose punitive taxation on wealth and luxuries; and he had done nothing to diminish the economic power of the bourgeoisie, though such accusations discounted the effect upon the merchants of the grain consortium and the impact on more wealthy townsfolk of both the limitation of rooms per family and the promotion of cooperative housing in Sofia. On the political front, the government's action against the transport strike of 1919–20 could not be forgotten and continued government action against the Communists kept the memory alive.

Like the workers, the civil servants – who formed another large element of the urban population – suffered from inflation. They also had other causes for complaint. The Agrarian government was inclined to circumvent the existing and at times obstructive administrative machine and rely rather upon party institutions. This was seen in recourse to the Orange Guard rather than the police or the army, and in the use of local party organisations, *druzhbi*, to work out the details of the land reforms; even the re-election of teachers was meant to put them under the influence of the local party *druzhbi*.

In reducing the size of the army the treaty of Neuilly had added yet another discontented element to Bulgaria's towns. Formerly proud members of a privileged caste, many officers had been forced to abandon their careers, and live either on pensions whose value was constantly depreciating or by taking up menial and demeaning jobs. Even those officers who managed to retain their commissions felt bitter, not only at the restriction of promotion prospects in the smaller army, but also because the Agrarians displayed an open contempt for the military and did not even maintain the army at the level permitted by the Neuilly treaty. The formation of the Military League in 1922 was an indication of solidarity amongst the soldiers and presented a long-term threat to the Stamboliiski regime, for the officers had the crucial qualities lacking in most opposition politicians: training, organisation, discipline and cohesion. Were the throne or the existing parties able to provide sufficient leadership and sense of political purpose they might secure the support of the officers and the Military League. Such a fusion of civilian and military virtues could generate formidable opposition to the Stamboliiski regime.

The soldiers were not the only discontented profession. The lawyers repaid Agrarian hostility and suspicion in handsome measure; journalists complained of censorship and intimidation; the medical profession quaked at Agrarian talk of dispersing doctors and ancillary personnel throughout rural Bulgaria. The teachers' grievances followed from Agrarian efforts to rid their profession of Communist influence, whilst at the apex of the education system the university and the government were in bitter dispute. The minister of education, Omarchevski, tried to limit socialist influence in institutions of higher learning. This the academic community resented as an attack upon the university's autonomy and upon academic freedom, and in the spring of 1922 the university was closed following strikes by its faculty members. Even the Academy of Sciences was at loggerheads with Omarchevski, this time over his almost obsessive determination to reform the Bulgarian alphabet by deleting two redundant but uniquely Bulgarian letters; the change was not in the event made until after the Second World War. The church too found reason to complain. Stamboliiski was an avowed free thinker and made no gestures towards religious belief. His government also reduced the amount of religious education in state schools, moved the Holy Synod to Rila so that its Sofia headquarters could be turned into an agronomic institute, and turned over some of Rila's property to an Italian commercial concern.

An entirely new feature in the Bulgarian political landscape in 1919 was formed by General Wrangel's 36,000 White Russians, almost half of whom were well-equipped with rifles and machine guns. They represented by far the largest armed force in the land, and it was not one well-disposed towards Stamboliiski, whom it saw as a dangerous radical hardly distinguishable from the Bolsheviks. Moreover, many wrangelist officers had had military experience in the Balkans before 1914 and therefore knew many of the pre-1914 political and military leaders. The danger to Stamboliiski was clear and in April 1922 he moved to neutralise it. Using somewhat questionable evidence he arrested a leading wrangelist on charges of conspiracy against the government. Other arrests followed until some 150 officers had been expelled, and in May the force was disbanded. His success against the wrangelists enabled Stamboliiski to parry some criticism from the left but it did not remove all the threats to his power.

Stamboliiski's position would have been strengthened if he had been able to rely upon a totally united, disciplined and faithful party, but for most of his period in office this was a luxury he did not enjoy. To his left Raiko Daskalov led a more radical group, whilst a new faction formed on the right under Turlakov and Tomov. In the face of increasing political discontent this group favoured more cooperation with the old established Sŭbranie parties. Turlakov had in fact attempted to seize the leadership from Stamboliiski when the latter was ill in 1921, and in March his group was strengthened when it was joined by Omarchevski. The opposition factions were, however, mainly confined to the leadership circles, and in the party congress of May 1922 they found almost no support amongst the rank and file.

By the spring of 1923 the weaknesses in Stamboliiski's position were more real than apparent. His regime had begun with a struggle against the left which had preoccupied him in 1919 and early 1920, after which he had for two years felt secure enough to concentrate on his reforming programme. In 1922 he set about the defeat of the right, dealing first with the wrangelists and later once again with the Macedonians.

Earlier in that year he had lifted the state of siege imposed during the transport strike of 1919–20. Immediately a new opposition paper, *Slovo* (*Word*), appeared, to voice the opinions of a new amalgam of bourgeois parties. These had formed the Constitutional Bloc but had realised that a grouping of old Sŭbranie parties would have little popular appeal, and therefore the Bloc had been aligned with the newly-formed Naroden Sgovor (National Alliance), which linked party politicians with members of the professions, especially academics, and the Military League. The National Alliance was itself an exclusive organisation of *prominenti* and never numbered more than forty-eight, but its existence was the first step in the galvanising of the demoralised right of Bulgarian politics.

In August 1922 one of the leaders of the National Alliance, Atanas Burov of the Nationalist party, announced that his followers would stage three large meetings, the first in Tŭrnovo on 17 September, the second in Plovdiv on 1 November, and the final one (imitating recent events in Italy) to take the form of a huge march on Sofia a fortnight later. The government's response was to mobilise the Orange Guard in Tŭrnovo and to call for a congress of sugar-beet growers to meet in the ancient capital on the same day as the National Alliance's rally. The scene was set for a confrontation between the government and the right. After addressing a large gathering of supporters in Sofia on 16 September the leaders of the Constitutional Bloc boarded the night train for Tŭrnovo. They did not arrive. Before they reached the city they were taken from their places, and, but for the intervention of a leading Agrarian politician who was also on the train, would have been executed on the spot. For their own protection they were placed in Shumen gaol; meanwhile the Orange Guard had taken possession of Tŭrnovo. The government then banned all public meetings. It was now clear that Stamboliiski would if necessary use force, that the prospects of a constitutional resolution of the differences between his regime and the right were minuscule or non-existent. The National Alliance, its leaders imprisoned and its followers forbidden to foregather for meetings or demonstrations, seemed irreparably weakened.

At this point the Macedonians came to the aid of the government's opponents. Already much angered by the steps which Dimitrov had taken against them in 1921, they were driven frantic by Stamboliiski's visit to Belgrade in November 1922 and by his denunciation of them in the 'enemy' capital. IMRO had to respond. On 4 December 1922 it occupied Kiustendil. Stamboliiski replied by sending his war minister, Tomov, to the town but the latter could do nothing and had to sit passively by as IMRO leaders fulminated against and then passed death sentences upon the minister president and others who had shown signs of friendship towards Yugoslavia. This the government could not ignore and units of the Orange Guard were therefore sent into Kiustendil. The Macedonians retreated to Petrich and the Orange Guard returned to Sofia where it indulged in a bacchanalia of violence against the bourgeois parties and their property. So great was the destruction that the representatives of the allies sent a collective note of protest. A chastened cabinet attempted to parley with IMRO but the latter was completely alienated and expressed its contempt for the government by attacking Raiko Daskalov on 15 December. Daskalov was uninjured, but Macedonian outrages continued, and on 9 February 1923 an unsuccessful attack was staged upon Stamboliiski himself.

Stamboliiski took immediate note of this and moved to secure his own position. The first victims were his opponents within the cabinet, Turlakov, Tomov and Manolov, who were deprived of office and dismissed from the party. Having purged his cabinet Stamboliiski set about securing a totally pliant Sŭbranie. A general election was called for 22 April, but not before the electoral system had been reformed, with the end of proportional representation and the reintroduction of single member constituencies. The poll was not entirely free of irregularities, with Stamboliiski at one point threatening to confiscate the property of all peasants who voted Communist. There was still good reason to fear the Communists, for they had done well in the municipal elections in February when they had taken control of Samokov, Lom, Kalofer, Yambol, Nova Zagora, Gorna Djumaya and Dupnitsa (Stanke Dimitrov). In April, however, BANU benefited from the new electoral system, and with 53.92 per cent of the vote won 212 Sŭbranie seats; the Communists with 19.30 per cent of the poll had sixteen seats, one more than the Constitutional Bloc with 18.28 per cent of the total vote. The Social Democrats reaped only 2.64 per cent of the votes and had only two representatives in the new Sŭbranie.

In March Stamboliiski had concluded the Nish agreement which promised further action against IMRO, action which came in May with the outlawing of all terrorist organisations and the confining of many of their members to camps in eastern Bulgaria. This was followed by a purge of the administration, with Stamboliiski hoping if not to contain corruption then at least to limit criticism of it. A week later mass party meetings were held throughout the country to consolidate support for the government, with members swearing oaths on religious relics and the party flag to give their lives for the organisation. In the same month there were yet more arrests of Communists, these being prompted by the discovery of arms on a Soviet merchantman bound for Varna. The first days of June saw more action against the Macedonians after Stamboliiski had received letters threatening his life and informing him that his killers were already in Sofia.

By now Stamboliiski had, it seemed, neutralised his main domestic opponents, purged and disciplined his own party, and won notable success abroad with the lessening of the reparations burden in 1923. He did not hesitate to exploit this apparent supremacy. He declared that BANU would hold its next congress to coincide with the dedication of the new Alexandŭr Nevski cathedral, the construction of which had been interrupted by the war, and he also announced that a mammoth party meeting would be held in Sofia later in the year and that the city would be policed by the Orange Guard, a body he meanwhile reviewed ostentatiously seated upon a white charger. Such posturings fuelled the worst fears of his opponents. Since the clashes in Tŭrnovo no-one had believed in the possibility of a peaceful or a constitutional end to the disputes between the government and its critics, and now it seemed that Stamboliiski was building a personal dictatorship, and could, it was feared, use the forthcoming party congress to announce another round of radical social reforms and perhaps to declare a republic.

The very strength of Stamboliiski's attack on his opponents, both of right and left, had at last forced a powerful section of them into cohesion. Shortly after the elections of 22 April a conspiracy had been hatched to which the Military League, IMRO, the National Alliance and even some Social Democrats were party. There is little doubt that the palace was aware of what was afoot, though it is equally probable that Boris had no idea of the horrific turn which events were about to take. The conspirators knew that they could count upon the help of the army; they did not have much reason to fear opposition from the allies, and last but by no means least, they were rightly convinced that the Communists would not contest their action.

At 3 a.m. on 9 June 1923 the conspirators moved. Sofia was in their hands within half an hour, the entire bemused nation within a day or so. Resistance was strongest in the Pleven area, where for a short period local Communists joined the Agrarians, but orders from the BCP central committee in Sofia soon put an end to such cooperation. Stamboliiski himself went into hiding and was not found until 14 June. His ears were sliced off before his Macedonian captors cut off 'the hands that had signed the Nish agreement'; finally he was decapitated and his head taken to Sofia in a tin box. Stamboliiski was by no means the only casualty and many other Agrarians were arrested, the new government admitting to at least 3,000 detainees.

The amazingly rapid collapse of a government which could undoubtedly command the confidence of the majority of Bulgaria's peasants marked the victory of the town over the countryside. The defeat of the Agrarian regime came about partly because its supporters were for the most part unarmed and dispersed in small communities, whilst their opponents, though few in number, were well-armed, well-organised and above all tightly disciplined. Furthermore, the Agrarians had no allies. Stamboliiski had cracked down so hard upon his opponents of both left and right that none was prepared to support him; the Communists saw the struggle between the Agrarians and the plotters as one between two arms of the bourgeoisie, whilst the allies, although they approved of Stamboliiski's anti-Bolshevism and his foreign policy, were unlikely to lift a finger to help him because of his attitude over reparations and the grain consortium. In any case the allies were almost as suspicious of Agrarian radicalism as they were of Bolshevism. Stamboliiski himself may well have reached the point where he had done all that could be done under existing conditions. For further reform he would have to break out of the present political system, declaring a republic and breaking up the Tŭrnovo constitution with its guarantees of free political activity. If he did not act to give more reform, would his followers, and more importantly the party, tolerate such stagnation? Before he could break this deadlock his opponents acted with as little regard for constitutional propriety as Stamboliiski would have had if he had marched further along his radical path. There was, however, a terrible price to be paid for the events of 9 June 1923. The Macedonians were to have another eleven years in which to threaten, to kill and to blacken Bulgaria's name even in a decade when political gangsterism was becoming more the rule than the exception. The Agrarian movement was shattered. After the coup it fragmented and could never again, except for a brief and heroic interlude after the Second World War, be considered a viable alternative to whatever group held power. And the corollary of this was that as long as the majority of the Bulgarian nation consisted of small peasant proprietors that majority would never be reconciled to those who held political power. With the radical parties at each others' throats and the old bourgeois parties lacking any substantive popular support, it was in the long run the army and the crown which had become the arbiters of the nation's political life.

TSANKOV, LIAPCHEV, AND THE DEMOCRATIC ALLIANCE, 1923–31

The army, which had played so important a role in the coup of 9 June 1923, was deeply suspicious of the old politicians, and therefore the new administration was headed by Alexandŭr Tsankov, a professor of economics who also became minister of the interior. Support for the regime was provided by the Democratic Alliance formed by Tsankov and consisting of the National Alliance together with the Nationalists, Democrats under the leadership of Liapchev, Tsankovists, Radicals, the Military League and IMRO. A small group of Democrats headed by the party leader, Malinov, and a section of the Radicals under Stoyan Kosturkov refused to enter the Democratic Alliance, which lacked both social and ideological cohesion and served little purpose other than to guarantee the government a dependable majority in the assembly.

Initially Tsankov's regime attempted to win support through concessions. Land redistribution continued – indeed succeeding administrations redistributed more land than did the Agrarian government, although those in receipt of such land now had to pay more, and proprietors were allowed a more generous allocation of land if their holdings were 'modern and rational'. Support for the cooperatives was also continued by both Tsankov and his successor, Liapchev, both of whom also encouraged the Bulgarian Agricultural Bank to fund agricultural improvement. Urban Bulgarians benefited from the retention of the eight-hour day and from an increase in official salaries, pensions and disability allowances for the war-wounded, whilst refugees were given government grants. The right of workers to form associations was recognised and many of those sacked after the strike of 1919–20 were reinstated. On the political front the new government showed favour to all non-Agrarian groups, allowing them full participation in the Sŭbranie, ending censorship, and even releasing a number of Communists held in detention.

This truce was of short duration. In Moscow the Comintern had been angry at the passivity of the Bulgarian Communists during the coup of 9 June, and a change of policy was ordered. In August the central committee of the BCP therefore decided to reverse its line and launch an armed attack upon the Tsankov government. The date set for the rising was 23 September, but the government had received information of what was afoot and it therefore arrested a number of leading Communists and imposed martial law before the rising began. The revolt won widespread support only in the Plovdiv, Vratsa and Stara Zagora areas – in the latter because there was real cooperation between the Communists and BANU supporters – and by 28 September it had been suppressed. Its leaders, though well-trained in organising strikes, lacked experience in armed confrontation; they were not well-equipped with weapons, and with less than a month to organise the rising they were inevitably ill-prepared. The party had not had time to make the psychological adaptation to the change of policy by which the Agrarians were to be regarded as heroes and allies only weeks after they had been written off as a doomed section of the petit bourgeoisie. Some Communist strongholds (Sofia and Pernik were prominent examples) saw little action and no strikes, the railways were kept working by their Social Democratic minister, and subversive activity, as in the *haiduk* days of old, seemed to be concentrated in the hills and forests. Even more damaging, especially in Sofia, were the breaches of security before the rising and the lack of any support in the army. Finally, the rising was hopeless because had it seized power it was more than likely that the Western powers would have allowed the neighbouring states to suppress a Bolshevik government in Sofia as they had done in Budapest in 1919.

The September rising of 1923 provided Tsankov with the excuse to strengthen and change the nature of his regime and to pose in the West as the defender of Balkan virtue against Marxist seducers. In November he passed a defence of the realm act which banned terrorism and which enabled the government to use as much as, if not more influence than usual in the elections held that month. The government coalition of the Democratic Alliance and the Social Democrats won a comfortable majority of 58.96 per cent of the poll with 201 seats; the Agrarians could still raise 12.05 per cent of the vote and return thirty deputies, whilst the Communists in alliance with some Agrarians polled 8.17 per cent and took eight seats.

The Communists did not have long to enjoy their modest electoral success. On 1 April 1924 the party was banned and its property confiscated. The government also invoked the new defence of the realm act to end the right of association and to disband Communist trade unions, and on 18 March 1925 the eight Communists elected in 1923 were expelled from the Sŭbranie. The effect of these measures was to strengthen those elements in the BCP dedicated to violent action. This faction had first appeared in 1922 and had solidified after the Comintern's condemnation of the party for its pacific stance in 1923. After the failure of the September rising the old Blagoev faction was discredited, the new official leaders, Georgi Dimitrov and Vasil Kolarov, were in Moscow and therefore the *enragé* element at home increased in power. Its growing influence resulted in an escalation of violence culminating in the appalling outrage in Sofia's Sveta Nedelya cathedral on 16 April 1925. A huge bomb detonated in the roof of the building just before a state funeral service attended by the king, his cabinet ministers and high-ranking officers. One hundred and twenty people died but neither the king nor any leading politician was among them.

This atrocity provoked the most savage wave of repression that Bulgaria had yet witnessed. Martial law was declared, all organisations calling for revolution were proscribed, and thousands of people were arrested, one estimate putting the number of detainees, many of whom were patently innocent, at a minimum of 6,000. Many were never seen again and some of them, it was reported, had been fed into the central heating furnace in the headquarters of the security forces; on one occasion the authorities even resorted to public executions, but the effect was the opposite of that required and the disgusting experiment was never repeated.

Macedonian violence kept pace with that of the Communists and the government. In August 1923 Raiko Daskalov was murdered in Prague by Macedonians, and in 1924 a new complication arose when a call for cooperation with the Communists was issued by a splinter group within the Macedonian movement. Their manifesto, published in Vienna, was signed by Todor Alexandrov, general Protogerov and Petŭr Chaulev; the first two were killed in the summer of 1924, and although Chaulev survived until 1927 the introduction of more internecine strife in the Macedonian camp could only mean more insecurity and terrorism within Bulgaria itself. Meanwhile IMRO continued to maintain a virtual state within the state in Petrich and to carry out operations abroad which complicated Bulgaria's foreign relations. In October 1925 the Greeks actually occupied areas of south-western Bulgaria for a few days, for which the League of Nations later required them to pay 30 million *leva* in compensation.

Despite the vindication of Bulgaria by the League the government's savage repression was earning more distaste than approval. In September 1925 the king had told leading army officers that it was time that more relaxed policies were introduced, but as yet neither Boris nor the officers felt strong enough to act on this conviction. More substantial pressure came from abroad. By the autumn of 1925 Tsankov's government was in need of money, and attempted to raise a loan which was to be spent on the refugees in Bulgaria. This was an astute move. The refugees, it was argued, represented a deprived section of the population amongst whom Macedonian and Communist extremists would easily find recruits, and these extremists would in turn threaten the stability not only of Bulgaria but of the Balkans as a whole – and since 1914 Europe had known well enough what price it might pay for Balkan instability. If, on the other hand, the refugees were settled on their own land they would acquire a stake in preserving social and political stability. The League responded enthusiastically, but in London, where most of the money was to be raised, it was made clear that no loan would be extended to a government under Tsankov's leadership. In January 1926, therefore, Liapchev became minister president and Tsankov left the cabinet to become president of the Sŭbranie. The loan was then granted. It was to be used for draining marshes, irrigation, road building, etc., but only Bulgarian citizens were to benefit from it; thus the refugees would be required to renounce their official links with areas now under foreign jurisdiction if they were to receive grants to buy land. As a result of the loan some 669 village communes set aside land for refugee settlement, and though corruption did much to vitiate the scheme the refugee problem had eased slightly by the end of the decade.

Liapchev was more keen than his predecessor to open Bulgaria to foreign investors, especially the Germans, and in 1927 he negotiated another large foreign loan, the so-called stabilisation loan which was intended to alleviate Bulgaria's growing problem of coping with the costs of reparations and of previous loans. Liapchev also did much to lessen the severity of Tsankov's rule. A series of amnesties was enacted and many detainees released, whilst censorship was relaxed and the trade unions allowed to function once more. In 1927 the Communists were permitted to reappear under the guise of the Bulgarian Workers' Party (BWP), which rapidly and skilfully developed its own trade union and youth organisations. Liapchev's more tolerant attitudes did also mean, however, that the Macedonians – of whom he was one – were even more indulged than before.

In October 1927 IMRO incursions caused the Yugoslav government to close the frontier, and at home the killings of opponents and of members of rival factions continued with depressing frequency and openness. But it was not merely the murders that sapped public confidence, for the Macedonians demanded and received jobs, many of them sinecures, in the public sector, with over a hundred being employed in the Pernik mines alone; they also continued to levy exorbitant taxes within their Petrich enclave, and they even interrupted a performance of Shaw's *Arms and the Man* because of its unflattering portrayal of Bulgarian society and soldiery. At a much more serious level it was the Macedonians too who were responsible for the Marinopolski affair in 1930, which did much to anger the army. Marinopolski confessed that after horrible tortures at the hands of the Macedonians he had given false evidence against a senior officer, who was, on that evidence, condemned to death as a spy. The officer had been a leading critic of IMRO, and this public acknowledgement that

Macedonian irregulars had the power to remove hostile officers both impaired the army's public image and affronted the *amour propre* of the officer corps.

In addition to the seemingly endless problem of the Macedonians, Liapchev's administration was also faced with the great economic difficulties of the late 1920s and early 1930s. Bulgaria had a foretaste of the Great Depression when tobacco prices fell substantially in 1926. Nor was the country well-served by the pressure from Western financiers which resulted in its return to the gold standard in 1928; this move forced the government to cut back on pubic expenditure to support an overvalued currency, so that when the great economic crisis broke the opportunities for retrenchment were already much reduced.

Macedonian activities and economic depression undermined Liapchev's position, which had already been weakened by splits within the Democratic Alliance. The leader of his own party, Malinov, still refused to enter the Alliance, and Tsankov, after he left office, had placed himself at the head of the 'internal opposition', criticising Liapchev for his lack of firmness towards the Communists and the Macedonians, and for agreeing to the terms of the stabilisation loan. That loan also worried other members and supporters of the government; one minister resigned from the cabinet in protest and forty government deputies voted against the loan in the Sŭbranie. More tensions within the cabinet and the Democratic Alliance were generated over the post of the minister of war. Its incumbent, general Vŭlkov, an architect of the 1923 coup, had very close connections with the palace but had shown great indulgence towards the Macedonians. This became so blatant that his colleagues pressed for his resignation, but Boris refused to listen, whilst in the assembly itself even Liapchev's own supporters within the Democratic Party argued that ministerial appointments were the prerogative of the king and not the cabinet. Technically this was true, but it was on control of the ministry of war that Ferdinand had based his personal regime, and indications that this unwholesome animal might still be alive in the later 1920s angered and frightened many outside the Democratic Party. By 1930 Liapchev seemed to be losing control of the Sŭbranie and of the Democratic Alliance.

The Alliance was falling victim to the progressive parcellisation of party politics which affected Bulgaria during the 1920s and early 1930s. The Agrarians were amongst the first to suffer this indignity. Stamboliiski had forced a form of cohesion on his party, but with his murder the fissures immediately widened. On the left were to be found Obbov and Kosta Todorov, now in exile, and Petko Petkov, the son of the prime minister murdered in 1907 who was himself to fall victim to a Macedonian assassin in 1924. The left Agrarians, the Vrabcha faction, were eventually marshalled into some semblance of cohesion by Dimitŭr Gichev and G. M. Dimitrov, nicknamed 'Gemeto' ('the G.M.') to distinguish him from his Communist namesake. On the right wing of the Agrarians were Tomov, Georgi Markov, Nedialko Atanasov and Hristo Stoyanov. The Agrarians, with the influence which personal and regional factors had always exercised in the movement, were predictable victims of political parcellisation. This was not true of the Communists, with their tradition of obedience to the central committee, yet they too found it difficult to maintain unity and discipline. After the September rising the centrist leadership of Dimitrov and Kolarov had been opposed by the *Zvezda* (*Star*) group, which wanted to leave the third international and by the *Lŭch* (*Ray*) faction, which was even further to the right and adopted revisionist views on cooperation with other parties. On the other side of the leadership were the men of violence, the 'left sectarians', whose following grew during the Tsankovist repression until in 1929 they won control of the party; this they were to retain until the mid-1930s when the Popular Front doctrine demanded their conversion or, more frequently, their liquidation.

The bourgeois parties suffered even greater fragmentation and by 1926 there were, including the BANU factions, no fewer than nineteen identifiable groups within the Sŭbranie. An electoral reform obviously based on Italian experience gave an automatic majority in the assembly to whichever group secured most seats at an election. This produced a scramble to form new alliances in time for the poll of 29 May 1927. The BWP found other groups on the left who would join a 'Labour Bloc' whilst some Agrarians and Social Democrats formed the 'Iron Bloc'; both of these campaigned against the Democratic Alliance. The opposition did succeed in cutting the Alliance's vote to only 38 per cent of the total, but the process of forming these new electoral pacts had involved a good deal of back-stairs intrigue and bargaining. It had also caused yet more divisions within the parties, for in a number of cases one faction would accept a proposed alliance whilst another would resist it and therefore find partners elsewhere, and thus yet more parties would be formed. By 1934 the nineteen groups of 1926 had become twenty-nine. Since the end of the nineteenth century the parties had been held together less by principle than by allegiance to a particular leader, yet in the 1920s even that cohesive element began to weaken both because of the frequent realignments and because party leaders tended to commit their organisations to electoral or parliamentary compacts without consulting their members. By

1930 the general sense of disillusionment was so widespread and deep that even the annual budget was passed through an inquorate assembly. Party politics and the Sŭbranie had become all but irrelevant.

Disillusionment with the established system was seen in the excited reception given to a policy statement by Zveno (Link), in the summer of 1930. Founded in 1927, Zveno was a supra-party pressure group with little organisational structure beyond a newspaper of the same name, a small but élite membership, and an office in Sofia. Zvenari who were already members of a political party were encouraged to remain in that party and to influence it from within – this despite the fact that the Zvenari believed that most of Bulgaria's ills derived from the nature of its political life, where, they believed, party considerations took precedence over the national interest. Zveno feared that eventually the parties might coalesce into two implacably opposed federations of right and left, and hoped, before that came about, to convince the parties of the error of their ways and to persuade them to put country before party. It was also much in favour of better relations with Yugoslavia, and therefore called for action to discipline IMRO. This, initially at least, complicated its relationships with the palace. Its detestation of party politics, its centralism and its avowedly élitist, étatist and authoritarian attitudes did, however, mean that Zveno had powerful support in the army and the Military League, although both these bodies also had strong monarchist factions. Outside the ranks of the military Zveno's call for a 'new and competent supra-party authority', which would both send the politicians and the Macedonians packing and use the power of the state to promote economic growth, was one which found many receptive ears.

Zveno did not participate in political actions such as demonstrations or polls, yet its criticism of the existing political structure cannot but have played a role in determining the results of the election of 21 June 1931, though the impact of the Depression and the wave of strikes it occasioned in 1930–1 also had a profound effect on the voting. This election, for which proportional representation was reintroduced, was unique in inter-war Bulgaria and rare in the modern history of the country, for it was, like that of 1901, the prelude to rather than the consequence of a change in government. This was, however, the swan song of the Tŭrnovo system.

The election was called because Liapchev's ministry, though it lasted longer than any other between the wars, had finally lost control of the Sŭbranie. The collapse of its authority was caused by a typical squabble over the distribution of cabinet posts after which Liapchev found himself unable to stitch together another coat of many colours. In the elections the Democratic Alliance joined with a faction of the Radical Party, but they could secure only 30.7 per cent of the votes and seventy-eight seats, whilst the People's Bloc, consisting of Malinov's Democrats, Kosturkov's Radicals, some National Liberals and the Vrabcha Agrarians emerged with 47 per cent of the votes and 150 seats. The BWP joined with a number of local Agrarian groups and took 13.2 per cent of the votes with thirty-one seats, whilst the Social Democrats could scrape only 2.04 per cent of the votes and five seats; the Macedonians organised the return of the eleven deputies from the areas under their domination. After the election the Democratic Alliance fell apart, and in 1932 Tsankov and his supporters decamped whilst the military element of the alliance moved towards Zveno.

THE GOVERNMENT OF THE PEOPLE'S BLOC, 1931–4

The People's Bloc formed a ministry under the Democratic leader Malinov, who, however, pleaded ill health and gave way to his party colleague Nikola Mushanov in October 1931. The government consisted of a Radical, two National Liberals, four Democrats and three Vrabcha Agrarians; it was the last hope for the Tŭrnovo system and Bulgarian democracy. The Malinov/Mushanov Democrats, by remaining outside the Democratic Alliance, had retained as much respect as could now be afforded to an established political party, and the readmittance of the Agrarians to the governmental fold could mean that the wounds of 1923 might finally be healing, that the mass of the nation's peasantry might at last be reconciled to those who ruled them.

That this opportunity for a national healing was lost was not entirely the fault of the new government. Like Maniu's Peasant Party in Romania it came to office at the least favourable of moments, for its first and most pressing task was to try to alleviate the effects of the Depression. The contraction of the export market sent the price of primary produce tumbling, and the peasants therefore held back their surpluses waiting for the usual upturn in prices. This caused a shortage of goods in the cities which was made good only by the purchase of 5,000 wagons of food from Yugoslavia, at great cost to the nation's foreign currency reserves. When it was obvious that the decline in agricultural prices was not the usual cyclical downturn and that peasant purchasing power would not recover, the market for industrial goods shrank and anxious creditors attempted to call in their loans. The factories lost both markets and the chance of further credit. Unemployment swept through the cities and for those workers left with jobs wages fell by 27 per cent between 1929 and 1933. At the same time peasant *per capita* income was halved.

In the towns the Communists were the natural beneficiaries of the new social pressures. In the local elections of November 1931 the BWP achieved considerable success, and in February 1932 it won nineteen of the thirty-five seats on Sofia city council. The government's reaction was to declare that 'The capital of Bulgaria is not and cannot be Red', but it waited a year before invalidating the election of fifteen of the councillors; in April 1933 the same fate befell twenty-nine of the thirty-one BWP deputies in the Sŭbranie; the remaining two renounced their links with the party.

Despite popular, and particularly urban discontent, the government had attempted to alleviate the impact of the economic crisis. Debts had been reduced by up to 40 per cent and repayment periods extended, whilst some taxes had been cut and for the peasants there was an assurance that no holding of five hectares or less could be taken for non-payment of debts. In 1930 the Liapchev government had set up an official purchasing agency, Hranoiznos, to guarantee peasants a market for their grain. Other responses by the government to the Depression included encouraging the growth of more diverse crops with greater concentration on export commodities such as wine, fruit and vegetables. These measures did something to soften the impact of the Depression upon the countryside, which was also helped to some degree by its very backwardness. Many Bulgarian peasants could easily revert to subsistence farming, and if families which could produce virtually all they consumed except coffee and salt would not grow richer, neither would they be devastated by a contraction in world trade. And withdrawal into the self-contained village had excellent historical precedents.

If the peasants did not expect economic miracles from the People's Bloc government they did look for maturity and a sense of responsibility in the political conduct of their own leaders. This they did not find. The Vrabcha leaders indulged in the most unseemly disputes for office and influence. The worst evils of *partisanstvo* were now practised by those who had previously railed most vociferously against them, whilst the pace and intensity of self-enrichment amongst Agrarian leaders surprised even the Bulgarians, who were not unaccustomed to such sights. After eight years out of office it seemed as if the Agrarians were determined to make up for lost opportunities, and, squirrel-like, to garner riches for further political winters; they seemed more anxious to profit from the political establishment than to reform it, and their supporters were sickened and once again alienated from the existing system. Another disappointment for BANU sympathisers had come over the question of an amnesty for Agrarians in exile since 9 June 1923. This had been promised during the election, but before being placed on the statute book had been much diluted by the

Democrats. Those Agrarians who accepted the amnesty bill and thereby condemned 'Stamboliiski's true disciples' to continued exile were rejected by a group within Vrabcha, a group which emerged under the leadership of Gichev as the Pladne (Noontide) Agrarians, the name being taken from their newspaper. In fact this split, which increased the number of BANU factions to five, was unnecessary, for in 1932 the amnesty bill was amended to allow the return of the exiles. They remained only until 1934.

The People's Bloc government was unable to balance these internal embarrassments with successes abroad. Tsankov had accused Liapchev of placing Bulgaria too much under Italian influence by letting IMRO have such a free hand, and a similar accusation could have been levelled against his successor. The Macedonian problem also bedevilled attempts made between 1930 and 1933 to bring about some degree of Balkan unity. Bulgaria could never sign an agreement which sanctioned existing boundaries, and the other states would not sign one which did not. Each of the four conferences held in the early 1930s was wrecked by this problem and by disagreements over the question of national minorities. All that came of the conferences was a Balkan agricultural chamber, a Balkan chamber of commerce, a Balkan medical union, and fatuous agreements to recognise a Balkan flag and a Balkan hymn.

The most important diplomatic development in the Balkans in the early 1930s, the signing of the Balkan entente in Athens on 9 February 1934. stressed Bulgarian isolation. Yugoslavia, Turkey, Romania and Greece agreed to guarantee existing borders and admitted that they saw the threat coming not from any great power but from within the peninsula. As Albania could threaten no-one the signatory powers could have meant only Bulgaria. The alliance of the second Balkan war had been recreated at a time when the advent of a new regime in Germany signalled greater international instability than had been known for a decade.

The Balkan entente had come about because Bulgaria would not renounce revisionism. This it would not do for fear of IMRO's reaction. IMRO and federalist terror had continued unabated despite the fact that it had increasingly alienated Bulgarian public opinion. In 1932 an IMRO congress in Gorna Djumaya had voted for a change in the organisation's objectives: the goal was now to be independence not autonomy for Macedonia, a region which they defined as including Dupnitsa, Kiustendil and areas to within a few miles of Sofia, a ridiculous assertion in terms of both geography and politics. In June 1933 IMRO's leader, Mihailov, shocked Bulgarians by calling for an attack upon the Yugoslav embassy in Sofia, which he described as 'a nest of vipers'. To prevent such an attack the city was occupied by troops, an operation which proved surprisingly easy, effective and popular. Yet nothing more was done to contain the Macedonians.

By the summer of 1933 the People's Bloc had lost much of its previous standing, its political credit dissipated in sordid squabbles over the spoils of office and in craven cowardice in the face of the Macedonians. But where could responsible critics turn? On the left the Agrarians were split, the Communists would be suppressed and the Social Democrats were no longer an effective force. There were some new groups on the right. Even before 9 June 1923 Bulgaria had seen its first fascist organisation, Kubrat. A more successful fascist group appeared in Rodna Zashtita (Defence of the Fatherland), which included the usual fascist paraphernalia of parades, uniforms, salutes, and so forth, but like any Bulgarian political party it soon split. In fact the histrionic posturings of fascism did not suit the down to earth and somewhat phlegmatic character of the Bulgarians, and Rodna Zashtita and similar organisations of the 1920s excited more ridicule than respect, whilst those who were consumed by the passions of violence and extreme nationalism could already find a congenial political home in one of the Macedonian organisations. In the 1930s, however, a more serious fascist group emerged under Alexandŭr Tsankov. After his departure from the Democratic Alliance he founded the National Social Movement (NSM), whose uniforms and methods were copied from Hitler's. Initially Tsankov's group exhibited the characteristic dynamism of a young fascist movement and it attracted a good deal of attention amongst the urban intelligentsia; its ideology owed little to anti-semitism but stressed the need for a social and economic restructuring, in which capital and labour should be equal partners in the service and under the control of the nation acting through its natural expression, the state. But Tsankov faced insuperable difficulties in Bulgaria. As the man who had replaced the martyred Stamboliiski he could never win peasant support, and his oratory could not equal that of Hitler, for Tsankov could never quite shed the style of the professor, a major encumbrance for a would-be demagogue.

For those who found solace neither on the right nor on the left there was the traditional option of total dissociation from politics, and Bulgaria, like many other states in the 1930s, saw an increase in allegedly non-political movements. The most popular of these was Dŭnovism, a widespread sect with a typical 1930s hotch-potch ideology which included hiking, sun worship, voluntary nudism, communal camping in the country, and, it was whispered, free love. No such attractions were on offer from the YMCA. Receiving large sums of money from its parent body in America, it was able to stage a growth so rapid that it occasioned a severe dispute in the Bulgarian Orthodox church as to how far the established religion should cooperate with the expanding organisation.

THE COUP D'ÉTAT OF 19 MAY 1934

The march of events since 1923 had meant the destruction or self-destruction of almost all political groups in Bulgaria, whilst of the new forces Tsankov's movement was not ready and Zveno was not willing to seize the initiative. There remained only the army and the king. In 1934 the former acted.

The engineers of the coup were pro-Zveno officers led by colonels Damian Velchev and Kimon Georgiev, who had decided in November 1933 to put an end to the existing system. The implementation of this decision was prompted by yet another cabinet dispute over the distribution of office, although it was also provoked by fears that the king might use the newly-appointed minister of war, Vatev, to limit Zveno influence within the army. Further motivation was provided by growing fears for Bulgaria's internal political stability. In February the NSM had performed surprisingly well in local elections, and on 21 May its leader planned to hold a huge rally which at least 50,000 of his followers would attend; the rally was to coincide with a private visit to Bulgaria by Goering. Added to this sense of internal insecurity came details of the Balkan entente which had just become known in Sofia, and which had to be considered in conjunction with the London convention of July 1933, which had included in its definition of aggression the support of or the failure to take measures against armed subversive groups which operated outside the borders of the state. Velchev decided the moment had come to put the country out of the misery inflicted upon it by its discredited politicians. In an excellently planned and executed operation on 19 May 1934 his supporters took control of Sofia, and within hours the country was in their hands. Velchev preferred not to take power himself and Kimon Georgiev was nominated minister president.

The government brought to power on 19 May 1934 accomplished a great deal in its short term of office. In foreign affairs its first objective was to improve relations with Yugoslavia. Signs of a relaxation in tension between Sofia and Belgrade had been apparent since 1930, and Velchev did all he could to encourage further development in this direction. Exchanges of cultural groups were organised, and before his murder in Marseilles in October 1934, King Alexander both invited Boris to Belgrade and paid a return visit to Bulgaria. An extension of this policy was to seek better relations with Britain and France, and Velchev spoke of the latter replacing Mussolini's Italy as the great power upon whom Bulgaria would rely for support in international affairs, though he was careful not to alienate either Rome or Berlin. Another foreign policy initiative by the Velchev–Georgiev government was the opening of diplomatic relations with the Soviet Union in July 1934. Successor governments saw no reason to break with this innovation.

The improvement in relations with Yugoslavia was helped by action against the Macedonians, which was an important facet of the new regime's domestic programme. Velchev and Georgiev sent the army into the Petrich area and moved swiftly against the Macedonians in the rest of the country. It was an extremely popular and entirely successful operation. IMRO was not destroyed and later in the decade it could still stage impressive demonstrations and carry out spectacular assassinations, but the organisation was never again the power it had been before 19 May 1934; also, the vicious feuding between federalist and autonomist no longer disgraced the streets of Sofia, and terrorism ceased to be a constraint upon the conduct of Bulgarian foreign policy. The organisations which had taken at least 884 lives in the decade between 1924 and 1934 had been little more than associations of terrorists and gangsters, and their lack of social and political purpose meant that they fell an easy prey to Velchev's soldiers.

The political parties were attacked with equal vigour. The Velchev–Georgiev government dissolved them all, closed their newspapers and confiscated their property. The teaching profession was purged of Communists and all known opponents of the new regime. Government employees were no longer allowed to belong to trade unions, whilst in those unions which were still permitted officials had to be approved by the government, and no-one who had preached dislocation of the social order would be eligible for office in such a union. In 1935 the regime established the Bulgarian Workers' Union, a voluntary organisation which was to be the only permitted labour organisation; it soon attracted large numbers and by 1936 120,000 out the nation's 145,000 industrial workers had joined. The Bulgarian Workers' Union, although actually inaugurated by the succeeding government, was organised not on the basis of participation in a common production process but rather around the estates into which Zveno and the Velchev–Georgiev group divided society; much in imitation of the Italian model, the estates were workers, peasants, craftsmen, merchants, intelligentsia, civil servants and members of the free professions. This was one of a number of reforms of the 19 May 1934 government which were not rescinded after that government had fallen.

The estates were also to provide the basic units for a reconstructed Sŭbranie. The new regime had dissolved the existing assembly and transferred its powers to the executive, declaring that in future the central place in the parliament would be held by the professional or estate organisations, which were to fill three-quarters of the seats; the remaining quarter would be allocated to the 'political element'. At the same time civil rights were suspended. The Tŭrnovo constitution, though not officially abrogated, had ceased to function.

Velchev and his allies wished to rationalise the administrative and political structures of the country and to create an authoritarian, efficient and centralised state. These designs were clearly visible in the reform of local government, where rationalisation and centralisation were very much the guiding principles. The sixteen regions were merged into seven new provinces, with an eighth being added after the reacquisition of the southern Dobrudja in 1940; the 2,600 village communes were amalgamated into 837 larger units. Elected mayors were all dismissed and replaced by men appointed by the central government, and all new mayors had to have legal training or a civil service rank equal to that of officer status in the army. The elected local councils were to be replaced by new ones, half of whose members were to be nominated from above and half elected, with the local electorate being divided into the seven estates used in the organisation of the new trade union. The new mayors and nominated council members were all too frequently civil servants with few commitments to the locality other than to use it as a stepping stone to higher things or as a means to self-enrichment, and inevitably these 'Flying Dutchmen' became extremely unpopular. More serious was the fact that the Velchev–Georgiev regime was the first ever to dare to abolish the local councils, some of which went back to pre-liberation days and were held by many to embody the true democratic traditions of the peasant nation.

There was administrative reorganisation at the centre too. The economic ministries were merged into one unit, and this and other reforms led to the sacking of almost a third of the country's civil servants, most of whom were replaced by supporters of the new regime. In an attempt to rationalise the credit and banking systems the new government merged the Bulgarian Agricultural and the Central Cooperative Banks, whilst nineteen Bulgarian-owned commercial banks were amalgamated into the Banka Bŭlgarski Kredit (Bulgarian Credit Bank) in an effort to bring provincial banks under unified, central control.

The reforming broom swept into education with a programme designed
to put more emphasis upon technological subjects. This effort at modernisation did not enjoy conspicuous success, nor did another typical move in
the same direction: a competition to produce a new city plan for Sofia.

The vehicles through which the Velchev–Georgiev government intended
to purvey their ideas to the nation were the new trade union and the
Directorate for Social Renewal. This large public organisation was 'to
direct the cultural and intellectual life of the country towards unity and
renewal', and thus it was given great influence over the press, the theatre,
public meetings, and publication. It was also given the vitally important
task of organising and caring for the nation's youth, and it organised
lecture campaigns which attempted, with little success, to ignite the
populace with enthusiasm for the ideology of the new regime.

BORIS'S PERSONAL REGIME, 1935–9

Although the activities of the 19 May government were wide-ranging its
support was not. Part of Velchev's problem was that despite the careful
preparation of the coup itself and despite fairly clear ideas of what policies
were to be followed thereafter, there had not been a great deal of thought
as to how these policies were to be implemented, and how power, once
seized, was to be maintained. A major debate developed within Zveno over
whether the regime should create a mass organisation to sustain
governmental authority. Opposition to the idea was based on the fear that
it would lead to the rebirth of the party system, which had not been
entirely destroyed. The parties had been declared illegal and their organisations broken up, but most were so personalised that as long as their leaders
were in circulation they could easily continue a form of shadowy
existence. Another difficulty for the Zvenari was that there had been
insufficient consideration for the future position of the king, an issue on
which the Military League was divided, particularly when rumours began
to circulate that the republican Velchev intended to promulgate a new
constitution in which royal power would be much reduced.

Velchev, despite the skill with which he had contrived the events of 19
May 1934, was not an accomplished political intriguer, and in January
1935 he was out-manoeuvred by his critics and his royalist opponents,
who secured the appointment of the non-Velchevist general Zlatev as
minister president in place of Georgiev. From the monarchist wing of the
Military League to civilian government was but a short step, and by April
1935 Boris and his accomplices had removed Zlatev and replaced him with
Andrei Toshev.

When civilian rule was reintroduced on 21 April the king issued a manifesto declaring that the objective of his new government was 'to restore orderly and peaceful life'; this did not mean, the document continued, the abolition of all recent reforms or the complete rejection of the ideas of 19 May 1934, but the Directorate for Social Renewal was dissolved and there was a promise of a new constitution which would enshrine Bulgaria's national and democratic traditions. Toshev's functions were to devise such a constitution, to create a popular movement which would ensure support for the regime, and to contain the political ambitions of the soldiers. After much discussion of contemporary systems in Italy, Poland, Portugal and elsewhere two draft constitutions were prepared, but neither was found acceptable by the king or by Toshev's colleagues in the government. A similar impasse was reached over the question of a mass organisation. The minister president accepted the need to establish a national youth movement but he would go no further, believing that the best solution would be to include a few representatives from the Agrarian factions and from the NSM in the cabinet but to retain an essentially non-party system. His colleagues from the monarchist section of the Military League, on the other hand, wished to create a Bulgarian National Front of Agrarians and the NSM, a synthesis of the historic left and the new right. In dealing with the military Toshev was more successful, for Velchev, who had gone into exile in July, played into his hands by staging a clandestine return in October; but even this could not overcome the differences within the cabinet on the other issues, and in November Toshev resigned, to be replaced by Georgi Kioseivanov. A diplomat by training and a poker and bridge player by inclination, Kioseivanov was to remain minister president until early in 1940, his long tenure of office being primarily the result of his pliability.

When he came to office Kioseivanov was more specific and realistic than Toshev, telling a Greek newspaper-man that his function was to restore normality by removing the military from politics. To do this he exploited the Velchev affair. After his capture in October Velchev was accused of plotting against the king and the government. In February 1936 he was condemned to death, his life being spared by the use of the royal prerogative of mercy, which he, ironically, had wished to abolish.

The Velchev trial illustrated the dangers of military intervention in Bulgarian politics, and in March 1936 Boris and Kioseivanov seized upon it as an opportunity to dissolve the Military League and to dismiss or transfer a large number of Zveno sympathisers in the officer corps, after which the king, together with his minister of war, general Lukov, assiduously toured the nation's major garrisons.

The neutralisation of the army, though there was no guarantee that it would be permanent, had important effects. The coup of 9 June 1923 had eliminated Agrarian radicalism; Tsankov's repression had emasculated leftist extremism; the government of 19 May 1934 had crippled the old parties; and now it seemed that the army too had been removed from the political stage. Only the king was left as a factor of any importance. Yet Boris did not aspire to a royal dictatorship. It is sometimes alleged that he looked with envy upon King Alexander of Yugoslavia, who had assumed full control of his country in 1929, but if that were so then in the context of the political instability of Bulgaria in the early 1930s Boris delayed an unconscionably long time before acting. In fact from the removal of Velchev early in 1935 to the local elections of 1937 Boris groped and edged his way to a form of benign control, without ever fully knowing what type of political system would emerge. If he had a model, which is unlikely, it was more probably that of King Carol of Romania, whose careful manipulation of existing civilian politicians was much more in the pattern followed immediately south of the Danube. The 'controlled democracy' which evolved in Bulgaria was much the same as Carol's 'guided democracy'.

In 1936 Boris, like Velchev before him, faced the problem of how to consolidate power. The king sought the middle ground of Bulgarian politics, where he hoped to be able to defend himself against attacks from three possible sources: the left, the right and the army. The threat from the latter had not entirely disappeared, and Boris believed that as long as his army had, in his own words, 'no toys to play with', it would be tempted to dabble in politics, whereas if it were given modern weapons and a realistic prospect of furthering the nation's interests abroad its energies would be diverted into the proper professional channels. Until then the danger remained, and would be much greater if the army were to join with Boris's opponents on the right or the left. This was not an idle fantasy: in 1935 the Communists had boasted that they had established cells in almost every barracks in the land, and during the 1936 tobacco workers' strike in Plovdiv officers in the city's garrison threatened to support the strikers.

In his search for this middle ground Boris was hampered by the simple fact that no-one knew whether it still existed. There had been no election since 1931, and Velchev's muzzling of the press and dissolution of the parties had destroyed the means by which the mood of the public might be judged. Although his manifesto of 21 April had promised elections and consideration of constitutional reform, Boris could not tell how democratic he could afford to be; he and Kioseivanov were searching for a political security based upon what they considered to be the centre ground of Bulgarian politics, but they had to face the prospect that this treasured centre could have disappeared.

That this might be so was indicated in 1936 by an enthusiastic celebration of May Day, and by a spate of industrial unrest which, though not as violent as that in Greece, did mean that the number of working days lost in 1936 equalled the total for the preceding five years. 1936 also saw the promulgation of the doctrine of 'the Popular Front from below', by which the Communists hoped to create a network of apparently innocent committees – for example, that for the promotion of Esperanto – which they would dominate and upon which they would build social and political power. Even if recent purges within the Bulgarian and the Soviet parties dented Communist prestige and took the gloss off Dimitrov's heroic stance in the Reichstag fire trial two years earlier, the Communists remained a force to be feared. And the election of 1936 in Greece had shown that the Communists did not have to win a majority of seats to exercise dominance within a divided parliament.

The threat to the middle ground did not come from the left alone. Tsankov's movement was active in the cities, its self-confidence and assertiveness growing with every fresh Nazi triumph, and in the summer of 1936 its congress saw the adoption of new statutes which intensified the fascist nature of the organisation and made it a more serious contender for popular support.

Whilst the king feared that an election might return an assembly dominated by the extremes and outwith his control, the leaders of the established parties feared the opposite: that any assembly which the king might allow would be totally under his sway. The party leaders therefore called for the restoration of the Tŭrnovo constitution by constitutional means, a cry last heard in 1883, and attempted to move closer together in pursuit of this objective. In May 1936 the Petorka, or 'Five', was founded by leaders of the non-Malinov Democrats, the Social Democrats, the Liberals, a Radical faction, and the non-Pladne Agrarians. Later Malinov, the Pladne Agrarians and – in obedience to the Popular Front doctrine – the Communists joined the group which became known as the People's Constitutional Bloc.

Boris too had seen the advantages of coalitions, and in the early months of 1936 had explored the possibility of a government bloc based upon the Tsankovites and Gichev's Pladne Agrarians. These explorations had led nowhere, for to the Agrarians Tsankov would always be the murderer of Stamboliiski, and Tsankov was not prepared to submit to royal domination. Lukov, Boris's minister of war, favoured a quick election and then the founding of a mass pro-government party crystallised around the Tsanko-vite movement (but not under its present leader), but this Boris rejected in favour of the policy advocated by Kioseivanov: that there should be no immediate attempt to move back towards an assembly dominated by party organisations, that the promised election should be postponed, and that the constitution should be gradually modified rather than reformed. He defined this as the road of 'slow though steady progress'.

The local elections of January 1937 formed the first milestone along this road. This was an occasion to test the new electoral regulations which were the first of the projected modifications of the constitution. Before the poll candidates had to attest in writing that they were not Communists; the voting was to be staggered over three separate Sundays so that police could be concentrated where they were needed; later the franchise was widened allowing married women and widows to vote for the first time; and educational qualifications were introduced with rural voters having to have had primary and the urban electorate secondary schooling. For men, but not women, voting was to be compulsory. The government was not, said its apologists, opposed to democracy but wished to create 'a tidy and disciplined democracy imbued with the idea of social solidarity'. This necessitated the continued ban on party organisations but large social movements would be allowed to emerge later when 'the soul of the people is completely healed'.

In March of the following year these regulations were applied to the first general election held since 1931. Also the new Sŭbranie was to consist of only 160 deputies; proportional representation was once more discarded in favour of single-member constituencies, whose boundaries were determined by government officials who lost few opportunities for gerrymandering. The minimum age for election to the assembly was raised from twenty-five to thirty. Though political parties had remained illegal the leaders of the People's Constitutional Bloc had fought a reasonably unified campaign on the slogan of the restoration of the Tŭrnovo constitution. The government argued that it was working for a 'new democracy' devoid of parties, and that as proof of its good intent the election of 1937 was the first in which the government did not have its own party and its own candidates. That did not prevent the use of influence on the part of the government, which thereby secured the return of about ninety-five of its own supporters, but the Bloc had over sixty deputies, though five Communists and six Agrarians were soon to be expelled. Clearly the new assembly would be dominated by the government, but it was by no means entirely quiescent, and in the autumn of 1939 so disturbed Kioseivanov's peace of mind that he dissolved it and went to the country. In the elections of December 1939 and January 1940 only ten days were allowed for campaigning, and non-government candidates were placed under various restrictions, including prohibitions on their travelling between villages, and upon their having assistants during the campaign. Kioseivanov secured the expected easy victory and was promptly dismissed.

His departure was not the result of his conduct of internal affairs but was a consequence of his attitudes towards foreign policy, the issue which by 1940 naturally dominated political life in Bulgaria as elsewhere. And foreign policy was an area where Boris's control was absolute.

FOREIGN POLICY, 1935–41

After the fall of Stamboliiski the immediate objective of Bulgarian foreign policy was to escape from isolation; alleviation of the peace treaty terms had not been forgotten, but this was to be achieved by 'peaceful revisionism' based upon article 19 of the League of Nations charter. Such a policy demanded a foreign patron, and this both Tsankov and Liapchev found in Italy, which could not only act as a protector in the League but would also turn a blind eye to the government's clandestine links with IMRO, for Mussolini was by no means averse to increasing Yugoslavia's difficulties. The close ties with Italy were symbolised by Boris's marriage to an Italian princess in 1930. Despite Italian sponsorship the 1920s saw little advance in the Bulgarian cause. A treaty of friendship was signed with Turkey in 1925, but as Atatürk's regime was as yet insecure and internationally without influence this was no great gain. The liquidation of disputes with Greece over the property rights of refugees, on the other hand, helped to dispel the bitterness left by the invasion of 1925, thus making relations with Athens correct if cool.

At the beginning of the 1930s important changes took place in Bulgaria's foreign policy alignments. In Rome there were distinct signs that Italy was becoming less interested in Bulgaria and paying more attention to Greece and Yugoslavia, a development which reawoke fears of isolation in Sofia. This encouraged efforts to improve relations with the neigbouring states. In 1932 the Romanians agreed to allow the teaching of Bulgarian in schools in the Dobrudja if Bulgaria permitted Romanian to be a subject of instruction in various Bulgarian schools. This was as far as matters could be taken with the Romanians, but prospects with regard to Yugoslavia appeared better. In 1930 the Pirot agreement regulated passage over the frontier and settled a number of problems concerning property rights. In September 1932 Kings Boris and Alexander met for the first time and a second encounter was soon arranged.

Bulgarian hopes of escaping isolation by forming closer relationships with her neighbours received a sharp setback when Yugoslavia, Romania, Greece and Turkey signed the Balkan entente in 1934, and the severity of this blow was increased by the fact that the League of Nations, in which Bulgaria had hoped to find support and succour – as it had at the time of the Greek invasion in 1925 – was in obvious and rapid decline after the withdrawal of Germany in October 1933. 'Peaceful revisionism' would offer little chance of success without a strong and respected League.

As Bulgaria could neither join nor destroy the Balkan entente it attempted to circumvent it by coming to an agreement with Yugoslavia. As a measure of his earnestness Kioseivanov in 1936 reaffirmed Bulgaria's commitment to peaceful revisionism, and as proof of this he banned all demonstrations calling for the destruction of the Neuilly settlement. The Yugoslavs were pleased to be courted. They had never been entirely happy at the exclusion of Bulgaria from the Balkan entente and had been positively disturbed by the aggressive interpretation put upon that agreement by the Greeks. Yugoslavia knew that an isolated Bulgaria would be easy prey to one of the two great-power blocs into which Europe was becoming increasingly polarised. The murder of King Alexander in Marseilles in October 1934, despite Macedonian involvement, did not impede efforts to improve Bulgaro-Yugoslav relations; in 1935 Zlatev was able to conclude an agreement increasing the number of frontier crossing points, and so bright did the prospects appear by the middle of 1936 that Boris would accept neither an offer of closer ties with Turkey, which was anxious to revise the regimen in the Straits, nor an approach from the Balkan entente itself; in January 1937 his patience was rewarded with the signing of the Bulgaro-Yugoslav pact of friendship.

The signing of the pact was an important symbol of changed attitudes but it made little real difference to inter-Balkan relationships. It was no more than a declaration of friendship, although the Bulgarians hoped that it might create a better atmosphere which might in turn lead eventually to revision through peaceful means. Initially such hopes appeared justified. Cultural exchanges between the two countries increased, frontier regulations were relaxed, and a joint Bulgarian–Yugoslav cooperative institute was established, as was an air link between the two capitals.

In the late 1930s, however, the relations between smaller states were becoming less important in view of the developing confrontation between Germany and the Versailles powers. Inevitably the great powers sought to intervene in the Balkans to seek support for themselves, or at least to deny it to their foes. By early 1938 the British were pressing for the inclusion of Bulgaria in the Balkan entente, and in July of that year came an apparently significant step in that direction when the Balkan states, in the Salonika agreements, pledged themselves to abjure the use of force; such is the way of international politics that it was taken as proof of their earnestness in this regard when they further agreed that Greece should remilitarise Thrace and that the Bulgarians should be allowed to disregard, as they had for some time been doing, the military restrictions imposed upon them at Neuilly. The Munich settlement caused a further shifting of alignments in the Balkans. The Yugoslavs lost the security of the little entente, which the dismemberment of Czechoslovakia wrecked, and therefore moved yet closer to Bulgaria. In October the two premiers met at Nish, where the Yugoslavs offered a customs union, a military alliance and the return of some frontier districts in return for Sofia's renunciation of all claims upon Macedonia; even though Kioseivanov rejected the proposed exchange there was no doubting the better relations between Sofia and Belgrade.

At the outbreak of war in September 1939 Bulgaria immediately declared its neutrality. There were those, especially in Germany, who believed that King Boris inclined towards Britain, both sentimentally and because he believed it would win, but there were powerful factors pushing Bulgaria towards the axis camp. During the 1930's Germany had played an increasingly important role in Bulgaria's trade, and commercial reliance on the Germans, especially for arms, induced political dependence. There was also the inescapable fact that Germany was a revisionist power, and since 1936 an increasingly successful one. After the Munich settlement Bulgaria was the only defeated power not to have benefited from recent territorial changes; the temptation to look to Berlin for help grew with every German success. The Nazi–Soviet pact conveniently made Bulgaria's traditional friend an ally of the now mighty Germans and helped many Bulgarians to accept a closer relationship with Berlin. From the restoration of diplomatic links in 1934 to 1939 relations with Moscow had been correct but distant; collectivisation decreased the Soviet Union's attractiveness for a nation of peasant proprietors, and from the mid-1930's the purges, particularly those of the armed forces, and then the Finnish war placed a sizeable question mark against its effectiveness as an international partner. However, after the Nazi–Soviet pact Bulgaria did conclude a commercial treaty with the Soviet Union early in 1940 which made possible the import of Soviet films, books and newspapers, all of which proved hugely popular; in 1940 the Soviet Union was also represented for the first time at the Plovdiv exhibition. Equally popular was the visit to Sofia in August 1940 of a Soviet football team.

The increasing power of Germany in Bulgarian political life was registered in 1940 by the removal of the pro-Western Kioseivanov and his replacement by Bogdan Filov, a distinguished academic who had studied in Germany and who retained a slavish affection for the land of his educators. To win German approval, Filov's cabinet decreased cultural links with the Western powers, closed the masonic lodges to which most of Bulgaria's political figures belonged, and set up a new youth organisation, Brannik (Defender), the function of which was to train Bulgarian youth in loyal service to 'king, fatherland, state and national aspirations'. A more sinister gesture was the appointment to the ministry of the interior of Petŭr Gabrovski, one of Bulgaria's few rabid anti-semites.

The concessions were meant, by the king at least, to buy off German pressure, not to indicate Bulgarian support for the German cause; they were intended as a final settlement rather than a down payment. Had Boris wished to throw in his lot with the axis he could easily have done so in 1938 or 1939 or even earlier. What he did, however, was to strive to maintain Bulgaria's neutrality and keep his country out of the war, despite the many domestic pressures upon him to do otherwise, pressures which led him to complain that, 'My army is pro-German, my wife is Italian, my people are pro-Russian, I alone am pro-Bulgarian.' To preserve Bulgarian neutrality Boris refused a number of attractive offers. In October 1939 Molotov suggested a Bulgarian–Soviet pact of mutual assistance with hints of Soviet support for Bulgarian claims in the Dobrudja; Boris refused and informed Bucharest of Stalin's designs on Romania. In February 1940 the foreign ministers of the Balkan entente met in Belgrade and decided to offer Bulgaria membership of their organisation and even some territorial concessions. The offer was refused because it would have aligned Bulgaria too closely with the Western powers who were backing the Balkan entente – this Boris wished to avoid not least because it would have angered Hitler, Stalin, and, very importantly, Mussolini, who was now moving fast into the Nazi orbit; alignment with the Western powers was useless for Bulgaria if Italy were on the opposing side because the Italian navy could, it was believed, deny the Western powers access to the eastern Mediterranean.

The dramatic military events of May 1940 in western Europe had profound repercussions in Bulgaria. The probability of involvement in the war, which all but a few wished to avoid, grew greater, and a series of preparatory measures were introduced. The compulsory labour service was placed under military control, and in May the cabinet established a

Directorate of Civilian Mobilisation to which all industrial enterprises could be subjected in time of war. The ministry of agriculture was to enjoy wide powers to control prices and to enforce commassation and the requisitioning of food and other agricultural produce; further legislation enabled the government to impose similar controls upon incomes and foreign trade. As in the First World War, however, civilian economic administration was later to be contested by the army, which, in 1943, set up the Directorate for the War Economy.

A further parallel with the events of the First World War was that the military successes of Germany greatly increased its attraction for Bulgaria's policy makers, though again the extent of the king's conviction is dubious. German victories also brought Bulgaria its first territorial gains. Greater Romania, the creation of Versailles, could hardly survive the collapse of that system in central and then in western Europe, no matter how deeply Bucharest's politicians might bow before Hitler. In the summer of 1940 Russia, Hungary and Bulgaria all pressed their claims, and on 7 September Bulgaria received satisfaction in the treaty of Craiova, by which it repossessed the southern Dobrudja, an area of some 4,300 square kilometers with 400,000 inhabitants, half of whom were Bulgarian, a quarter Turks and 70,000 Romanians; Craiova, it was hoped, would show a Russophile peasantry the value of German friendship. In the same month Turkey offered Bulgaria and Yugoslavia a defensive alliance, but this they dared not accept for fear of antagonising the mighty powers of Rome, Berlin and Moscow. A month later Boris reaffirmed his dedication to neutrality when he rejected an overture from Mussolini; the Italians were about to launch their assault upon Greece and offered Bulgaria access to the Aegean if it would join in the attack. A more chilling offer came in November 1940 when the deputy commissar for foreign affairs, the aptly-named Sobolev, appeared in Sofia. He talked of a mutual assistance pact under which the Soviet Union would have use of Bulgarian Black Sea naval bases, and hinted at a joint descent upon Turkey from which Bulgaria would receive Thrace and the Soviets the Dardanelles. Again Boris refused, not least because he knew that Sobolev's language did not correspond entirely to that which the Russians had recently used in Berlin, where they had designated Bulgaria as a 'Soviet security zone'. Nevertheless, the supposedly secret offer of a pact occasioned a massive campaign of posters and graffiti by Bulgarian Communists in favour of the proposed agreement with the Soviet Union.

By November 1940 Boris had very little room for manoeuvre. The game which he had played with dedication and consummate skill was all but over. Since September German troops had been moving into Romania preparatory to the coming campaign in Russia. Early in December Mussolini's embarrassments in Greece led him to seek German military assistance. Hitler had already decided upon operation 'Marita', the diversion of some German troops in Romania to Greece, for with the Italians crippled in southern Albania and in headlong flight across the north African desert, he feared an allied landing in the Balkans which could threaten the campaign in Russia. 'Marita' would mean the passage of German troops through Bulgaria; on 8 December forty German staff officers arrived in the country and thereafter the number of German troops entering Bulgaria disguised as businessmen and single male tourists increased rapidly. In January 1941 Filov went to the Reich to discuss details of the forthcoming German operation. The Americans made a last attempt to persuade the Bulgarian leaders that ultimate victory must lie with a Britain backed by the moral and economic strength of the United States, but German pressure in Sofia was now enormous and Bulgaria no longer had any real freedom of choice. In February it was agreed with the Germans that a pontoon bridge should be built across the Danube and that on 2 March German troops should begin their journey from Romania to Greece.

The day before the German operation began Filov had arrived in Vienna to sign the tripartite pact. Britain withdrew its diplomatic representative in protest. Bulgaria was therefore effectively a member of the axis camp although a formal declaration of war on Britain and the United States was not made until after Pearl Harbour. Boris's attempt to keep Bulgaria neutral having failed, he bowed to the inevitable, chosing cooperation with the Nazis rather than hopeless resistance to them and hoping perhaps that the eventual declaration of war would both prevent further German pressure and secure favourable consideration when the final peace terms were decided. Few who compared the condition of Sofia and Belgrade in April 1941 would have questioned his decision. From now on his efforts were directed at preserving as much independence for his country as the grim circumstances would allow.

BULGARIA DURING THE SECOND WORLD WAR, 1941–4

Bulgaria's alignment with Germany brought short term benefits, the most obvious of which was the occupation of Thrace and Macedonia; the axis powers had only been able to make the latter available to Bulgaria after the Belgrade coup of 27 March had seemingly placed Yugoslavia in the allied camp; its previous non-availability had been yet another reason for Bulgaria's refusing to commit itself to the German side. The boundaries of the occupation zones were not precisely defined, which led to some tension with Italy in 1942, and Bulgaria was not allowed onto the Aegean coast, which remained in German hands; furthermore, full ownership of the occupied territories was not to be conferred until the end of the war, lest Bulgaria defect from the axis taking its newly acquired lands with it. The gains were received with great enthusiasm in Bulgaria, and, initially at least, in Macedonia, where long years of domination from Belgrade had made Bulgarian rule seem an attractive alternative, and the new authorities did introduce a number of improvements, most particularly in the field of education with the building of over 800 new schools and the establishment of a university in Skopje. The Bulgarians, however, soon fell into the same vice as the Serbs: over-centralisation. In March 1942 the council of ministers was given absolute power in the new territories, which all too rapidly were subjected to bureaucratic corruption and exploitation, whilst the insensitive domination by Sofia of all features of Macedonian life, especially the church, led to resentment and a strengthening of separatist or autonomist thinking; Bulgarian bishops in Macedonia became as unpopular as Greek ones had been in Bulgaria a century before. In Thrace there was never any honeymoon between occupier and occupied. The Bulgarians conducted a ruthless campaign to encourage the resident Greeks to leave and a local rising in September 1941, which was suppressed with extreme savagery, was thought by many to have been provoked by the Bulgarians to provide an excuse for incarcerating or exterminating large numbers of Greeks.

The initial excitement felt in Bulgaria at the acquisition of the new territories was soon overlaid with perplexity and anxiety at events elsewhere in Europe. Hitler's attack on the Soviet Union on 21–2 June 1941 ended the comfortable situation in which alignment with Germany did not conflict with the traditional feelings towards Russia; no longer could business be so easily combined with pleasure. Filov's government reacted initially by tightening internal controls. The number of offences for which the death penalty could be imposed was increased, and fear of Communist demonstrations led Filov, an academic and rector of the university, to become the first ruler ever, Ottoman or Bulgarian, to ban the celebration of St Cyril and St Methodius day, 24 May. Between 1 January 1942 and 4 September 1944 15,000 persons were interned, 11,000 were sent to labour battalions, and 6,000 were herded into the concentration camps at Gonda Voda and Enikyoi and the women's camp at Sveta Nikola. Communists were prominent amongst the victims of the regime, as it had been the landing and parachuting into the country of Bulgarian exiles from the Soviet Union after 21 June which had encouraged Filov to introduce tougher controls; in 1942 suspicions that he had surreptitious connections with the Soviet Union were enough to bring general Zaimov, a veteran conspirator of 1934, within the executioner's grasp. Yet it was not the Communists alone who suffered. In January 1942 the newspaper of the Legionnaires, the fascist youth organisation, was suppressed for advocating that Bulgaria should take part in the war on the eastern front, and on the extreme right neither Tsankov nor Lukov were allowed to hold public meetings. This was a product of Boris's fear that the Nazis would use an active fascist group to supplant him. The right, for its part, was confident that it would soon be in office, for it believed that Boris's non-party regime, which lacked any cohesive ideology, must give way to a group more in tune with Europe's new order.

A major demand of the right was for a Bulgarian commitment to the German war effort in Russia. This Boris steadfastly refused, forbidding even the formation of a Bulgarian volunteer legion, and throughout the war in the east Bulgaria's contribution amounted to little more than voluntary contributions to the *Winterhilfe* scheme and a single Red Cross train, which, in theory at least, could be of benefit to both sides. The refusal to fight on the eastern front was understandable. A volunteer legion, if it returned victorious, might, as Boris feared, join with local fascists to threaten the king's position. Resistance to the commitment of regular troops could be justified by less cynical arguments, all of which were skilfully deployed before the Germans. The Bulgarian army had to be kept in the Balkans to counter three possible dangers: an attack by Turkey, the allies' client in the eastern Mediterranean; a Soviet descent upon the Black Sea coast, an important consideration in 1942 when the Germans were storing oil-drilling equipment in the Bulgarian Black Sea ports for later use in the Caucasus; and after axis reverses in north Africa, a full-scale allied landing in the Balkans. In the summer of 1941 the Bulgarians also used the likelihood of future partisan activity to justify keeping their army in the Balkans. They argued, too, that the Bulgarian army was still not equipped with the modern weapons necessary for a campaign such as that on the eastern front, whilst the peasant conscripts, it was stated, could not be expected to fight efficiently if removed from their familiar, Balkan surroundings, particularly if they were required to fight against the Russians, for whom they retained a deep attachment. These arguments were sufficient to counter the Führer's suggestion that if the Balkan nations did not join in defeating the Communist menace they might one day suffer the fate of the Baltic states, and Hitler reluctantly accepted that the Bulgarian army would not be committed on the eastern front.

In successfully resisting pressure to commit Bulgarian troops to the Russian war Boris had been able to present a case based upon practical considerations. In the second of the two main issues at stake between Berlin and Sofia, that of the fate of Bulgaria's 50,000 Jews, the king, his ministers and the Bulgarian nation were face to face with the lunacy of Nazi doctrine and no rational arguments could be usefully deployed. This did not weaken resistance to what was widely thought to be wrong. In November 1940 and January 1941 a number of anti-semitic regulations, including the wearing of the yellow star, were introduced. Yet Bulgaria neither had, nor in this case wished to have, Teutonic efficiency and thoroughness. Jews with decorations for valour in battle were exempt from the regulations; the *numerus clausus* for the university and the professions was based upon the urban rather than the total population and therefore allowed many more Jews to enter the supposedly closed ranks. A shortage of electricity, it was explained, had meant that by October 1941 only a fraction of the total number of yellow stars that were needed had been produced. Later in the war the restrictions increased. In March 1942 Jews were placed outside the protection of the law, and a year later plans were made to begin deportations to the death camps. The plans were made public, as one of those involved in their implementation had revealed them to his Jewish mistress. The legislation of 1940 and 1941 had produced protests from professional organisations, from the Sŭbranie and from the church, but these were muted compared to the anger which greeted the deportation proposals. In street demonstrations, parliamentary resolutions, and newspaper articles a national outrage poured forth in which, perhaps, other frustrations were given a cathartic release. The deportation plans were abandoned. Though the legal restrictions remained in force and the plight of many Jews worsened in May with their expulsion from the cities to road-gangs or camps such as that at Somovit, the Bulgarian Jews, if not those in the occupied territories, had been saved from extermination. All sections of Bulgarian society except a tiny handful of inveterate anti-semites had been united in opposition to the deportations and their views had undoubtedly had the support of the king, for if Boris had wanted the deportations to go ahead they would have done so.

When, a little over a fortnight after a visit to Hitler, Boris died suddenly on 28 August 1943 at the age of forty-nine, it was widely believed that his refusal to comply with German requests for help on the eastern front and with Nazi plans for the deportation of Bulgarian Jews had led the Germans to poison him. This was almost certainly not the case. The official cause of death was recorded as thrombosis of the left coronary artery complicated by gall stones. Although some mystery still shadows the event, the Germans could hardly have gained from Boris's death; there was no guarantee that the succeeding regime would be amenable to

German wishes, and with Italy about to drop out of the war instability in the Balkans could only compound Germany's difficulties. For the Bulgarian people the king's death was a cruel blow, as was shown by the unprecentedly large crowd which gathered for his funeral. His skill in acquiring the new territories and more importantly in keeping Bulgaria out of the terrible war on the eastern front had earned him gratitude and respect. The personal or non-party rule which he had established in the 1930s could bear favourable comparison with many contemporary regimes in the Balkans and elsewhere. Political controls, especially on left-wing extremists, were tight, but his rule was neither fascist nor totalitarian. Tsankov never held public office after 1931, Lukov, who served as minister of war from November 1935 to January 1938 was always subordinated to the king, whilst in 1939 restrictions were placed upon the activities of the Legionnaires. There was no government party, Bulgaria was blessedly free from the public histrionics of a fascist leadership, the Sŭbranie, though highly managed, always contained at least a handful of opposition deputies, and even a moderately critical newspaper such as the pro-allied *Mir* could continue publication during the war. Communist activity was prohibited even during the period of the Nazi–Soviet pact, but May Day parades were allowed until 1941 and Boris's regime restored Bulgarian citizenship to some 500 veterans who had fought for the republicans during the Spanish civil war.

Boris's successor, Simeon, was six years old in 1943, and a regency was formed of Filov, general Mihov and Boris's brother, Prince Kiril. The regency was technically illegal in that it had not been endorsed by a grand national assembly and because Kiril, as a member of the ruling dynasty, was ineligible. As Mihov had few interests outside his profession and Kiril concerned himself with little else but self-indulgence real power rested with Filov. To make sure that this continued to be the case he secured the appointment of the pliant nonentity, Dobri Bozhilov, as minister president.

In the year which followed his death the war which Boris had done so much to keep at a distance crept ever nearer to his erstwhile kingdom. The German defeat at Stalingrad had already caused some Bulgarians, Boris included, to think of loosening ties with Germany. Secret soundings of the allies had revealed just how difficult this would be, for the allied conditions were harsh: unconditional surrender, the evacuation of all occupied territory and an allied occupation of Bulgaria. In 1943 the war was still too distant to make these terms acceptable, but it was rapidly coming closer, and on 19 November 1943 it arrived, with the first major air-raid on Sofia; two more followed before the huge bombardment of 19 January 1944. As a small and compact city Sofia made an easy target and the

January raid produced thousands of casualties. The population fled in terror. In March Sofia was subjected to a series of incendiary raids culminating in a massive blitz on 30 March.

The bombing produced severe social dislocation. In so centralised a system the flight of civil servants impaired the functioning of the administration, and after the January raids the government had to order bureaucrats to return to their posts in the capital. Industry and transport were also affected, whilst many villages were swamped with refugees they could not absorb; and it was the coldest time of year. The bombing had also shown that the Nazis could not protect Bulgaria from allied power, and inevitably German prestige suffered; even in November the bishop of Sofia, when burying the victims of a raid, had used the occasion to criticise the Germans rather than the allied airmen.

By the beginning of 1944 Bulgarian cities, or what was left of them, were beginning to experience food shortages reminiscent of the First World War. In 1940 too much grain had been sent to Germany and in the following year too much had been requisitioned for the Bulgarian army. In 1942 there was a serious drought. At the same time the peasants would sell only the minimum amounts required to official purchasing agencies, for much larger profits were to be made on the black market; and everywhere shortages were aggravated by German soldiers sending home more food than they should have done. By the middle of 1944 official food prices stood at 563 per cent of their 1939 level whilst on the black market the figure was 738 per cent. Shortages were not the only cause of inflation. The inability of the regime to find external loans to cover an expenditure which arose from 92 billion (U.S.) *leva* 1939 to 209 billion *leva* in 1944 also forced the government to print more money; so too did a hike of 50 per cent in official salaries in the summer of 1944.

Those who benefited from these intensifying problems were the opposition elements: the resistance movement and its as yet somewhat shadowy political organisation, the Fatherland Front. The resistance had some dramatic coups to its credit. In February 1943 general Lukov had been assassinated, and other killings followed as the Communists mounted a sustained urban guerilla offensive. There was political activity too, with demonstrations on San Stefano day stressing both friendship with Russia and opposition to participation in the war on the eastern front. In terms of armed resistance, however, there was nothing in Bulgaria to compare with that in Poland, Yugoslavia or Greece. The highest estimate for the number of partisans active at any one time is 18,000, most of whom were concentrated near Plovdiv, Varna and Burgas. Bulgaria was not, of course, occupied, and until late 1943 it was relatively little affected by the war itself. After Stalingrad the Communists, whose party had touched a nadir in 1941 with only 10,000 members, became more active and effective, and in March of that year they divided the country into twelve operational zones; but they were still to suffer major setbacks in the field and were always short of arms and equipment, partly because of poor relations between them and the chief supplier of such items, Britain's Special Operations Executive. In the spring and summer of 1944 partisan activity intensified as the Red Army fought its way into the Balkans, but the Bulgarian partisans were never in a position to topple the government in Sofia.

The Fatherland Front had first been mooted as early as 1941, when attempts were made to build a wide coalition on what remained of the 1938 electoral agreement. It failed, because other factions would not cooperate with the Communists, who demanded control of the coalition – an absurd stance in view of the weakness of the party at that time. In February 1942 a second and more successful attempt at engineering a coalition was begun, from which emerged in July a loose and clandestine association of Communists, Zvenari, the left Agrarians under Nikola Petkov, and Cheshmedjiev's Social Democrats. The Fatherland Front programme as broadcast by the popular Bulgarian-language Hristo Botev radio station in the Soviet Union included demands for absolute neutrality in the war, the withdrawal of Bulgarian troops from operations against the partisans in Serbia, the removal of the army from royal control, a ban on the export of food to Germany, the guarantee of a decent living to all workers in town and village, the restoration of full civil liberties and a ban on all fascist organisations. The Fatherland Front insisted that its programme was non-negotiable, and this, plus the hope that King Boris would soon switch to supporting the allied powers, meant that the legal opposition would not join the Front; moreover many Agrarians resented partisan activity, the major consequence of which, at this time, was to bring reprisals upon villages most of whose inhabitants were Agrarian sympathisers. By the summer of 1943 the Fatherland Front was strong enough to establish a central committee under Nikola Petkov, Kimon Georgiev, the Communist Dramaliev, Cheshmedjiev and another Social Democrat, Dimo Kazasov. Again an attempt was made to widen the base of the organisation by approaching the legal opposition, but the result was little different, the Democrats refusing to cooperate with the Communists and the Agrarians with the Zvenarist soldiers, who, before the formation of that group, had helped stage the coup of 1923. Not until the summer of 1944 did the Fatherland Front acquire a wide following and even in August of that year its membership was no more than 3,600.

By 1944 there were few politicians outside the ranks of the fanatical
pro-Germans who would not concede that sooner or later Bulgaria had to
switch to the allied side. Secret approaches in February and March revealed
that the allies' terms were unchanged; Bozhilov and Filov continued to
believe that the nation would not tolerate the loss of the new territories,
nor was unconditional surrender to be contemplated whilst German troops
were in the country and allied troops were still too distant to defend it;
Bozhilov said he would join the allies as soon as they joined him by landing
in the Balkans. The Bulgarians also tried to persuade the Western allies that
the bombing might produce a total collapse of morale which would lead
to German intervention and an eventual Soviet occupation. The British
and Americans refused to be drawn by this intimation of future instability
in the grand alliance. Meanwhile in March Hitler warned Filov that a
Soviet victory would mean implementation of a plan which Stalin had
talked of in 1940, by which Bulgaria would be incorporated into the Soviet
Union. The Führer also spoke of having to deal with the problem of
Horthy's Hungary; when he did so by detaining its leader and occupying
his country the lesson was not lost upon Filov.

Soviet pressure in the meantime was intensifying. Moscow had refused
to intercede with the Western allies for a cessation of the bombing, and
after the capture of Odessa the Soviets demanded with increasing
persistence that Bulgaria's Black Sea ports be cleared of all German
shipping and personnel; in a note of 18 May 1944 the Soviets reported
that there were 2,000 German troops and fifty to sixty naval vessels,
including submarines, in Varna, where boats and barges for use by the
Wehrmacht were under construction, all of which, said Moscow, infringed
Bulgaria's supposed neutrality in the Russo-German war. The Soviets
therefore demanded strict application of neutrality, and, most importantly,
that Bulgaria break off diplomatic relations with Germany.

Bulgarian policy had been founded on the assumption that the present
balancing act between Berlin and Moscow could be sustained long enough
to find an agreement with the Western allies. The Soviet note intimated
that this might not be the case and that Bulgaria might find itself facing
war with and probable occupation by the Red Army. To make matters
worse Bulgaria was rapidly losing the military value it had once had for
the allies. That value had been predicated on the assumption that
Bulgaria's eventual defection would seriously damage the axis cause in the
Balkans. Bulgaria's strategic value would be enormous if the allies opened
the second front in the south-east of Europe, but the Normandy landings
finally dispersed the lingering, and always misplaced, hopes that this might
come about. At the same time the advance of the Red Army made it more

and more probable that the German position in the Balkans would be irrevocably damaged whatever the Bulgarians might decide. Bulgaria seemed doomed to military irrelevance and political impotence.

This, after the Soviet threat of 18 May, produced a deep political crisis. Gichev wanted to form a government of national consolidation to avoid the extremes of right and left, but the Fatherland Front would join only if their left-wing policies were fully endorsed, a condition which if accepted would have vitiated Gichev's plan for avoiding extremes. Change, however, did take place, when Bozhilov resigned and gave way on 1 June to Ivan Bagrianov. The change of minister president marked the first real shift from Bulgaria's pro-German policy, because the new premier, though he had been educated in Germany and had served in a German artillery regiment during the First World War, was pro-Western and had proved his pro-Western credentials in secret negotiations with the allies earlier in the year. Bagrianov now intensified his search for a settlement with the allies, who in turn let it be known that although their terms were unchanged the evacuation of the new territories would not prejudice decisions on their future; it was also hinted heavily that the southern Dobrudja would remain Bulgarian. Bagrianov decided to stall and wait for better terms: a fateful decision.

Bagrianov looked everywhere for support for his regime, even making a vain effort to persuade the Communists to join his cabinet. This he followed with a series of promises to dismantle most of the apparatus of the previous regimes, though not all these fine words were translated into deeds. His already weakened position became even less tenable on 2 August, when Turkey severed diplomatic relations with Germany. This lessened yet further the importance of Bulgaria to the Western allies, and at the same time posed the danger that the Germans would occupy Bulgaria to counter any forward move by the Turks. At home the government was inundated with petitions, organised by the Communists, demanding the declaration of strict neutrality. On 17 August Bagrianov not only conceded this demand but granted an amnesty to all political prisoners, repudiated the policies of his predecessors, and repealed the anti-Jewish legislation. Yet he still insisted that Bulgaria could not conclude peace with the Western allies until the middle of September when the harvest had been gathered; action any earlier would invite German reprisals which might include seizure or destruction of the crops. Hardly had he made the declaration of 17 August when another thunderbolt struck the hapless Bagrianov. On 20 August the Red Army invaded Romania and three days later a royal coup brought about a surrender; the Russians were on the Danube. Bagrianov rushed to make further concessions, and said that Bulgaria had now withdrawn completely from the war. On 26 August he assured the Russians that all foreign troops on Bulgarian soil would be disarmed, Bulgarian troops would be withdrawn from Yugoslavia, allied prisoners of war would be released, the Gestapo would be driven from Bulgaria and the Sŭbranie would be dissolved to allow the election of a regime enjoying popular confidence.

These concessions did not satisfy the Soviets, who retorted that Bagrianov was still persecuting the Communist partisans and that the disarming of foreign troops might one day be applied to their own forces. Above all Moscow demanded that Bulgaria declare war on Germany, which Bagrianov refused to do on the grounds that it would infringe Bulgaria's recently declared neutrality. In the meantime Bagrianov pressed new urgency into the negotiations with the allies, which had now shifted from Ankara to Cairo. Should these negotiations succeed the Soviets would have no direct part in the determination of Bulgaria's political future, and such a consideration can hardly have been absent from Stalin's mind when on 30 August he announced that the Soviet Union would no longer respect Bulgarian neutrality. A despairing Bagrianov resigned and was replaced by the Agrarian Konstantin Muraviev, a nephew of Stamboliiski. Muraviev made a vain attempt to include the Fatherland Front in his government, but the former, hardening its demands, was now insisting upon the formation of a purely Fatherland Front administration. Muraviev granted yet more concessions, but despite clashes between Bulgarian and German soldiers he still refused to declare war on Germany lest the Red Army use this as an excuse to come to Bulgaria's aid and occupy the country. At the same time he clung to the hopes that negotiations would be successfully concluded in Cairo and the Germans would leave Bulgaria, thus ending any pretext for a Soviet occupation. On 4 September a series of strikes and demonstrations organised by the Fatherland Front added to the pressure on Muraviev, pressure which was intensified two days later by large scale desertions from the army to the partisans.

On 5 September Muraviev at last decided to sever relations with Germany, but his minister of war, Marinov, persuaded him not to declare war for seventy-two hours, in order to complete the evacuation of Bulgarian troops from Yugoslav Macedonia. Before war could be declared upon Germany the Soviets, to the amazement and consternation of the Western allies and the Bulgarians alike, declared war on Bulgaria. Any hopes that the Cairo talks might succeed and that Bulgaria might conclude a peace without the Soviet Union being involved were dashed; from that moment the USSR became an inescapable force in the determination of Bulgaria's destiny. This did not prevent Bulgaria going to war with

Germany on 8 September, a step which meant that for a few hours the Bulgarians had the dubious distinction of being the only nation to have been technically at war simultaneously with Germany, Britain, the United States and the Soviet Union. In what now seemed an irrelevant gesture, Filov resigned as regent on 8 September.

Soviet troops entered Bulgaria on the same day, but they met with no resistance. They were joyously welcomed in town and village whilst in Sofia their political allies put a rapid end to the Muraviev administration. With the help of Marinov units of a partisan brigade took Sofia during the night of 8 to 9 September and installed a Fatherland Front administration headed by Kimon Georgiev and including five Zvenari, four Agrarians, two Social Democrats, and four Communists; the latter held the ministries of justice and of the interior.

The deposition of Muraviev had taken hardly more than an hour, had involved nothing more dangerous than entering the ministry of war after an accomplice had unlocked the door, and was carefully organised by those past masters in the questionable art of the coup: the Zvenari Damian Velchev and Kimon Georgiev. The coup had become a traditional feature of Bulgarian politics, as too had violence. The second was to follow inexorably upon the first.

Between the wars Bulgarian culture had inevitably been affected by the political vicissitudes of the state. In literature, Bulgaria shared the general experimentalism of the early 1920s but in the later years of that decade indulged in the fragmentation which was at the same time affecting the political parties; and in the 1930s ideological commitment in literature declined, partly in response to tightening political controls. The novel increased in stature, although the inter-war years produced nothing to equal Vazov's *Pod Igoto*, and the Bulgarians, like the Greeks, were still readers of newspapers rather than books; in 1934 one estimate put the number of newspapers printed in Bulgaria at 642 and the number of periodicals at 380. Of the literary journals the most important was *Zlatorog* (*Golden Horn*) whose editor from 1920 right through to 1944 was Vladimir Vasiliev. The most important writers of the inter-war years were Elin Pelin and Yordan Yovkov, both of whom had begun publishing well before the First World War. Pelin, who wrote sympathetically about the peasants, particularly those of his native *shop* region around Sofia, and who had been called the 'singer of rural misery' by Krŭstev, in fact wrote little in the inter-war years besides a number of children's stories. Yovkov too had strong regional ties, in his case with the Dobrudja; his work also reflected on social problems, but in a calm and conciliatory fashion and with a much greater aesthetic consciousness than most of his contemporaries. Another writer who had been active before 1915 and whose work continued after 1918 was Todor Vlaikov, who had been heavily influenced by the Russian Narodniks. So too had Georgi Shishmanov, who abandoned his early mentors in the 1920s for the murky by-ways of Freudianism. More wholesome fare, and one much in tune with the escapism or withdrawal from politics of the 1930s was provided in the historical novel, which flourished between the wars with expert exponents of the art such as Stoyan Zagorchinov, Stiliyan Chilingirov, Fani Popova-Mutafova, who continued writing after 1944, and Nikolai Rainov, the symbolist poet who, after a brief flirtation with Freudianism, indulged his own fascinations in and delighted his readers with his recreations of Bulgaria's medieval past. From a very different mould were the Communist writers, particularly poets. Geo Milev, another former symbolist, left a masterpiece, *Septemvri* (*September*), which praised the rising of 1923 but which cost him his life after he disappeared during Tsankov's reign of terror. Hristo Smirnenski began publishing verse of lasting quality in 1918, although he was to die in 1923 of natural causes. An early death also befell Nikola Vaptsarov. Born in Macedonia, Vaptsarov had espoused Marxism when a naval cadet, and he continued to spread the Communist gospel when working on the railways and in factories during the 1930s. He was shot in 1942 for partisan activities. Another prominent author who ended his life in front of a firing squad was Dimitŭr Shishmanov, but this time the executioners were Communists; Shishmanov, a son of the dramatist, had written, though not always in complimentary vein, about Bulgaria's *haute monde*.

By 1939 there were thirteen theatres in Bulgaria, including the National Theatre in the capital and municipal theatres in Plovdiv, Varna and Russe. There was little new of quality to show in them, however, Stefan L. Kostov being the only dramatist of any stature at work between the wars, although Yovkov also produced a handful of notable plays. Political control over the theatre was strict, besides which there was the new medium of the cinema in which frustrated playwrights might wish to take refuge. Bulgaria had 213 cinemas by 1939, and although most of what was shown was imported, about fifty Bulgarian feature films and a few hundred 'shorts' had been produced by 1944.

SOCIAL AND ECONOMIC DEVELOPMENT, 1918–44

During the inter-war period, as in the years 1878–1918, Bulgaria's social structure underwent few changes. The departure of almost all the country's Greeks paralleled on a lesser scale the emigration of the Turks

Table 2 *Distribution of land by size of holdings, 1926–46*

Size of holding in hectares	Percentage of total holdings		
	1926	1934	1946
Below 2	24.3	27.0	29.8
2 to 10	60.7	62.3	63.3
10 to 30	14.7	10.3	6.8
Above 30	0.6	0.4	0.1
Total	100.3	100.0	100.0

Source: Adapted from Joseph Rothschild, *East Central Europe between the Two World Wars* (Seattle and London, 1974), p. 330.

after the liberation, and together with the inflow of Bulgarian-speaking refugees meant that by the census of 1934 the Bulgarian element of the population had risen from the 81.23 per cent of 1910 to 86.7 per cent, whilst the Greeks had declined from 1.17 per cent to below 0.4 per cent and the Turks from 11.63 per cent to 9.8 per cent.

Whilst remaining predominantly Bulgarian, the country also preserved its status as a land of the small peasant proprietor, despite some growth in the industrial sector. By 1937 approximately 12.5 per cent of the total population of 6,300,000 lived in settlements of over 20,000 inhabitants, between a quarter and a fifth of them in Sofia; a further 10 per cent, living in communities of between 2,000 and 20,000, were also classified as urban dwellers, leaving 77.5 per cent to form the rural population. As will be seen from table 2 the strength of the medium and small peasant proprietors was in no way diminished. In fact they became even more prominent, holdings of under ten hectares increasing from 85 per cent of the total in 1926 to 90.2 per cent in 1934 and 93.1 per cent in 1946. As a percentage of the total area of agricultural land, holdings under ten hectares rose from 58.1 per cent in 1926 to 66.9 per cent in 1934 and 76.7 per cent in 1946; and of the land worked in 1934 only 10 per cent was rented from other land-holders. Until the disappearance of the traditional system of farming the large estate remained a rarity, and in 1944 holdings over twenty hectares accounted for only 1 per cent of the total agricultural area. Landless families and full-time agricultural labourers were also rare. In 1926 the former numbered only 100,000, and in 1937 for every one adult employed in agricultural labour there were 520 proprietors and a further 404 members of the proprietors' families.

There was nevertheless some pressure on the traditional system. The population, despite a decline of one-third in the birth rate between the wars, was increasing, and with little prospect of alternative forms of economic activity the demand for land strengthened. There was not much marginal land that could now be put under the plough, and even though the division of communal property continued apace supply could not match demand. Between 1920 and 1940 the agrarian population increased by 18.4 per cent whilst the number of holdings increased by 38.4 per cent. Inevitably the size of individual holdings shrank; the average 5.73 hectares of 1926 had fallen to 4.31 hectares by 1946. With more and more people subsisting on the land agricultural over-population became increasingly apparent, and by the late 1930s towards one and a quarter million, or nearly two-thirds of the rural population, were in excess of minimum requirements. Pressure on the land was also reflected in the tendency towards greater parcellisation, and the average number of strips per holding had risen from eleven in 1908 to seventeen by 1926. Measures to encourage commassation had been taken by the Agrarian government of the early 1920s, and the import of agricultural machinery in the late 1920s encouraged moves in the same direction, but by the late 1930s the myriad patchwork of small strips remained characteristic of Bulgarian land distribution.

Adaptability to new crops was a distinct feature of Bulgarian agriculture in the inter-war years. The First World War had shown the value of tobacco, and this was reinforced immediately after 1918 by a number of factors, including the loss of the former British market for wheat, the loss of the grain-growing Dobrudja, the decrepit state of the transport system and of the land itself, the lack of storage facilities for grain which meant a loss of quality, and a series of poor harvests. Between 1907 and 1911 tobacco had accounted for 1.3 per cent of the total export value, but from 1926–30 the figure was 38.5 per cent, whilst grain exports in the mid-1920s were at only a third of their pre-war levels. In 1926 tobacco suffered a setback following a poor harvest and a fall in world prices, but the threat to it encouraged a switch to other profitable industrial plants, primarily sunflowers and sugar-beet. By the late 1920s the real value of industrial crops was 235 per cent that of 1911 whilst in cereal production the figure was 92 per cent.

The Depression showed the weakness of the inter-war system of world trade, and thus forced Bulgaria into greater self-reliance for industrial as well as food and fodder crops, and in this respect the Depression did a little to repair the faults in Stoilov's pre-war industrialisation programme. Import substitution was most noticeable in cotton, where domestic production expanded by 900 per cent between 1929 and 1939, with home-produced yarn and fibre rising from a quarter to two times the weight of imported material. In the export trade pressure on wheat and tobacco encouraged moves to more specialised commodities such as vegetables, fruit and wine; from 1936 to 1938 vegetable production was 75 per cent higher than in the years 1926–30 and wine production 38 per cent higher. Cereals, however, were still important export commodities, but at 13 per cent of total export earnings in the late 1930s they were much less significant than before 1915.

During the Second World War cereal production fell, with the 1944 volume being only 60.2 per cent of that of 1939. In the same years fruit and wine production increased by 3.6 per cent and that of vegetables by 31.2 per cent, the peasants being encouraged to produce such crops first because government interference was less than with grain, tobacco and other items, and secondly because of the high profits which these products could bring, especially on the black market.

If governments, wittingly and unwittingly, had encouraged crop diversification, so too had the cooperatives, which purchased approximately one-third of the agricultural produce processed in 1943 and 1944. Equally important was the cooperatives' work in maintaining supplies of credit in the 1930s. Membership of the cooperatives increased by 71.36 per cent from 199,000 in 1928 to 341,000 in 1939, and those families which had dealings with credit cooperatives made up approximately three-fifths of the total population. That the cooperatives were an essential prop to the fortunes of the small farmer was seen in the fact that the average holding of peasants belonging to the cooperatives in 1945 was 4.3 hectares whilst those who did not belong to the cooperatives had estates averaging 8.7 hectares. The only agrarian enterprises to make a legal profit in the final years of the war were the fifty-eight cooperatives with consolidated fields and mechanised implements.

Efforts to modernise Bulgarian agriculture had continued throughout the inter-war period. Stamboliiski's government had encouraged education, commassation and the use of modern machinery. After 1923 the Liapchev administration attempted to diversify and improve cereal production by encouraging the growth of new crops such as lucerne and vetch, and by continuing to foster the import of agricultural machinery; between 1925 and 1929 the number of metal ploughs in Bulgaria increased by 40 per cent, and the amount of modern agricultural machinery more than doubled. Any strategy to improve home production through the import of machinery naturally collapsed with the Depression, but imports were resumed when relative economic stability returned in the mid-1930s.

Despite undeniable progress in crop diversification and considerable success in weathering the worst effects of the Depression, Bulgarian agriculture remained backward. Although the percentage of worked land devoted to industrial and garden crops in 1938, 13.9 per cent, was higher than that in Romania, Yugoslavia, Hungary and Austria, the proportion devoted to cereals (67.2 per cent) was the highest in eastern Europe, the nearest contenders being Romania (61.9 per cent) and Hungary (57.3 per cent); the proportion of meadows, pastures and feed crops (8.4 per cent), was the lowest in the region, the next lowest being Romania (27.4 per cent) and Hungary (28.6 per cent), whilst Bulgaria's 10.5 per cent of land left fallow was by far the highest in eastern Europe, the nearest being Poland (4.5 per cent) and Yugoslavia (2.7 per cent). (Albanian statistics are not recorded.) Between 1930 and 1940 the Bulgarians used on average 0.01 kilos of nitrates per hectare, whilst the use of phosphates and potash was too small to be measured in international statistics; in Czechoslovakia the figures were 4.4, 8.9 and 5.0 kilos per hectare and in Denmark 10.7, 24.1 and 7.9 kilos per hectare. Shortly after the Second World War it was estimated that in the U.S.A. the production of one acre of cotton absorbed fifty-seven man hours; in Bulgaria it was 605 man hours plus 405 ox hours or 262 horse hours; maize demanded thirty-five man hours per acre in the U.S.A. but 305 in Bulgaria, whilst the production of wheat in Bulgaria consumed six times more labour than in the Soviet Union. Nor did small, peasant Bulgaria see a rural electrification scheme similar to that in the Irish Free State, for by 1941 only one in nine Bulgarian villages had electricity. In the early 1930s Bulgaria had the highest tuberculosis mortality rate in Europe, a reflection of the country's woefully inadequate medical provision with only 4.9 doctors and twenty-two hospital beds for each 10,000 of the population, though in this respect Bulgaria fared better than both Yugoslavia and Poland.

Between 1911 and 1929 industrial output more than doubled, with some sectors showing very rapid growth (see table 3), but this was not because of any significant change in government strategies towards industry. Stamboliiski extended the encouragement of industry legislation for a further ten years and allowed cooperatives to qualify for encouraged-industry status, and Liapchev altered some details of the scheme, making railway carriage rates even more attractive and in 1926 introducing a swingeing tariff on imported manufactured goods. By 1930 Bulgaria had 263 joint stock companies compared to 128 in 1921, and the average number of workers per enterprise had risen from thirty-six to forty-one during the decade, though only in textiles did the average number of workers per plant exceed a hundred. Textiles still accounted for the highest proportion of industrial production, 65 per cent, with metals and

Table 3 *Industrial growth in the 1920s*

	Production index 1930 1911 = 100	Average annual growth in output, 1921–30
Metals and machinery	702	29.4
Chemicals	514	27.9
Non-wood building materials	601	18.2
Cement	1,160	24.6
Paper	172	12.1
Textiles	297	23.5
Sugar	961	12.6

Source: John R. Lampe and Marvin R. Jackson, *Balkan Economic History, 1550–1950* (Bloomington, Indiana, 1982), pp. 404–5.

machinery providing only 8 per cent of total industrial output. And profits on industrial investment were still at least 10 per cent lower than those on banking or commercial capital. Fifteen per cent of Bulgarian industry in 1929 was owned by foreign capital, and a similar proportion of banking capital was in foreign hands. The state and the cooperatives owned a further 15 per cent of Bulgarian industry, and their share in the 1930s tended to increase, whilst foreign investment declined by about a third during the decade.

Whilst industrial production rose by 52 per cent between 1929 and 1939, Bulgarian-produced goods rose from 61 per cent to 88 per cent of the total of industrial goods consumed in the country. Taking 1929 as the index of 100, by 1938 manufacturing output stood at 152 and the extraction industry at 128; the average annual increase in industrial output during the same period was 4.8 per cent, below Greece's 5.7 per cent but well ahead of the European average of 1.1 per cent.

The role of the state in Bulgarian industry declined slightly in the years before the Second World War. In the 1920s Liapchev had made the management of the Pernik mines autonomous, but much more significant was the restriction of the encouraged-industry category in the 1930s. In 1936 some seventeen areas of light industrial production, accounting for almost half of all industrial output, were denied further privileges under the encouragement of industry scheme, though they continued to benefit from general tariff and price regulations, and some derived advantage from one or more of the twenty-five new cartels which sprang up in the 1930s, though most of these were ineffective and ephemeral. By 1939 state-owned enterprises were responsible for only 9 per cent of total industrial production, and by 1944 the figure had fallen to 5 per cent. Public ownership dominated in coal mining, however, with 84.8 per cent of production, and in electricity generation, where 61.3 per cent of output was from state or municipal plants. State and cooperative banks were responsible for 81.3 per cent of deposits and 78.2 per cent of loans, and, of course, the railways remained firmly under government ownership and control.

Neither the relaxation of direct state involvement nor the expansion of production brought about significant structural change in Bulgarian industry in the 1930s. Although much of the expansion in capacity had taken place in food-processing, that segment of industry accounted for only a fifth of total production in 1937, and textiles (60 per cent) remained the dominant sector; the remaining figures were clay and building materials (12 per cent), iron and steel (10 per cent), chemicals (9.5 per cent), paper (3.6 per cent), leather (3.5 per cent) and timber (1.4 per cent); of these only iron and steel and chemicals were not essentially related to agrarian production. Nor did home production always relate most effectively to home needs; in 1944 Bulgarian chemical plants produced glue, paint, soap, glycerine and cosmetics, but not fertilizers.

By 1938 Bulgarian industrial production was no more than 5.6 per cent of gross national production, the lowest proportion in south-eastern Europe, Albania excepted, and one not much different from the 5.1 per cent of 1926. The size of Bulgarian industrial units, like that of farms, remained small. In 1934 only 322 out of some 88,000 workshops and factories employed more than fifty people, and between 1926 and 1938 the share of workshops in the total of manufactured production rose from 5 per cent to 9.3 per cent, whilst the average number of employees per firm declined from 32.5 in 1931 to 28.6 in 1938; by 1944 the average had fallen to 26. The number of small, non-encouraged enterprises rose by 218 per cent between 1931 (643) and 1937 (2,042) whilst that of the larger, encouraged firms fell by 26.2 per cent from 1,145 to 845.

If the industrial sector during the 1930s saw the withdrawal of the state from some of its former activities, this was not the case in finance and commerce. The chaos produced by the collapse of the Vienna Creditanstaltverein in the summer of 1931 forced the Bulgarian government to impose foreign currency restrictions in October. These, together with subsequent control over foreign trading, restored to the Bulgarian National Bank much of the authority it had lost when Western pressure forced Bulgaria on to the gold standard in 1928. By 1933 the BNB had to authorise all imports, and by 1936 it was allocating quotas and issuing

Table 4 *Relative income per category of workforce, 1934*

	Distribution of the population	Distribution of income	Relative income per capita
Agriculture, forestry and fishing	69.1	42.6	0.62
Manufacturing, mining and building	14.0	15.9	1.14
Transport and communication	2.3	4.2	1.83
Commerce and finance	4.1	24.6	6.00
Public administration	3.9	9.5	2.44
Services	6.6	3.2	0·49

Source: Colin Clark, *The Conditions of Economic Progress* (second edition, London, 1951), p. 449.

import licences. In December 1930, under the impact of sliding world prices for agrarian produce, the government established the grain-purchasing agency, Hranoiznos, which began operations in February 1931. As Hranoiznos was buying at above the world price and selling to local consumers it needed protection against undercutting by external concerns operating in the Bulgarian market; it therefore acquired exclusive control over the sale as well as the purchase of grain, and its powers were later extended to sugar-beet, where it could determine the area to be sown, and to other commodities such as flax and hemp. With the revival of trade in the late 1930s Hranoiznos lost much of its relevance, but this was immediately restored by the outbreak of the Second World War; by 1943 twenty-three items were under its control, the only major commodities outside its jurisdiction being tobacco and fruit. Hranoiznos had set a powerful precedent for state control of the economy in peace as well as war.

This was recognised in 1939, when Hranoiznos was used as a skeleton around which to fashion the body of state economic control, this being effected primarily through the Directorate of Civilian Mobilisation, established in 1940. The problems of directing the war economy were much the same as between 1915 and 1918, the relations between civilian and military authorities being uneasy and the attitude of the German ally frequently obstructive. The policies adopted by the Directorate and by its short-lived successor, the Directorate for the War Economy, were similar to those of the First World War. So too were their consequences – resistance to requisitioning, circumvention of the official distribution system, and hoarding. This together with grain shortages and the drought of 1942 forced the government to introduce bread rationing and later a number of meatless days. And yet some lessons had been learned from 1915–18, and Bulgaria's experiences on the home front during the Second World War, though uncomfortable, did not produce deprivation and social unrest as profound as that seen in 1918.

Throughout the inter-war period Bulgarian trading links with Germany had been close. These links had been forged in the First World War, and were maintained in the 1920s, when Germany took a quarter of all Bulgaria's exports. The crisis of 1929, and more so that of 1931, further impelled Bulgaria towards Germany, which was prepared to allow the purchase of German goods in non-convertible currency, a vital consideration when, despite the decline of foreign currency earnings, the French were still demanding payment of reparations and loan obligations in convertible currency. The first formal agreement between Sofia and Berlin was signed in 1931, and thereafter exports to Germany grew at an exponential rate with the major expansion coming at the end of the decade; by 1939 Germany was buying 67.8 per cent of Bulgarian exports, compared to 48 per cent for Germany and Austria in 1934, and providing 65.5 per cent of Bulgarian imports, compared to 44.9 per cent in 1934. By 1944 Hitler's Reich purchased 87.7 per cent of Bulgarian exports and provided 72.2 per cent of its imports.

With the quickening of economic activity in the mid-1930s and the intensification of governmental control over many sectors of the economy during the Second World War came yet greater dominance by Sofia. In a heavily centralised political system such as Bulgaria's the administrative power of the capital was inevitably great, but in the inter-war period Sofia entrenched itself also as the industrial centre of the nation, primarily because investment funds were easier to find in the capital than in the provinces. By 1934 62 per cent of Bulgaria's joint stock companies were in Sofia, which accounted for no less than a third of the nation's industrial production: that the city's revenues trebled in the 1930s was due largely to the growth of industry within its borders, a process measured also in the decline of officials from 28 per cent to 14 per cent of the capital's workforce. The concentration of industry in the capital was halted only by the savage bombing of 1943 and 1944.

The economic growth without substantial structural change which had characterised the Bulgarian economy in the 1930s did little to solve the nation's basic social problems. Although the peasants could withdraw into a form of frugal self-sufficiency this did nothing to alleviate the hardships of the urban population, who by the late 1930s were spending up to 56 per cent of their income on food. Taxation now fell more heavily upon the townsfolk, as food, which the peasants could provide for themselves, was subject to indirect levies. Also, whilst social differences in the countryside were minimal and disguised by the fact that almost all rural Bulgarians were engaged in similar occupations, in the towns disparities of wealth were considerable and palpable. These differentials in economic reward are revealed in table 4.

Bulgaria thus emerged from the war politically adrift and disillusioned, economically backward, centralised and over-dependent upon one large foreign trading partner, and, in the towns at least, socially divided. The old political order was again near collapse, and the patronage of Germany had again failed; but after this war Russia was not the ruined, racked and introspective power of 1918–19. In that difference were to be found many of the determinants of Bulgaria's future development.

4

Bulgaria under Communist rule

THE SEIZURE OF POLITICAL POWER, 1944-7

The coup d'état of 9 September 1944 did not create Communist power in
Bulgaria. That formidable edifice was built gradually and with much effort
between September 1944 and December 1947. The process involved the
elimination of effective political opposition, the destruction of the social
power of the bourgeoisie and the isolation of Bulgaria from hostile foreign
influences; it was a process affected by the dynamics of internal evolution
and by developments in the international sphere.

The cabinet formed on 9 September 1944 included representatives of
the four main groups within the Fatherland Front. Kimon Georgiev
became minister president with his Zveno colleague Velchev as minister
of war. There were four Communists, including Anton Yugov and Mincho
Neichev who occupied respectively the vital posts of minister of the interior
and minister of justice. There were four Agrarians, the most prominent
of whom was Nikola Petkov, and three Social Democrats led by Grigor
Cheshmedjiev. The three new regents were professor Venelin Ganev, a
Radical Democrat; Tsvetko Boboshevski, an independent with conservative
leanings; and the Communist philosopher Todor Pavlov.

In addition to the posts held by party members the Communists had a
number of advantages after 9 September 1944. In the first place there was
the Red Army, which was to remain in Bulgaria until the end of 1947.
In the armistice agreed on 28 October the Soviet Union was allowed
permanent chairmanship of the allied control commission which was to
remain in Sofia until the signature of a peace treaty, an arrangement
which bestowed upon the Soviet commissioner, Biriuzov, almost viceregal
powers. This arrangement had been suggested by London and suited a
British government that was about to dictate the political future of Greece.
Eden also parried American suggestions of intervention in Bulgarian
affairs with the argument that disagreement with Moscow would cause
more problems than it solved, especially if the Bulgarians, with Soviet

approval, refused to withdraw from the territories they had occupied in Macedonia and Thrace. The West, therefore, had no real prospect of intervening in Bulgarian affairs until the end of hostilities in Europe. By then much had been done to entrench Communist power.

Eden's fears that Moscow would back Bulgarian defiance of the West were well-founded, for the Soviets willingly provided Sofia with that great power patronage which had nearly always been considered essential to Bulgarian national security, and they even gave initial support to Bulgarian hopes for the retention of Thrace and for the securing of a port on the Aegean. Also, the Soviets gave immediate and much-needed aid to soften the impact of the poor harvest of 1944, and provided Bulgaria with oil and raw materials such as cotton fibre which were essential if the nation's industry were to be quickly re-established; in addition, the Soviet Union provided a welcome market for Bulgarian tobacco. Bulgaria's traditional Russophilia, a feeling assiduously nurtured by visits of Russian priests and the holding of a pan-Slav congress in Sofia, ensured that the Communists would profit from Soviet patronage and generosity. Nor was it without significance that Bulgarian Communists such as Dimitrov and Kolarov had played so prominent a role in the Comintern, for this could flatter the nationalist vanity of even non-Communist Bulgarians.

The party itself had recovered well from the decline which had affected it until the summer of 1943. Its tradition of discipline, together with the new enthusiasm born with the advent of the Red Army, created an organisation which was far more cohesive and controlled than any of its rivals. Morale was also boosted by Bagrianov's release of large numbers of political detainees in September 1944. These elated prisoners formed the kernel of the local party organisations, which now began the rapid expansion which was to take party membership from 15,000 in October 1944 to 250,000 a year later. By 1948 it was 460,000.

As in other parts of Europe, the general atmosphere of the initial post-war days favoured left-wing groups. The Communists' record of resistance, at least after June 1941, was as good as and usually better than those of the other parties, a fact which to many legitimised Communist participation in the government; the Soviet Union, and particularly the Red Army, were widely respected, and it was assumed that a government which included some Communists would be favourably regarded by Moscow and thus make Soviet patronage more secure and effective, and this was a powerful factor as long as the peace terms were still to be decided. The notion of a planned economy was generally attractive to a generation whose only experience of capitalism was its dismal failure in the 1930s, and even if Bulgaria suffered less in economic terms than almost any other European state, it still faced considerable problems. There was also the hope that if the Communists were to experience real coalition government and the genuine democratic process then they would shed their aspirations to monolithic control on the Soviet pattern.

The delusion that the Communists might become 'house-trained' in this fashion was soon dispelled by the rapid and systematic manner in which they began both to weaken their opponents and to consolidate their own power.

Immediately after 9 September 1944 the army was neutralised. Soldiers' councils were formed in many regiments and party zealots removed some 800 officers, including forty-two generals. The Soviet high command eventually stepped in to halt a process which might impair the fighting efficiency of the Bulgarian army, but not before it had frustrated attempts by the non-Communists to end the military purge; this was the first, but by no means the last occasion on which the local Communists came to rely on Soviet influence for the implementation of their policies. The attack upon the army involved not only the removal of unreliable officers but also the introduction of political commissars, many of whom had years of service in the Red Army. In December 1944 the very highest echelons of the Bulgarian army were reorganised, with colonel Ivan Kinov, a Bulgarian-born Soviet officer being appointed chief of staff. By this time a large proportion of the army was outside the country. After October, when Tito had lifted his embargo on its operation within his territory, the Bulgarian army had joined the Third Ukrainian Front in the campaign in Hungary and Austria. The troops which moved west with the Red Army were the trained elements of the regular army; the highly politicised units of the partisan detachments were formed into the new people's guard division, and were kept at home and in Macedonia where they could provide useful support for their civilian political allies.

More important than the people's guard divisions were the local Fatherland Front committees. In September 1944 they numbered about 700, but by November there were over 7,000 of them with a total membership of about 25,000 in which the Communists outnumbered the Agrarians by two to one and the Zvenari by thirty to one. Yet the Fatherland Front committees were not easily controlled and could embarrass the party leadership with their excessive zeal. The committees did, nevertheless, strike fierce if uncoordinated blows at the apparatus and the personnel of the old regime. Priests and other suspect elements were removed from any position of influence; teachers who were too devoted to established practices were replaced by men and women of the 'new era'; school textbooks and curricula were drastically revised, and public institutions were stripped of all the appurtenances of the old regime – in Lom, for example, all books in the town library published before 1944 were burnt. Most important of all factors in the consolidation of Communist power within local government, however, was the party's control of the ministry of the interior. By the end of 1944 30,000 bureaucrats had been dismissed, their dependable replacements receiving crash courses in administration and accounting and being exempted from educational qualifications needed for the civil service.

Other institutions were taken over in similarly energetic fashion. The Bulgarian Workers' Union created by the Zveno regime in the 1930s was purged and then disbanded, to enable the Communists to create a new General Workers' Professional Union consisting of the former BWU and a number of white collar unions; by March 1945, when it held its first congress, the new union could boast 264,000 members. Even more influential in the social sector were the workers' councils established in most enterprises after 9 September. A decree of December 1944 increased the powers of the councils, which now had to check all company accounts, a very powerful weapon and also useful training for the cadres who in later years would manage the newly nationalised industrial concerns. The power of the employer was further weakened by other economic and social controls exercised by the new authorities. The properties of all Germans and Italians and of Bulgarian fascists were confiscated and handed initially to the Soviets; a long term of imprisonment or even the death sentence could be handed out to any employer who failed to honour delivery quotas set by the authorities; profits were to be limited to a set percentage of capital; shares could be confiscated if possession of them were not publicly acknowledged; and anyone found guilty of profiteering since 1935 would face a similar sanction. It was left to the Fatherland Front committees and to the workers' councils which were represented on them to search for profiteers.

Two institutions born immediately after the liberation, the people's militia and the people's courts, helped carry out the purges which racked Bulgaria after 9 September 1944. The people's militia was formed when the former police force collapsed with the old regime; the new body was entirely dominated by the Communists, who held every post of importance at national or local level. Closely allied to the people's militia were the people's courts, created by a decree of 6 October 1944 to try 'collaborators' and 'war criminals'. Since Bulgaria had retained its own administration and had refused to participate in either the war on the eastern front or the final solution, the number of citizens in either of these categories was not large, but this did not prevent the new Bulgarian authorities from indulging in a purge which, per head of the population, claimed more victims than any other in eastern Europe. Official figures admit to the trial of 11,667 persons within six months of the 6 October decree, but unofficial estimates number the victims at anything between 30,000 and 100,000.

Partisanstvo had accustomed Bulgarians to the notion that the party which enjoyed political power would pack the administration with its supporters, but it had not prepared the nation for the social revolution which it was now experiencing. The bloodletting which engulfed Bulgaria in the months after 9 September 1944 had many causes. In the first place it was inevitable that the thousands of political detainees, recently released from gaol and handed wide-ranging social and political power, should take revenge upon their former tormentors. Inevitable too was the mixing of personal vendetta and political vengeance in which not a few innocent victims were persecuted. Such a process was of course useful to, and used by, the Communists, for it allowed an attack upon potential or actual opponents to be subsumed into the understandable, European-wide reaction against defeated fascist power. But the extent of Bulgaria's attack upon the 'collaborators' was in itself a function of the relative quiescence of the war years. Bulgaria had not experienced the human destruction which other states had had to endure. It had seen little of the elemental violence or the calculated brutality inflicted upon Yugoslavia or Poland, and therefore the forces of the old regime were stronger in Bulgaria than in many other states; in Bulgaria the local, non-Communist intelligentsia had not been pruned either by native fascists or by Nazi occupiers, and therefore the potential pool of opposition was greater than in those countries which had suffered more. It was also felt that a strenuous persecution of those responsible for Bulgaria's pro-axis policies might do something to soften the peace terms which the allies would impose on the country. For some Bulgarians their nation's lack of resistance, even to the relatively mild authoritarian regimes of the 1930s and 1940s, demanded some form of dramatic expiation; thus would guilt be expunged by blood.

Whilst Communist supremacy was established within the framework of local government an attack was also launched upon former leaders at the national level. Immediately after 9 September 1944 the Soviets or the new authorities in Bulgaria had quietly removed Boris's body from its final resting place at Rila and then proceeded to arrest two of the regents (Filov had disappeared temporarily), together with a number of royal advisers, all those who had held cabinet office since 1941, and all members of the existing Sŭbranie. Their trial began at the end of December. On 1 February 1945 the chief prosecutor demanded the death sentence for fifty of the accused. In a gesture of warning to all potential opponents of the Fatherland Front the supreme penalty was inflicted upon precisely twice that number; they were shot in batches of twenty that very night. The old right and centre of Bulgarian politics had been irrevocably destroyed.

The removal of the right and centre meant that the only forces remaining to oppose the Communists were on the traditional left, and it was in this much-troubled region that battle was now joined. The first confrontation was with the Agrarians, though the first target of Communist attack was only those sections of BANU which had not joined the Fatherland Front. In the summer of 1944 Gichev and his supporters had refused to become part of the coalition and had joined the Muraviev cabinet, hoping thereby to form the centrist-dominated block which would achieve Gichev's objective of containing the excesses of both right and left. After 9 September 1944, with the Pladne Agrarians within the Fatherland Front, Gichev had been imprisoned, and leadership of the Agrarian party had been taken up by G. M. Dimitrov, 'Gemeto'.

Gemeto, however, did not join the government, and from his position as party leader concentrated upon rebuilding and strengthening the Agrarian party as a bulwark against increasing Communist influence. After being smuggled out of Bulgaria in their diplomatic luggage Gemeto had spent much of the war advising the British, and in the summer of 1944 had attempted to negotiate a peace with the Western allies. This and his war experiences provided convenient sticks with which to beat him. Soon after the British suppression of the Athens rising of December 1944 he was accused of being a British agent, and after fierce pressure from the Communists Gemeto resigned the leadership of his party in January 1945. By April he had been placed under house arrest, from which he was to escape to find refuge in the home of the American representative in Sofia, whence he eventually slipped out to exile in the West. In July 1946 a Sofia court sentenced him to life imprisonment.

Gemeto's successor as leader of the Agrarians was Nikola Petkov, the son of the minister president assassinated in 1907. Petkov's credentials as an anti-fascist and an opponent of Bulgaria's pro-German alignment were unassailable, and to these advantages he added a fearless and attractive personality, a compelling oratorical style and a shrewd sense of political tactics. By the end of 1944 he had become an outspoken critic of Communist methods and was calling for an end to Communist domination of the local Fatherland Front committees. With the Social Democratic leaders, Cheshmedjiev and Kosta Lulchev, he had been prominent in opposing Communist attempts to unite all youth organisations under that run by the Communists, and had condemned decrees of December 1944 and January 1945 by which the government used the shortage of newsprint to increase its control over newspaper publication and distribution. In March 1945 Petkov's relations with the Communists were strained yet further, first by the decree for the defence of the people's power, which attempted to confer a political monopoly upon the parties of the Fatherland Front, and secondly by the election to the executive committee of the Fatherland Front of the veteran Communist leaders Dimitrov and Kolarov, both of whom were still in Moscow. At BANU's congress in May, proponents of collaboration, led by the former Pladne leader Alexandŭr Obbov and much encouraged by Dimitrov in Moscow, outvoted Petkov, who then resigned the leadership of the Agrarian party. The Obbov group took control of the party paper, *Zemedelsko Zname*, after which Yugov, the Communist minister of the interior, ruled that the property and all the assets of BANU belonged to the Obbov faction. Petkov, though still a member of the government, was forced to organise his own party outside the Fatherland Front. Similar methods were to be employed in September to remove Lulchev and Cheshmedjiev from the leadership of the Social Democratic Party, which fell to the pro-Communist Dimitŭr Neikov.

Communist tactics within BANU and the Social Democratic Party had three important results. In the first place they secured Communist domination within the Fatherland Front, and once that domination had been established the Communists could feel confident enough to go forward to the elections which the Yalta conference had said must be held, though they were still careful to insist that the coalition should present a single list. Secondly, the Communist takeover of the old BANU apparatus highlighted Petkov's increasingly important role as the nation's bulwark against total Communist domination. There was a general nation-wide distaste for the excesses of the purges, but to voice such distaste could be hazardous when denunciations and rapid dispensation of justice were so common. Those who themselves felt under threat from Communist functionaries at the lower levels saw in Petkov's position a national reflection of their own predicaments, and heard in Petkov's words an echo of their own aspirations. This was especially the case for many of Bulgaria's peasant proprietors, who instinctively looked to a BANU leader for protection. The peasants had survived the war without too much discomfort; casualties had been lower than in the First World War, and peasant incomes had not fallen as much as those of their urban compatriots. Now their security was threatened by the over-assertive Communists and the odour of collectivisation which inevitably hung around them. Petkov seemed the peasants' best defence against the loss of their land.

In the third place the manoeuvres against Petkov were so transparent that they galvanised him and his sympathisers to effective counter measures against the Communists in the elections which had been arranged for 26 August. Petkov concentrated his criticism on the government's insistence that the coalition should go to the country with a single list; this, he maintained, was unfair, not least because it would mean the Communists having more candidates than the Agrarians despite the fact that in the country at large the latter outnumbered them by five to one. Petkov demanded separate lists for each constituent party of the Fatherland Front, and on 2 August resigned from the government. At the same time he appealed to the Western powers for help in pressing the Soviets to prevent the carrying out of the single-list election, and for assistance in reducing the illegal pressures which, he said, were being put upon the electorate by the Communists. At the very last moment Moscow accepted postponement of the elections until 18 November.

Petkov, with Western backing, seemed to have scored a notable victory, and the Communists had been forced to recognise that Soviet influence was not unlimited. Nor was the postponement of the elections Petkov's only victory, for the government soon announced that it was willing to allow oppositionists to stand as representatives of parties and not merely as individuals, as had been the original plan. Four opposition parties were to be allowed to enter the contest: Petkov's Agrarians, the independent Social Democrats under Lulchev, the United Radical Party of Stoenchev, and the Democrats, now led by Mushanov and the historian Aleksandŭr Girginov. There was also some relaxation in the government's control over the press, although the radio remained a government monopoly.

This was not enough for Petkov. He still wanted the parties of the Fatherland Front, like those of the opposition, to run on separate tickets in the elections. He also wanted an end to Communist intimidation through the local committees of the Fatherland Front, the complete elimination of political influence in the law courts, the restoration of twenty-one as opposed to eighteen for the minimum voting age, the resignation of the government, and an end to Communist tenure of the ministries of justice and the interior. In this, as in his demand for the annulment of the decisions of the rigged Agrarian congress in May, he had the support of the Western powers. Petkov's was a bold programme and his audacity grew from two roots. The first was the apparent increase in the strength of his own party, to which Gichev's faction had attached itself, and which had been joined by the Social Democrats in a loose 'federation of rural and urban labour'. The second was his conviction that after the postponement of the elections the Communists were a much weakened force: Soviet influence had been checked, and the local Communists themselves, Petkov believed, would not have sufficient internal support to make their own way to power. Petkov also declared that if his conditions were not met he would have to tell his supporters that active participation in the election would be too dangerous and that they should therefore boycott the poll. Should that happen, he believed, the result would be without any validity and any government that might be built upon it would never receive recognition from the Western powers. This the government could not afford. Non-recognition, as in the 1890s, would make it difficult to find the loans which were necessary to pay, *inter alia*, the occupation expenses of the Red Army, and might also mean the exclusion of Bulgarian representatives from discussions on the country's borders. Moreover, as long as an unrecognised government held office there could be little prospect of a peace treaty, and until a peace treaty was signed the Western powers would retain their commissioners in Sofia. That the Western powers were clearly important in Petkov's plans was illustrated when on 10 October the United States announced that it had reason to believe that Petkov's fears for the impartiality and freedom of the coming polls were justified; the U.S. government had already decided to send Mark Etheridge, editor of the Louisville *Courier–Journal*, to the Balkans to make sure that American diplomatists there were not misleading the secretary of state, but now his chief function was to observe Communist behaviour with regard to elections in Bulgaria and Romania. On 11 October Petkov ordered his supporters to withdraw from the election campaign.

The political contest around the elections of 1945 ended in a draw. The Communists, strengthened by the return to Bulgaria on 7 November of Vasil Kolarov and the legendary Georgi Dimitrov, were able to lift martial law on 10 November and claim a sweeping victory in the poll of 18 November, in which the government coalition received 86 per cent of the votes as opposed to the 12 per cent cast for the oppositionists; a cabinet was formed, again under Georgiev, containing most of the leading figures from the previous administration. On the other hand, Petkov too could claim success. The poll was not recognised as valid by the United States, for, as expected, Etheridge had reported unfavourably on the elections. Petkov could now not only demand all the concessions he had insisted upon before the vote, but also the annulment of the elections. At the end of the year the powers, meeting in Moscow, agreed that two oppositionists should be included in the Bulgarian cabinet, and this seemed yet another indication of Petkov's strength. In January 1946 Vyshinsky, the Soviet deputy commissar for foreign affairs, paid a visit to Sofia in an effort to persuade Petkov and Lulchev to join the government and thus settle the dispute between the Fatherland Front and the oppositionists. He failed completely. Petkov and Lulchev remained adamant that the Communists must relinquish their hold upon the ministries of the interior and of justice, that the Sŭbranie should be dissolved, and that free elections should be held immediately.

Petkov and Lulchev had proved the equal of their Communist opponents and the political impasse was not to be broken for another year. In the meantime battle could be joined on other fronts. On 24 February 1946 Krŭstiŭ Pastuhov, a prominent Social Democrat and life-long opponent of the Communists, was arrested after he had written an article in the Social Democratic newspaper, *Svoboden Narod* (*A Free People*), criticising a speech Dimitrov had made to army officers. Pastuhov was charged with attempting to sow discord in the ranks of the army and sentenced to five years' penal servitude. The incident was used to make another attack upon the political power of the army. Shortly before Pastuhov's trial ended the Communist former minister of justice, Neichev, declared that there would be a thorough purge of 'fascists' within the army, and on 3 July the Sŭbranie enacted a bill for the leadership and control of the army. The bill was reminiscent of the debates of the early 1880s, for it decreed that authority for the control of the army was to pass from the ministry of war to the cabinet as a whole. This weakened Velchev and his Zveno colleagues and strengthened once again Communist influence over the armed forces; Velchev's position was further undermined because the Pastuhov trial had connected him with the murder of Stamboliiski in 1923, and with Mihailović, whose trial had just ended in Belgrade. In September Velchev resigned as minister of war to become Bulgarian ambassador to Switzerland; his political career had ended. The events of the summer of 1946 not only impaired the political strength of Zveno but further weakened the old professional officer corps of Bulgaria. It had lost its most powerful spokesman in the cabinet, control of the profession had been passed to the party politicians which it had always despised and distrusted, and, last but by no means least, its own ranks had been drastically reduced by the sacking of some 2,000 'reactionary' officers. For a generation at least the Bulgarian army had been removed from the political arena.

These decisions on the army were followed by two important votes. Early in September, in a referendum on the future of the monarch, 92.32 per cent of the 92.1 per cent of the electorate who voted declared in favour of a republic. This was proclaimed on 15 September; the nine year-old King Simeon immediately went into exile. The second vote was to elect a grand national Sŭbranie which was to decide upon the future constitution of the republic.

The assault upon the old officer corps and the polls of autumn 1946 were closely connected with developments in the international sphere. In August the Paris peace conference had begun discussion of the Bulgarian treaty. Kulishev, the Bulgarian foreign minister, had asked the conference for recognition of Bulgaria as a co-belligerent, a plea which all the major allies, the Soviet Union included, refused. Kulishev also argued against the severe limitations upon Bulgarian armed strength which the draft treaty proposed, and the destruction of the political power of the old officer corps had been meant in part to persuade the Paris conference that the Bulgarian army need no longer be feared as a bastion of nationalist, royalist or pro-German sentiment. Kulishev was more open in his propagandising over the referendum, and, with much sense of occasion, he announced its result to the conference on 9 September, declaring that 'the war-mongering Coburgs' had been removed from Bulgarian political life for ever. As for the elections to the grand national Sŭbranie, they would allow the expression of all opinions other than those of monarchism and fascism, and the powers could therefore have every confidence that the new system of government which the assembly would devise would enjoy full popular support and would therefore be worthy of recognition.

The elections to the grand national Sŭbranie took place on 27 October. After the Paris debates, in which the Western powers had shown little sympathy towards Bulgaria, the opposition was less confident of British and American support, and for this reason Petkov and the other non-governmental parties not only decided to join the election but also chose to fight it as a combined force with a single list of candidates. They received 22 per cent of the votes cast and 101 of the 364 seats; the distribution of votes showed that there had been massive defections from the non-Communist parties of the Fatherland Front; this weakening in the cohesion of the Fatherland Front was to gather pace in the coming months. One reason for this was the naked assertion of Communist dominance within the coalition, as seen, for example, in the distribution of Fatherland Front seats in the new assembly; the Communists had 277, the coalition Agrarians sixty-nine, the coalition Social Democrats nine, Zveno eight and Kosturkov's Radicals one. The Communists were not only overwhelmingly the largest single party, they had all but annihilated their partners in the Fatherland Front; Bulgarian politics was now visibly what it had been since 9 September 1944, a life-and-death struggle between the Communists and their opponents.

Neither Petkov nor the Western powers were satisfied with the election. Petkov told foreign journalists that interference and intimidation had decreased the opposition vote by at least three-fifths. The opposition parties, he said, had not been allowed either a free press or an unrestricted right of assembly, and the meetings they had held had not infrequently been disrupted by Communist activists. He complained further that a number of opposition supporters had been kept in prison, that protagonists of the government had been allowed to vote more than once – most of the new, pro-Communist army officers had been given at least two ballot slips – whilst many anti-government activists had not received their voting cards or had been prevented from reaching the polling stations by military road-blocks. His scepticism about the result was shared by the Americans and the British.

Despite these misgivings there was nothing which Petkov, the Social Democrats or the Western members of the allied control commission could do to prevent the formation of a new government reflecting 'popular opinion' as expressed in the election. In November Georgiev, having failed to gain a seat in the grand national Sŭbranie, resigned the premiership, though he was soon made minister for foreign affairs. Georgi Dimitrov became minister president. With him in a much enlarged cabinet were seven fellow Communists, including Traicho Kostov, a minister without portfolio, Anton Yugov, who remained minister of the interior, and general Georgi Damyanov, who, as minister of war, consolidated Communist influence over the army. The cabinet also contained five Agrarians, including Obbov, two Social Democrats, two Zvenari, and one independent, Dimo Kazasov, who had, however, run on the Communist ticket in October. Vasil Kolarov had since September been acting president.

The elections of October 1946 had cleared the ground for the decisive struggle of Bulgaria's post-war history, that between the Communists and Petkov. Before the main battle, however, there were a number of minor skirmishes. In December 1946 Mushanov's small but respected Democratic Party was dealt a severe blow when its newspaper, *Zname* (*Banner*), was closed down. At the close of the year the government turned its attention to another arm of the old state when it ordered all Bulgarian diplomatists serving abroad to return to the country by 15 March 1947 on pain of losing their rights of citizenship. In March 1947 the central committee of the BWP (Communists) ordered a major offensive against the opposition parties with the specific objective of dividing them from within. By April such tactics had succeeded in removing Petkov's devotee, Dimitŭr Stoyanov, from the post of organisation secretary of BANU and replacing him with the more pliable Asen Stamboliiski, son of the great leader, and by the early summer there was also rising tension, much of it fomented by Communist supporters, between the Petkov and Gichev wings of the party. In May the two most important opposition newspapers, the Petkovist *Narodno Zemedelsko Zname* (*National Agrarian Banner*) and the Social Democratic *Svoboden Narod*, were suspended, when workers in the Strela company refused, on instructions from the Communists, to print or distribute opposition newspapers. As Strela enjoyed a state monopoly on newspaper distribution this meant that opposition journals were at the mercy of the Communist-dominated unions.

This sudden intensification of the campaign against the opposition had several causes. The first was the increasing strength of the opposition itself. The slaughter of the innocents within the Fatherland Front caused a number of small groups to leave the coalition and join the opposition. In December Yurukov, leader of a sizeable Zveno faction within the Front, attacked 'doctrinaire Marxism', and transformed his group's newspaper, *Izgrev* (*Dawn*), into an opposition journal. The Radicals too began to reconsider their attitude to a coalition now totally dominated by the Communists. The nakedness of Communist ambition, together with the defections from the Fatherland Front which it caused, did much to reactivate the old bourgeois parties of Mushanov, Burov and others; it also put the Bulgarian church on its guard, for its synod rejected a proposal from the national committee of the Fatherland Front for the democratisation of the church. If these parties and the church could not exercise much individual power they could at least combine with one another, and in the spring of 1947 there were signs of an emerging opposition coalition which would include not only the church and Yurukov's supporters but even disaffected elements from the right-wing of Obbov's Agrarian Party, which was still within the Fatherland Front. At the same time Petkov had a good deal of support in the mass organisations, particularly the youth and the women's movements, which were affiliated to the Fatherland Front; the Front seemed to be on the point of dissolution. The bourgeois parties, the church and the disaffected groups within the Front would constitute a powerful force if they could combine with Petkov's adherents, who by now numbered between 90,000 and 100,000.

Such support for Petkov's independent Agrarians is easily understood and reflects the social transformation which Bulgaria was undergoing. Peasant suspicion of attempts to collectivise the land was ineradicable. The government moved cautiously. In Bulgaria the new socialised form of agriculture, the TKZS, was cooperative rather than collective.* Membership was voluntary and those joining did not have to contribute all their land,

---

* Socialised agriculture in Bulgaria was cooperative rather than collective but the distinction had disappeared by the late 1960s, and because of the familiarity of English readers with the term 'collective farm' I have used this as well as the more accurate 'cooperative'.

but for whatever land they did bring into the cooperative they received a ground rent, an arrangement which was unique in eastern Europe, and which (in that it looked back to Stamboliiski as well as to Lenin) could be seen as an individual Bulgarian solution to the problem of how the land was to be socialised. Yet despite the voluntary nature of the TKZSs there was some pressure on the private farmer, particularly in regulations concerning maximum holdings and in the setting of compulsory delivery quotas. Pressure on the private sector increased in 1948, but until then the new collectives attracted only a few very poor peasants, most of whom were already committed Communists. The main body of the peasantry remained instinctively and doggedly opposed to the Communists and their plans for agriculture.

The commercial and manufacturing sectors of Bulgarian society had already been put on their guard by the compulsory registration of assets, the confiscation of the property of 'fascists', and the punishment of profiteers. The local committees of the Fatherland Front were empowered to investigate any enterprise or person considered suspect, and by 1947 137 enterprises had been confiscated, 1,941 cases had been reviewed by the people's courts, and a further 3,282 cases had been dropped, not through a sudden access of mercy or compassion, but in most cases because more effective ways of dispossessing or weakening their owners had been found. There were also some instances of nationalisation. The coal, rubber, and fur industries had been taken into public ownership shortly after 9 September 1944, and in 1947 it was the turn of the much more widespread alcohol and soft drinks concerns. Government control was also exercised by its considerable purchasing power in the domestic market. In the commercial sector, in fact, private enterprise was still much restricted in that the government, partly because of the rains of the autumn of 1944 and the droughts of the two subsequent springs, retained much of its wartime powers to regulate the supply of foodstuffs and other commodities, the machinery of Hranoiznos and the Directorate of Civilian Mobilisation being incorporated into the new Higher Economic Council (VSS). In 1946 new tax laws hit at capitalists and Bulgaria's few remaining private financiers, who were given a painfully short period to clear arrears outstanding since 1942, whilst Bulgarian shares in foreign companies were confiscated; the one major foreign financial concern still extant in Bulgaria, Paribas, sold out in the same year. In March 1947 the monetary reforms which introduced a new currency also blocked all private bank accounts holding over 20,000 *leva* and imposed a once-and-for-all tax on all other accounts; the accumulation of new deposits was made impossible by a progressive tax on incomes and savings. By

1947 Bulgaria's small bourgeoisie felt itself to be under an ever-intensifying siege, and would naturally support any efforts to break free of Communist encroachment.

Suspicion and hostility from the peasants, private employers and investors could have been anticipated by the Communists, who were, however, less prepared for opposition on the part of the industrial workforce. Bulgarian industry had suffered considerably both during and after the war. The bombing had forced many plants to move out from the cities, and after 1944 deficiencies in the transport system meant that they could not be reassembled rapidly enough, on top of which Bulgarian industry had to search for new markets in a generally hostile and impoverished world. These factors, together with demobilisation and the return to Bulgaria of many workers who had been sent to Germany during the war, caused unemployment, and by 1947 38,000 workers, some 20 per cent of the country's industrial labour force, were without jobs. As half of them were in the tobacco industry, traditionally a Communist stronghold, it was sometimes asked how effective the Communists could be if they were unable to defend their own best friends in the working class. Whilst unemployment increased real wages were being forced down by food-price inflation caused by the severe winter of 1947 and by the export of food to the Soviet Union. Strikes were increasingly frequent, but many workers found relief not in political action but, as soon as the weather allowed, in leaving their place of work in order to cultivate the family plot; this recrudescence of the ancient habit of withdrawal into the village deprived one mine of two-thirds of its labour force. Although this was an extreme case, mining in general was much affected by this return to the countryside, and the resulting coal shortages impaired the effectiveness of the railways and made food distribution yet more difficult.

In addition to these short-term difficulties the Communists faced a serious long-term problem in the industrial sector. The persecution of 'war profiteers' had removed a considerable proportion of the pre-1944 manufacturers, but the state sector had not replaced them all. Here was a golden opportunity for private enterprise, and such enterprises founded after 9 September 1944, as long as they conformed to recent legislation, had nothing to fear from the people's courts. Furthermore, the dispersal of industry during the air-raids meant that there were scattered around the country many small plants which could themselves be developed and could in turn stimulate the growth of more local, private enterprises; between 1944 and 1947 the number of employees in plants with over twenty horsepower of energy supply grew by 30.63 per cent from 111,000 to 145,000, whilst those employed in smaller plants increased by 58.75 per cent from 80,000 to 127,000. The Stalinist variant of Marxism made no provision for the building of socialism in a society whose petty producers were growing stronger, and these economic and social developments, which naturally alarmed the Communists, must be taken into account when explaining both the rise of the opposition and the intensification of government attacks upon it in 1947.

It was not only internal factors that encouraged the sharpening political confrontation of 1947. In February the peace treaty had been signed in Paris. The boundaries of Bulgaria were fixed at their 1940 lines, thus preserving Bulgarian possession of the southern Dobrudja but ending any aspirations to Macedonia, Thrace or an Aegean port; Bulgaria's armed forces were to number no more than 65,500 persons and were to have no more than ninety aircraft; reparations were to be paid to Yugoslavia and Greece; all Bulgarian citizens were to enjoy complete equality and full civil rights; Bulgaria was forbidden a fascist or a military regime and was not to pursue policies hostile to the Soviet Union or any other member of the United Nations; and Soviet troops were to leave Bulgaria within ninety days of the treaty coming into force.

This last stipulation heartened the opposition and Petkov even talked in the Sŭbranie of Communist power collapsing as soon as the Red Army had quit Bulgarian soil. The Truman doctrine announced soon after the peace treaty provided even greater encouragement. On the other hand the signing of the treaty was not entirely to the oppositionists' advantage, for its ratification would mean the end of the allied control commission and the departure of their powerful Western supporters in it. The opposition needed to work fast, and therefore attacks upon the government intensified throughout the spring of 1947. There were sharp clashes in the grand national Sŭbranie over the proposed constitution. Petkov argued for a restoration of the Tŭrnovo system without the monarchy, but this the Communists would not accept. The constitutional debate opened out into a fierce confrontation in which the opposition even demanded a ban on the Communist party as a 'fascist' organisation, and Petkov taunted Dimitrov with accusations that present expenditure on prisons and the police was four times higher than in 1942. The climax of the struggle came in the summer of 1947, and once again internal developments were closely connected with external factors. On 4 June the United States senate ratified the peace treaty; on 5 June Petkov was arrested; on 20 September the peace treaty came into force; on 23 September Petkov was executed.

The final stages of the Petkov saga were grotesque. He had been arrested amid tumultuous scenes in the Sŭbranie and on 23 July was handed a 9,000 word indictment, the main charges of which were that he had attempted to form a military league to overthrow the government, that he had undermined military morale and discipline, that he had conspired with various BANU functionaries to organise acts of terrorism, that he wished to cooperate with 'monarcho-fascists' in Greece, and that he aimed to destroy Bulgarian–Soviet friendship and to divide worker from peasant in his native land. Such bizarre charges had to be invented because the fashionable and usually convenient accusation of collaboration could scarcely be invoked against one who had been resisting pro-German policies even during the days of the Nazi–Soviet pact; and if there had been but the slightest hint of collaboration between Petkov and the pro-German regimes it would have been eagerly seized upon and used against him. When the trial opened on 5 August neither Petkov nor any of the other accused – three officers and a bemused peasant – was allowed a defence lawyer or permitted to place evidence before the court; this, it was said, would not be 'of use or importance'. Prosecution witnesses, on the other hand, had been carefully prepared. Despite Petkov's amazingly dignified conduct the result was never in doubt, and on 16 August a verdict of guilty and a sentence of death were pronounced; to give the latter a ghostly patina of public endorsement the authorities bussed into Sofia hundreds of peasants primed to demand the death of the 'traitor' Petkov; meanwhile the trade unions chorused, 'To a dog, a dog's death.' When the desired sentence was carried out Petkov was not shot but hanged like the meanest of criminals, and in a final refinement of malice he was, although a practising Christian, denied both the final sacraments and a religious burial. The execution took place despite official diplomatic intervention from Britain and the United States, and private pleas for clemency from, *inter alios*, Herriot, Blum and Dimitrov's defence lawyer in the Reichstag trial.

Dimitrov had no time for such noble sentimentality and he was quick to turn foreign championship of Petkov against him; had it not been for such intervention, he said, Petkov need not have been executed. The Fatherland Front stuck to its insistence that the opposition had tried to overthrow the government by illegal means, and that such tactics could not produce the Western-style parliamentary democracy to which Petkov and his allies said they aspired. The Communists debated whether such a system was in any case practicable in a society as embittered and divided as Bulgaria's, especially when previous experience of theoretically representative democracy had meant only chaos, personal rule and eventual disaster; what Bulgaria needed, argued Dimitrov's camp, was the political stability necessary for massive social and economic restructuring.

Whether full Communist power was to bring political stability is doubtful, but what is beyond question is that the defeat of Petkov marked the end of the real battle between the Bulgarian Communists and their domestic opponents. Only mopping up operations remained and these began almost immediately after the arrest of Petkov. On 12 June the grand national Sŭbranie decided to unseat twenty-three Agrarians for writing 'unconstitutional letters of loyalty' to their arrested leader; on 20 June a number of prominent Agrarians who had rallied to Petkov's defence, including Asen Stamboliiski, were warned that disloyal opposition would no longer be tolerated in Bulgaria. On 26 August, ten days after the verdicts on Petkov had been declared, an official statement pronounced that his party had become 'a centre for fascist forces seeking revenge' and was therefore to be dissolved; its deputies were removed from the grand national Sŭbranie, its youth and other organisations were disbanded and its property confiscated. In effect the historic Agrarian party, which had contributed so much to Bulgarian political development and which had done so much to promote the well-being of the mass of the Bulgarian people, had ceased to exist. This was the most important single development in Bulgaria since the end of the war, for it removed the one sizeable and popular obstacle on the Communist road to power. The removal of that obstacle had had to be violent. The Communists could not hope to win over the peasants by programmes of land redistribution similar to those in Poland, Czechoslovakia, Hungary or even Romania, for there were no large estates or former German territories to carve up; nor could they rally the mass of the peasantry with an anti-kulak campaign, because Bulgaria's equitable land distribution meant that there were no kulaks. If the majority of the peasants could not be won over, then the existing focus of their loyalty had to be destroyed.

After Petkov's party had been smashed the others were easy prey. In September Yurukov's faction was excised from Zveno, and in the same month a further eighteen opposition activists were arrested on charges of helping 'diversionists' enter the country from Greece. Early in October any notions of resistance which might have arisen within the army were dispelled when thirty-nine senior officers went before the courts charged with attempting to form a military league to overthrow the government. The chief defendant was general Kiril Stanchev, a republican activist of many years' standing and the commander of the second army, which had fought against the Germans in 1944–5; in addition to the thirty-nine who stood public trial there were many other sackings in a purge which removed almost a third of serving officers on the grounds of their supposedly anti-Fatherland Front views. The Stanchev trial was used to link Petkov with the alleged military dissidents, and through them with figures such as Velchev, with whom Stanchev had cooperated in 1934 and 1935. After this accusation Velchev finally dissociated himself from Bulgarian public life, resigned his post as ambassador in Berne and went into exile.

By this time the division of Europe had solidified, with the rejection by the east European states, Bulgaria included, of the Marshall Plan in July, and with the formation of Cominform in October. Cominform policy, as set out in the Warsaw letter of October 1947, called for more rapid construction of socialism in the member states. One part of this process was the fusion of existing coalition parties into monolithic structures under Communist domination. The Fatherland Front was reconstructed accordingly. On 22 October its national committee accepted a proposal from the central committee of the Bulgarian Workers' Party that the worker–peasant alliance should be strengthened and that people's democracy should be transformed into social democracy. In December the XXVII congress of BANU (the Obbov wing) agreed upon a common programme with the Fatherland Front for the construction of a 'workers' democratic and socialist society in Bulgaria'. In same month the youth movements of the Fatherland Front's constituent parties were amalgamated into a single organisation completely dominated by the Communists; other mass organisations, for example women's associations, completed similar evolutions. In May 1948 the constituent parties agreed that they should reassess their ideologies in the light of Marxism–Leninism; in August the major acts of reconstruction were finally performed, the Socialists within the Front merging with the Communists, and the coalition Radicals and Zvenari being subsumed into the reorganised Fatherland Front. In deference to BANU's historic role Obbov's supporters were allowed to maintain a separate, Agrarian identity, but in July they had already renounced any aim of forming an independent Agrarian government and had recognised 'the leading role of the working class and the Communist party'. In addition to absorbing the political parties the Fatherland Front took over those parties' dependent social and trade union organisations; also incorporated into the Front were the large number of Bulgarian–Soviet friendship associations. By the summer of 1948 almost all Bulgarians belonged to one or other of the many societies now operating within the Fatherland Front or under its political domination.

The liquidation of Petkov's Agrarians and the fusion of the parties within the Fatherland Front into a monolithic structure left only a few weak opposition groups. Lulchev and his Social Democrats, despite crude threats from Dimitrov, courageously voted against the budget and were therefore condemned as traitors. In July 1948 Lulchev and six of the nine

Social Democratic members of parliament were arrested; their party was disbanded and Lulchev condemned to fifteen years in gaol, which, for a man of his age, was a virtual death sentence. The anti-government Radicals held out until March 1949, but their longevity reflected nothing more than their utter insignificance. Those parts of the Zveno movement which had remained outside or had been excluded from the Front transformed themselves into purely scientific and academic groupings before disappearing completely from Bulgarian political life.

The eventual defeat of the opposition was total, but its ultimate fate is not a true measure of its significance or its strength, for it was unparalleled in eastern and central Europe. Few political movements have had so many disadvantages. Communist power, backed by a party machine organised and disciplined to a degree which no other group could equal, had been deeply entrenched in the local committees of the Fatherland Front ever since the purges which followed 9 September 1944; the Communists could and did profit from the tradition of Russophilia, from the prominence their leaders had enjoyed in the world Communist movement, and from the presence of the Red Army. Whilst on the march to power the Communists were also careful to mask the nature of many of their policies; thus they avoided alarming phrases such as 'the dictatorship of the proletariat' or 'collectivisation'. The oppositionists also had to face the inescapable fact that in the last resort the Western powers would not complicate their relations with Moscow for a state so remote, so small, and, in Western eyes, so unpopular as Bulgaria. Besides, the West's moral position was weakened by British support for a Greek regime which was patently lacking in popular approval; at the same time this British involvement in Greece made the Soviets the more determined to hold on to Bulgaria, which, especially after the announcement of the Truman doctrine, was seen as the first line of defence for their newly-won zone of influence in south-eastern Europe.

Towards the end of 1947 it was suddenly announced in Sofia that a second confession by Petkov had been discovered. This implicated Professor Venelin Ganev, the former regent and a respected academic expert on constitutional law. Ganev was exiled to a remote village, but the measures taken against him showed clearly that the Communists were about to impose their will in the constitutional question. The grand national Sŭbranie had debated draft constitutions submitted by Petkov, by the Democratic Party, by the Bulgarian league for the defence of human and civic rights, and by the Fatherland Front. In fact none of these drafts was accepted, for in November there arrived from Moscow fresh suggestions for Bulgaria's future constitutional structure. These were accepted by acclamation on 4 December and the 'Dimitrov constitution' was born.

The new constitution declared Bulgaria to be a people's democracy. The people were to exercise their sovereignty through an assembly elected every four years by all citizens of eighteen or over; the Sŭbranie was therefore in theory the supreme organ of state. The Sŭbranie was to elect from its own members a praesidium which combined legislative and executive authority. The praesidium was to consist of the president of the republic, two vice-presidents, a secretary and fifteen others. The government was to consist of the chairman of the council of ministers, an unspecified number of vice-presidents and the ministers, along with the presidents of the state planning commission, the commission for state control, and the committee for science, art and culture. The president of the praesidium and most of its members were also members of the central committee of the party, and until 1954 the secretary general of the party was also chairman of the council of ministers. These devices, together with the fact that candidates for the Sŭbranie were approved by local party committees, guaranteed a Stalinist mingling of party and state.

The 1947 constitution promised Bulgarian citizens equality before the law, freedom from racial or religious intolerance and discrimination, welfare facilities for all, the complete emancipation of women, and liberty of speech, press, assembly, and conscience, together with the inviolability of the person, domicile and correspondence. These liberties were, however, qualified by the clause which proscribed any organisation whose purpose would in any way 'deprive the Bulgarian people of the rights and liberties gained with the national uprising of 9 September 1944'. The constitution contained a guarantee of work, but also an obligation that a citizen's occupation had to be socially useful. Unlike its Soviet model the Dimitrov constitution did allow the individual to retain private property, but again there was a catch-all qualification, namely that this privilege must not be exercised 'to the detriment of the public good', and although private property could be retained the constitution placed all the means of production in public ownership.

The constitution specifically rejected the notion of the separation of powers, and thereby allowed both the admixture of legislature and executive seen in the praesidium and the subjugation of the judiciary to the state at all levels; the supreme court and the public prosecutor were to be elected by the Sŭbranie, and all courts had lay assessors who played a considerable role in weighing evidence as well as in determining verdicts and sentences. At the local level the 1947 constitution was at least as centralist as the Zveno reforms of 1934. The old provinces or regions were dissolved, and the praesidium was given the right to review all acts of the remaining district and communal authorities, which were now to be formed by people's councils.

THE SOCIALISATION OF THE ECONOMY AND THE RISE OF CHERVENKOV, 1948–50

With the new constitution enacted the major preoccupations of the regime were to integrate Bulgaria into the Soviet camp and to construct a socialist society at home. The first objective was easily achieved and by the spring of 1948 Bulgaria had signed treaties of friendship and cooperation with all the other states of eastern Europe. Bulgaria was also a founder member of Comecon in 1949 and of the Warsaw pact in 1955. With regard to the second objective, progress was much more limited, not least because formidable obstacles were encountered within the agrarian sector. These obstacles were to be overcome only after the use of considerable force and only after a political upheaval as violent as that which had removed Petkov.

There were few difficulties, however, in bringing about the nationalisation of Bulgarian industry. On 23 December 1947 trained groups seized the country's 6,109 remaining private enterprises together with all their machinery, property, stocks and accounts. The sole exemptions from the nationalisation programme were the plants of some cooperatives and craftsmen. On the following day the grand national Sŭbranie sanctioned the takeover and ruled that the former owners should receive government bonds in compensation for their losses, but the compensation scheme was not to apply to anyone who had collaborated with the Germans, Italians, native fascists or post-9 September 1944 reactionaries, a category which was made to include the owners of nearly all the valuable, modern plants. By this device the government paid out in compensation no more than a tithe of the value of the property seized, and the nationalisation of industry amounted to little else than the final destruction of Bulgaria's small industrial bourgeoisie. Later in December the remaining thirty-two banks in Bulgaria were merged into the Central Bank, and two months later the state established a monopoly over foreign trade. At the same time the confiscation of large urban properties put an end to the existence of the Bulgarian private landlord.

The Dimitrov constitution had stated that the national economy would be planned. A two-year plan to repair the damage done by the war and to raise living standards had been introduced in April 1947, but plans for a radical restructuring of the economy and society were revealed in the first five-year plan, which was presented to the V party congress in December 1948, when the BWP also reverted to its original name, the Bulgarian Communist Party. The plan, which was to come into effect on 1 January 1949, set up the apparatus by which the Bulgarian economy was to be weaned from its over-long dependence on agriculture and was to develop a heavy industrial base. Industry was to receive 47 per cent of investment, almost half going to electrical power and chemical production; and industrial output was to increase by a total of 119 per cent with increases of 75 per cent in light industry and of 220 per cent in the heavy industrial sector. New metallurgical and fertilizer complexes were to be built, as were factories for food processing and for the manufacture of electrical apparatus, agricultural machinery, and construction materials. The balance between agricultural and industrial production, which at the beginning of 1949 stood at 70:30 in favour of agriculture, was to change to 45:55 to the advantage of industry. Private trading was to disappear and three-fifths of Bulgaria's food was to be produced on collective farms. As to the question of the land, the plan stated that it would not be nationalised but that conditions would be created 'in which the problem of the nationalisation of the land will be solved in practice'.

This was a formidable task. In 1946 Bulgaria was more than ever the land of the small farmer. Its 1.1 million holdings had, through parcellisation, decreased in average size to 4.31 hectares, with separate plots within each holding averaging only 0.4 hectares. Some land was already owned by cooperatives and by the state, but this and the small degree of voluntary collectivisation after 9 September 1944 involved a minute proportion of the total area. Legislation in 1945 set out the details on which the state farms (solhozes),* and the collectives (TKZSs) were to be based. Membership was to be voluntary and a minimum of fifteen holdings was necessary to form a TKZS, but once a peasant had joined he was obliged to remain a member for at least three years; all members were to receive wages in proportion to their work as well as the ground rent, which varied with the amount of land contributed. In 1946 more stringent regulations concerning private land were introduced. Henceforth members of a TKZS owned not actual areas of land but undemarcated percentages of the whole, and thus anyone leaving a cooperative was to receive bonds, not land, in compensation for the property he had originally contributed. The bill also placed a maximum on the area any one family might own, this being set at twenty hectares in general and thirty in the Dobrudja. Any

---

* Bulgaria had very few state farms. The proportion of land in such institutions was lower than anywhere else in eastern Europe.

farmer who had rented 40 per cent or more of his land for at least two years was entitled to only ten hectares, compensation being paid for the land taken from him. Minimum sizes for holdings were also set. The state was empowered to assume possession of holdings which were below the minimum size, and also to seize that part of the large holdings in excess of the maximum decreed acreage, as well as fallow land which the owner refused to cultivate, land belonging to disbanded organisations such as foreign churches or schools, and land reclaimed through publicly-sponsored improvement schemes such as drainage, irrigation, and the straightening of rivers. Of the land confiscated under the maximum holding regulations half was redistributed in small plots to some 129,000 dwarf-holders, the remaining half, some 3.6 per cent of the total land in use, being allotted to the TKZSs, which were also supplied with tractors and other machinery from the Soviet Union.

As long as the peace treaties had not been ratified there could be no official talk of enforced collectivisation, but there was, nevertheless, increasing pressure in that direction. Both in the 1945 and the 1946 legislation there had been clauses which allowed the enforced acquisition of private property if that property formed isolated islands within voluntarily formed TKZSs; when the two-year plan of 1947 organised the rationing of essential commodities into seven ranks of priority, members of collectives were in the third rank and private farmers in the seventh or last; and procurement prices and requisitioning quotas were skewed very much to the disadvantage of the individual owner. The collectivisation drive sharpened perceptibly after the Communists' political victory of 1947. In February 1948 all privately-owned farm machinery was confiscated and handed over to the machine tractor stations, the MTSs, which were now to enjoy a monopoly of mechanised equipment for use on the land. These pressures did achieve an increase in the rate of collectivisation and by the end of 1948 there were 1,100 TKZSs, although the government had aimed only for 800; on the other hand, the regime had hoped that by this stage 400,000 hectares would be in collective ownership, whereas the figure was only just over 292,000 hectares; it was, therefore, still the small farmer who was entering the TKZSs. In December 1948 the V party congress called for mass collectivisation and thousands of meetings were held throughout the country to explain and defend this policy; the five-year plan also allotted more investment to agriculture than had the two-year plan: 17 per cent as opposed to 6 per cent. Yet this was still a small proportion of total investment for a category which accounted for almost four-fifths of the population, and the increase of 59 per cent in agricultural production during the years 1949–53 laid down in the plan was an impossible imposition on a backward, disoriented and increasingly disaffected agrarian sector. The peasants registered their discontent by refusing to join the collectives and by such extreme measures as the slaughtering of their cattle.

It was not the rural population alone which was experiencing discomfort. The social changes initiated after 9 September 1944, which had greatly intensified after 1947, inevitably created widespread tensions. The causes of these tensions were various. Bulgaria did not have the energy supplies or the equipment to build a heavy industrial base at the speed which the wildly over-ambitious plan dictated, and the Soviet Union was not in a position to make good so wide a gap between intention and capability; the raw management cadres drafted in to run the recently nationalised industries and the rapidly expanding bureaucracy were in many cases neither experienced in nor equal to their new tasks; coordination between different sections of the economic plan was poor; the railways were run down after the war; and the neglect of the consumer industries and of social amenities, especially housing, caused widespread suffering. There was also some dissatisfaction at Soviet attitudes. For some there was a suspicion that the locomotives and rolling-stock sold to Bulgaria by the Russians had in fact been confiscated in the country in 1944, whilst others pointed out that when the Soviet Union took control of former German and Italian concerns it did not assume responsibility for their liabilities, and the five Soviet–Bulgarian 'joint stock companies' for lead and zinc processing, the extraction of uranium, the construction industry, ship-building and civil aviation, were unpopular. Far more unpopular were Soviet trading policies. A trade agreement signed in Moscow in July 1947 arranged that Bulgarian foreign trade should be conducted under Soviet auspices; it also provided for the exchange of Soviet cotton, rubber, railway rolling-stock, motor vehicles and machinery for Bulgarian tobacco, but it did not abolish the system, practised since 1944, by which the Soviet Union bought Bulgarian goods at 1933 prices. This had meant a substantial loss to the Bulgarian economy, as the Russians could purchase valuable goods at low cost and then dispose of them at great profit in the hard-currency market; in 1945 the Russians bought rose-oil at $110 per kilo and sold it at $1,200 per kilo.

Despite these complaints, however, the Soviet Union continued to provide the inspiration and the pattern for Bulgarian domestic policies. Soviet experience in the 1920s and 1930s had of course shown that rapid industrialisation and radical restructuring of property relations in the countryside would give rise to serious social and political tensions; but Soviet experience had also shown how these various tensions might be most effectively contained.

With the elimination of the non-Communist parties hostile opinion could now find refuge in only three areas: in religious bodies, in institutions connected with states outside the Soviet camp, and in doubting sections of the party itself. The Orthodox church had already been tamed. The Exarch Stefan, though willing to collaborate with the new regime, had been packed off to a monastery and his clergy had been required to choose between joining the Union of Bulgarian Priests or disappearing into a labour camp. In February 1949 the law on the organisation of churches codified state domination. The new law guaranteed freedom of conscience and recognised the Bulgarian Orthodox church as 'the traditional church of the Bulgarian people', though church and state were to be separated, and the lay authorities were to approve clerical appointments and supervise church finances; the churches were to be subjected to the 'will of the people' and the pulpit was not to be used to spread anti-government opinions.

In its dealings with the non-Orthodox churches the 1949 bill was much more severe, and the attack upon these institutions was an important part of the policy of isolating Bulgaria from all non-Soviet influences, a policy which fed on the fears and paranoias generated by the Cold War and Tito's breach with Moscow. In 1949 Roman Catholic influence in Bulgaria was weakened by the government's refusal to allow the newly-appointed apostolic delegate to take up his post. In 1948 Bulgarian churches whose headquarters were outside the country were deprived of their charitable institutions, and the 1949 act dissolved the churches themselves, whilst firm government control was also established over Bulgaria's Muslim communities and their religious institutions. Early in 1949 fifteen leading Protestant pastors were arrested. The Protestant communities in Bulgaria were not large but had contributed notably to the nation's history, not least through their educational institutions. Now their leaders were charged with espionage on behalf of Britain and the United States, and with complicity with both Petkov and Tito. The pastors' trial was a sorry spectacle. Naumov, the Baptist leader, wept in court, praised his interrogators as 'a school for the re-education of waverers', and, *sic transit gloriae ecclesiarum*, dismissed the world council of churches as a reactionary tool of American policy; Ziapkov, the head of the Congregational church, also sobbed in court, asking the judge, 'What will you make of me – a heap of dust or a new man?'

A much greater drama was about to be played out. At the end of March

1949 Traicho Kostov was removed from his posts as deputy minister president and chairman of the politburo's economic and financial secretariat, and appointed director of the National Library. He was arrested soon after, and in December, together with ten other prominent party figures, stood accused of a wide range of startling crimes, including left-wing deviationism and Trotskyism, spying for Britain and the United States, treason, collaboration with the fascist police, and conspiring with Tito to bring Bulgaria into a Yugoslav-dominated south Slav federation. On 14 December Kostov was found guilty. Although his life had once been spared by King Boris Kostov was executed two days later. He was partially rehabilitated in 1956 and completely exonerated in 1962.

The charges against Kostov were absurd. He had jumped from a pre-1944 police station window to avoid further torture, he had personally conducted the purges of the 'left-deviationists' in the 1930s, and as a consistent Stalinist he was an unlikely agent of London, Washington or Belgrade. But the charges, however absurd, reflected current developments within Bulgaria's political hierarchy, and the trial itself did much to determine the nature of the country's political life for years to come.

The trial was in part an episode in the struggle for the leadership of the Bulgarian Communist Party. Dimitrov had died in Moscow on 2 July; his body was brought back to Sofia and installed in a hastily-erected mausoleum, making Dimitrov the only non-Soviet leader to receive such treatment. As the other major figure of the older generation in Bulgaria and Dimitrov's successor as minister president, Vasil Kolarov, was far from well – he was to die in January 1950 – Kostov would have been a natural contender for the succession. Although in Bulgaria the distinction between 'Moscow' and 'home' Communists was less clear than in other east European parties, Kostov had spent much less time in the Soviet Union than had the other probable successor to Dimitrov and Kolarov, Vŭlko Chervenkov. After Kostov's removal Chervenkov had little difficulty in securing dominance.

In the pastors' trial foreign influence had been denounced by linking the accused with Western 'imperialist' interests; in Kostov's case the chief foreign devil was Tito. Yet the dispute between Bulgaria and Yugoslavia was more complicated than a case of Sofia following Moscow's example. After the end of the war Yugoslavia's Communist leadership had argued that Pirin Macedonia should join the Macedonian Federal Republic, a constituent part of Yugoslavia, for of what importance were state boundaries in the bright new dawn of proletarian internationalism? Bulgaria's old Comintern hands, who in the past had patronised their less influential Yugoslav comrades, found Belgrade's suggestion embarrassing.

In that it was supposed to be a step towards a Balkan federation it should have been enthusiastically welcomed by true Balkan radicals, yet the Bulgarian leadership was not prepared to alienate Bulgarian territory. This dilemma was solved when Tito and the Yugoslavs were placed outside the Communist pale; nationalist interests could again be squared with proletarian internationalism, and accusations of Titoism would blacken a person not only in party circles but in the nation as a whole – even in later years, when the Belgrade regime had relaxed its rigid controls, the association of Titoism with the loss of Bulgarian territory diluted any appeal which Yugoslavia's alternative form of socialism might have had in Bulgaria. In the meantime the possible danger from Yugoslavia's young, victorious and assertive partisan leadership would be contained by yet closer ties with Moscow.

Criticism of the Soviet Union in these circumstances was virtual treason which could only help the renegade Titoists. Kostov had in fact been critical of Soviet economic and commercial policies, especially over the purchase of rose-oil, but if external factors provided some of the causes of the trial, its main effects were to be seen, and were meant to be seen, in domestic politics. The destruction of all political organisations outside the BCP and the bullying of religious groups meant logically that the only political organism in which opposition might now breed was the party itself. At the same time the strains of industrialisation and collectivisation would mean that the causes of discontent were bound to multiply. To contain these discontents and to drive forward with the social revolution would require of the party an ever greater degree of commitment and resolve; would the party rank and file be able to comply with this demand when inevitably its quality had suffered as its numbers rocketed from 15,000 in 1944 to 460,000 in December 1948? The disciplining of one of its most prominent leaders would show the rank and file that dereliction of duty would not be tolerated at any level.

The Kostov example was meant not only for party members. Kostov had been disgraced in April, yet his trial and execution did not take place until mid-December. This timing, together with the fact that the trial was broadcast to the nation, is significant, for on 18 December Bulgaria held its first general election since the promulgation of the new constitution. If the mightiest in the land could be felled, individual resistance, however widespread the discontent might be, would be senseless. Not surprisingly, of the 98.89 per cent of the electorate who went to the ballot boxes 97.66 per cent voted for the single Fatherland Front list. The new Sŭbranie contained 156 Communists, forty-eight Agrarians, and thirty-five Independents. It was not an assembly which would challenge the new ruler of Bulgaria, Vŭlko Chervenkov.

THE CHERVENKOV YEARS AND THE BEGINNINGS OF
DESTALINISATION, 1950–6

The removal of Kostov and the election of December 1949 had consolidated and legitimised Chervenkov's power. His rule was to be characterised by severe repression, the isolation of Bulgaria from the non-socialist world, and the Sovietisation of the economy and of most other features of Bulgarian life. Chervenkov himself was a huge, haughty man of coarse demeanour and sarcastic wit, whose ability, subservience and relative youth – he was born in 1900 – made him popular in the Kremlin. At home his hold over the party and the party's domination in society were unchallenged.

As in other east European states the rapidly expanded bureaucracies of party and state created large numbers of posts, for which political conformity was a necessary qualification. The *nomenklatura* system thus became an important instrument of social power in Bulgaria as elsewhere in eastern Europe, but Chervenkov could not rely on this alone; terror and the purge were an integral part of his system. In October 1949 there had been major changes in the army high command, and in May 1950 the highest echelons of the security police were also purged. Immediately after the fall of Kostov the party itself had been subjected to a purge so fierce that by April 1951 at least 100,000 individuals, more than one in five of party members, had been expelled and many of them had been sent to labour camps. Amongst the victims were thirteen central committee members, six members of the politburo, and ten ministers. Amongst those who were particularly vulnerable were those 'left-deviationists' who had survived the liquidations of the 1930s, and those, including the veterans of the Spanish civil war, with experience of the world outside the Soviet bloc.

Non-party members who had connections with the non-socialist world were even more vulnerable. In February 1950 Shipkov, a former translator at the American embassy, went on trial for espionage. He was forced to make allegations in court against the U.S. minister in Sofia, as a result of which the United States broke off diplomatic relations. In September 1952 the leading Roman Catholic in Bulgaria, Mgr Evgenii Bosilkov, bishop of Nevrokop, together with twenty-seven Catholic priests and twelve others, were tried for spying for the Vatican and for France. Bosilkov and three other priests received death sentences and more priests were arrested in December. By then the power of the Catholic church in Bulgaria had been destroyed. The Orthodox church had seldom ventured to show the independence of which the Catholics were capable and for which they were persecuted, yet even its tenuous links with the outside world were cut. In 1951 the exarchate was raised to a patriarchate, which removed the last tie with the Orthodox community in Istanbul. In 1953 Metropolitan Kiril of Plovdiv was elected patriarch, and the national church was restructured to give more influence to lay elements and to the Union of Bulgarian Priests.

Chervenkov's suspicion of external, non-Soviet elements, and his Stalinist determination to limit diversity at home, were combined in his attitude towards Bulgaria's small minority groups. The Pirin Macedonian problem had shown what embarrassment could be caused by foreign claims upon Bulgarian citizens, but Yugoslav claims on Pirin could be rejected on the grounds that its populace was Bulgarian by race. No such claim could be made for the Jews, Armenians and Turks resident in the country. Chervenkov therefore allowed the Jews to leave, although this was in contradiction of the anti-Israel policies adopted in Moscow; by 1956 88.9 per cent of the Jews in Bulgaria in 1946 had emigrated, and in 1965 those remaining numbered only 5,000. Some 1,000 Armenians also left Bulgaria in the late 1940s and early 1950s. Neither Jews nor Armenians were numerous enough to constitute a serious minority problem, but this was not the case with the Turks. The 1925 agreement with Atatürk had allowed for a trickle of emigration, but in January 1950 the Bulgarian government announced that it would allow a quarter of a million Bulgarian Turks to leave for Turkey. The Turkish authorities protested vehemently. The condition of those entering Turkey was deplorable, said Ankara, and included amongst them were a number of gypsies who were as unwelcome in Turkey as they were in Bulgaria. In September the border was closed until an agreement later in the year, by which the Turkish side would accept 650 emigrants per day. By 1952, when the border was again closed, some 162,000 Turks had left Bulgaria. The sudden explosion of the emigration issue was directly connected with the collectivisation programme, for many of the Turks who left were from the Dobrudja and the grain-growing areas of the north-east, which the Chervenkov regime was particularly anxious to bring into the collectivised system. After 1952 softer policies towards the minority groups meant that the question disappeared into the background until the mid-1980s.

Dimitrov had once proclaimed that 'for the Bulgarian people friendship with the Soviet Union is just as necessary for life as the air and sun is for any living creature'. Under Chervenkov Sovietisation proceeded apace. Thousands of Russian advisors were in Bulgaria by the end of 1950, and they included at least 400 officers attached to the Bulgarian armed forces, the uniforms, training and command structure of which had been adapted completely to the Soviet pattern. In the cultural sphere, reform of the alphabet removed the two purely Bulgarian letters which had so exercised Omarchevski, and thus left the Bulgarian script almost indistinguishable from the Russian, and Soviet books were overwhelmingly predominant amongst those translated from foreign languages. After the V congress had decreed that Marxism–Leninism must dominate all spheres of science and culture dissent and individuality disappeared, and talented practitioners such as Radoi Ralin, the editor of the satirical weekly *Stŭrshel* (*Hornet*), and the singers Leshnikov and Vankova, were amongst the many who ceased to practise their art. In 1951 Dimitŭr Dimov published *Tabac* (*Tobacco*), a novel in which workers were shown to have human feelings as well as historic roles and economic functions; although the book was later to be proclaimed as the greatest Bulgarian novel since *Pod Igoto*, it was initially condemned and had to be revised before going into a second edition. Socialist realism was to remain unchallengeable in all departments of culture and the arts until 1956. In 1949 it was announced that the education system was to be remodelled in 'the spirit of socialism, proletarian internationalism, and indissoluble fraternal friendship with the Soviet Union'. The social services were similarly restructured, whilst in the factories wage differentials based upon piece-work and rewards for over-fulfilment of norms were copied from the Soviets. Foreign trade was almost entirely confined to the Soviet bloc, which in 1951 took 93.11 per cent of Bulgaria's exports, and provided 92.92 per cent of its imports.

Bulgaria was also the only east European state to copy the Soviets by declaring that their first five-year plan had been completed a year ahead of schedule. In industry considerable progress had been made and probably 80 per cent of the target had been fulfilled. In agriculture the story was very different and here growth had reached only 11 per cent as opposed to the plan figure of 59 per cent. Furthermore, although more households entered TKZSs in 1949 than in any previous year, the collectivised sector was not expanding as rapidly as hoped, and at the end of the year encompassed only 11.3 per cent of the total arable area. This was in spite of increased legal pressure on the individual owners during 1949, when criminal action was threatened against anyone who sold on the private market grain which had been earmarked for the delivery quotas, and in May a new land survey was undertaken after which all unrecorded land was to be handed over to the TKZSs. Yet peasant resistance was intense and contributed to the appalling harvest of that year. In October Chervenkov ordered a halt to the collectivisation programme, but it was only a case of *reculer pour mieux sauter*. In April 1950 individual holdings were ordered to hand over three-quarters of their grain, and in May new tax laws discriminated once more against the private farmer. In the same month came the model statute for the formation of collective farms, based largely but not entirely on the 1935 Soviet example. Members of the TKZSs were allowed to maintain for their own use small plots of between 0.2 and 0.5 hectares together with a few livestock; as in the Soviet Union all members had to contribute a regulated number of labour days to the collective, although the peculiarly Bulgarian ground rent was retained. The statute also decreed that henceforth the only permissible transfer of landed property would be from individual to cooperative ownership. In 1953 peasants were required to hand over to the cooperatives equipment for brick-making, carpentry, blacksmithing etc., whereas previously surrender of such items had been voluntary; also, from this point the TKZSs were to be the owners rather than the users of the property and equipment incorporated into them. Collectivisation was now inescapable, and over half a million households were subjected to the process both in 1950 and in the following year. Thereafter the pace slackened somewhat and the collectivisation programme was not completed until 1958. The inevitable peasant resentment was shown by the slaughter of cattle, the burning of crops, the hiding of produce from requisitioning agents and ultimately by acts of physical resistance. In 1950 troops had to be used to contain unrest in the Vidin and Kula districts.

Chervenkov continued his essentially Stalinist political policies until the death of his mentor on 3 March 1953. In January of that year a major show trial had sent Todor Hristov, a former officer in the royal army, to the gallows, and in the following month came a tightening of the already stringent regulations over labour discipline together with a fierce law against those attempting to leave the country without official permission, a law which included provisions for punishment of the relatives of anyone who succeeded in such an attempt.

After the death of Stalin Bulgaria was the first east European state to experience a popular outburst of anger against government policies. In Plovdiv in May tobacco workers rioted against new work schedules which demanded greater effort without commensurate increase in reward. The outburst encouraged the tentative move away from Stalinist orthodoxy which had already begun, most publicly in a willingness to settle the long-standing frontier dispute with Greece, an issue which had led to an exchange of artillery fire during the previous summer. By the time of his anniversary speech on 9 September 1953 Chervenkov was prepared to admit to a willingness to be on better terms not only with Greece but also with the U.S.A. and Yugoslavia, and full diplomatic relations were restored with the latter a few days later.

The anniversary speech was even more dramatic with regard to home affairs, for the Bulgarian leader now committed himself to a 'new course' much in conformity with that adopted in Moscow. Chervenkov talked of increases in the production of consumer goods together with a number of strategic price reductions, and he also promised a whole series of concessions to agriculture, though all of them were to go to the collectivised as opposed to the private sector.

The new course was at this stage still primarily an economic phenomenon, but changes in other spheres could not be far behind. By the end of the year the hated legislation of February on labour discipline and emigration had been softened and the police terror had been considerably reduced. There had even been an amnesty in September for a sizeable number of political prisoners who had been, in the new terminology, 'victims of departures from socialist legality'. Despite these concessions Sofia had not yet bowed to Kremlin pressure to dissociate party from state at the highest level. Chervenkov was wary, not knowing whether the current Moscow line would hold, and, at the same time, he felt the need to keep a watchful eye on potential opponents at home, especially Yugov and the younger element in the leadership which was coalescing around the former Sofia party boss, Todor Zhivkov. Not until the VI party congress in February-March 1954 did Chervenkov finally agree to relinquish one of his two posts, choosing – like Malenkov, Stalin's assumed successor – to retain the minister presidency rather than the secretary generalship of the party. The latter post was disbanded to be replaced by a secretariat of three. The newly-created office of first secretary of the central committee went to Zhivkov, who thereby became the youngest man to hold the senior post in a ruling party.

Zhivkov was distinguished neither by political acumen nor unusual intelligence. Born of peasant stock in 1911, he had become a printer, joining the party's youth organisation in 1928. During the war he served in the partisan movement and after 1944 worked his way up the Sofia party apparat. By the V congress in 1948 he had achieved a reputation sufficient to secure his election to the central committee, and by 1950 he was a central committee secretary and a candidate member of the politburo, of which he became a full member in the following year. The power-brokers of Moscow and the Bulgarian politburo, not least Chervenkov himself, welcomed Zhivkov's quiet reliability and apparent pliability, and he was also helped both by his strong backing in the Sofia party and by his youth, for he was not yet old enough to have created powerful friends, or, more importantly, enemies.

In 1954 Zhivkov, like Stalin in the early 1920s, had the instruments of power but had yet to play upon them. Chervenkov was still the most powerful figure in the land, and if he had lost his patron in Moscow then his new, more relaxed image had done something to win the sympathy of the Bulgarian party. If there were potential rivals to Chervenkov in the leadership after the VI congress they were either Generals Panchevski and Mihailov, who enjoyed strong Soviet backing, or Anton Yugov. The latter was the most likely contender for supreme power. He had earned a formidable reputation as minister of the interior from 1944 to 1949, and although he had been transferred to less powerful posts after the fall of Kostov he returned to prominence by calming the Plovdiv rioters in May 1953; his resurrection made him the natural focal point for the many party members who had been purged with Kostov and who were now being released from the labour camps; the central committee itself had been enlarged to ninety-seven full and candidate members partly in order to accommodate the returnees, who were now an important group within the party.

For the time being, however, there was to be no challenge to Chervenkov, and the regime moved cautiously in the destalinising direction already plotted by the Kremlin. The release of political prisoners continued, with over 10,000 returning from labour camps by the summer of 1955. Soviet advisors who had played so decisive and so prominent a role in many Bulgarian institutions packed their bags and left for home, and in October 1954 the transfer of the joint Soviet–Bulgarian companies to Bulgarian ownership began. The role of heavy industry was downgraded a little and slightly more attention and investment were devoted to the consumer. An improvement in social provision was also noticeable. Between 1952 and 1958 real wages rose by an estimated 75 per cent, whilst between 1953 and 1957 the consumption of meat increased by 48 per cent, that of fruit by 52 per cent and that of vegetables by 36 per cent, although for many households these advances succeeded only in restoring or nearly restoring pre-war levels of consumption. There was, however, real improvement in the provision of medical facilities, the number of doctors per thousand of the population rising from 0.87 to 1.33 between 1952 and 1958, and there was even progress in that most difficult of all social problems in post-war Bulgaria, housing, though here the improvement was much less apparent in the fast-growing cities than in the villages.

A more generous attitude towards the rural population was a distinctive feature of the Bulgarian new course. In 1957 Bulgaria was the first east European state to extend pensions and certain other welfare provisions to collective farm workers, and agricultural wages rose more rapidly than those in most industries. Investment allocation to the countryside rose in both relative and absolute terms, and there was even a relaxation of the collectivisation drive, the area in cooperative or state ownership increasing by only 2.5 per cent between 1953 and 1955. There were also attempts to win the political loyalty and respect of the peasants. In 1954 General Vŭlkov and six others found guilty of the murder of Stamboliiski in 1923 were sentenced to death, though this was commuted to twenty years' hard labour, and former peasant activists, including Asen Stamboliiski and a number of close associates of Nikola Petkov, were encouraged to tour the country urging cooperation with the government.

THE APRIL PLENUM AND THE RISE OF ZHIVKOV, 1956–62

Whether concessions to the agricultural community would have had any profound effect was never to be established, because the relative political stability established in Bulgaria after the VI congress was shattered in 1955–6. There were two main causes of this, both of them external. The first was Khruschev's *rapprochement* with Tito. The full rehabilitation of the former outcast caused considerable discomfort to Chervenkov, who had secured supreme power by branding Kostov as a Titoist and who in his numerous purges had always used alleged sympathy towards or association with Yugoslavia as a political crime. Chervenkov was already feeling somewhat uneasy, therefore, when the second destabilising factor burst upon the Bulgarian leadership with Khruschev's denunciation of Stalin at the XX congress of the CPSU in February 1956. The Bulgarian party had to react, and therefore a central committee plenum was held from 2–6 April, its unanimous resolutions being announced on 8 April. The 'cult of personality' which had grown up around Chervenkov was denounced as having departed from the party's 'traditional and tried methods of work', and two days later an amnesty for all those found guilty of 'flight abroad' was declared. On 11 April Zhivkov made a speech to Sofia party activists which at last addressed the question which recent events had pushed to the forefront of many minds: what now was the status of Kostov and the other victims of the purges? Zhivkov admitted that 'innocent comrades were accused and unjustly punished' and that all would be rehabilitated 'before the party and the people'. This was a complete refutation of Chervenkov and his career since 1949, and on 17 April the Sŭbranie unanimously accepted his resignation, voting with equal single-mindedness to appoint Yugov minister president in his place. A Yugoslav delegation watched from the visitors' gallery.

Ever since 1956 the Bulgarian party has celebrated the April plenum as its break with Stalinism. There is no doubt that the atmosphere of Bulgarian politics was much changed by the meeting and that after it more power resided with first secretary Todor Zhivkov. He had not been thought significant enough to be included in the Bulgarian delegation to the CPSU's XX congress, but immediately after it he had made himself known as an unwavering supporter of the Moscow leadership and of Khruschev. In 1957 Zhivkov's authority was increased with the purge of Dobri Terpeshev, General Yonko Panov and Georgi Chankov, the so-called 'counter-party group', by far the most important of whom was Chankov, an intelligent fellow-member with Zhivkov of the 'Chervenkov kindergarten'. The replacements on the central committee were all 'home' rather than 'Moscow' Communists, and two of them had been in disgrace after the Kostov trial; none, therefore, could be counted as Chervenkovites.

The fall of Chankov was followed by a wave of arrests which affected both party and non-party elements and filled the labour camps with the 'Hungarian prisoners'. The counter-party purge clearly followed the Soviet example, and was no doubt intended to show Moscow that the Bulgarian party would not tolerate the loss of control which had recently afflicted its Polish and Hungarian comrades. In fact there was little danger in Bulgaria that protests on the Polish or Hungarian scale might occur. Few Bulgarians felt the anti-Russian passions which consumed so many Poles and Hungarians, the economic impact of destalinisation was less in countries which were only on the threshold of industrialisation, and the Bulgarian authorities acted swiftly against any sign of unrest.

This is not to imply that Bulgaria, and especially its intelligentsia, was immune from the ferment which was sweeping eastern Europe after February 1956. Even before the XX congress of the CPSU there had been a noticeable enlivening of Bulgarian culture. A new generation of poets, the 'second call-up', had emerged, with figures such as Kosta Pavlov, Liubomir Levchev, Stefan Tsanev and Vladimir Svintila aching for the liberation of culture from bureaucracy and rigid political control, whilst a new form of satirical journalism practised by writers such as Valeri Petrov and Radoi Ralin had been seen in the weekly *Stürshel*. These were soon followed by new and more searching schools of literary criticism associated with Zdravko Petkov, Minko Nikolov, and the poet Svintila. The April plenum emboldened the adventurous spirit which now spread into such bastions of the cultural establishment as *Literaturen Front* (*Literary Front*) and *Otechestven Front* (*Fatherland Front*). The editor of the latter, Vladimir Topencharov, a brother-in-law of Kostov, had in May 1956 published a leader in which he argued that fear of independent thinking had stultified Bulgarian journalism, but for such boldness he was forced to make a public recantation and to resign his editorship. But even this did not end the 'Bulgarian thaw'. In November *Literaturen Front* carried short stories by the young writers Vasil Popov and Nikolai Haitov, both of whom explored the dangerous topic of alienation, and early in 1957 a younger group within the Writers' Union launched a new journal, *Plamŭk* (*Flame*), under the editorship of Emil Manov. For the authorities things had gone far enough, and whatever their differences they united in the face of continuing disrespect on the part of the intelligentsia. In February 1957 Chervenkov was brought back into the leadership and appointed minister of education and culture with a clear brief to restore order and control. By the end of the year criticism was far more restrained, and figures such as Manov were being accused by officials of sympathy with the Polish and Hungarian rebels, Topencharov had been removed from the presidency of the Bulgarian Union of Journalists and the literary élite had been subjected to a through purge. The 'thaw' had ended.

The upheavals of 1956–8 had strengthened the conservative wings of the leadership, that is both Chervenkov, who was recalled to stiffen official control, and Yugov, the strong-man of 1944–9. Chervenkov, however, was a good Stalinist now caught in the destalinist trap: he believed both in obedience to Moscow and in strict internal control, the primacy of heavy industry, and outright condemnation of Yugoslavia; yet if he were to remain obedient to Moscow he must now reverse or modify the other three articles of his faith. Yugov shared Chervenkov's taste for discipline at home, and, as a Macedonian by birth, his antipathy to Yugoslavia; but he was no Moscovite, and as a victim of the Chervenkovite terror he could not cooperate with the former party boss. This benefited Zhivkov, who had emerged essentially as a home Communist but in the paradoxical context of destalinisation had become a Moscow Communist to dissociate himself from the Stalinists at home; he was a Moscow Communist, but one 'made in Bulgaria'. He had undoubtedly increased his authority but he was still far from being the dominant figure, and it was quite possible that Yugov, like Chervenkov between 1954 and 1956, would use the minister presidency to exercise considerable power. Until 1962, however, the Bulgarian party enjoyed that true collective leadership which is founded upon the inability of any single faction to secure complete dominance.

This collective leadership hastened Bulgaria's economic and social reconstruction. The last steps towards the elimination of the private farmer were taken, and at its VII congress in July 1958 the BCP proudly declared that it had become the first socialist state after the Soviet Union to achieve full collectivisation. The VII congress also endorsed the third five-year plan, which doubled investment in light industry. At the same time the relaxation of international tensions and the need for modern equipment encouraged a widening of trade relations, and by the late

1950s Federal Germany was already a significant partner, providing 8.2 per cent of Bulgarian imports by 1959.

If these developments raised any hopes that Bulgaria was now to enter upon a period of gradual and measured transformation such hopes were short-lived, for the country was soon in the throes of further massive economic, social and administrative upheaval. Late in 1958 Bulgaria's 3,450 collective farms were amalgamated into 932 units with an average size of 4,200 hectares, by far the largest anywhere in eastern Europe outside the Soviet Union. It was decreed that party and government employees must work for between thirty and forty days per year in the fields or factories, and an extensive redefinition of both central and local government was enacted to give the latter more control over economic enterprises; it was even hoped, as it had been under Stamboliiski, that eventually the boundaries of economic and administrative units would become coterminous. These reforms were intended to make possible the extraordinary economic programme put forward in the Zhivkov Theses of January 1959, which called for a four-fold increase in industrial production by 1965 and a trebling of agricultural output by the end of 1960. The latter was to be helped by the economies of scale which the amalgamated farms would make possible and by ambitious irrigation projects, especially in the Dobrudja, whilst industrial expansion was intended to solve the embarrassing problem of the labour surplus created by rapid collectivisation in an essentially pre-industrial economy, a problem which until the late 1950s had been partly evaded by the export of labour to the Soviet Union. The 1959 plans had called for the creation of 400,000 new jobs by the end of 1962, and in this respect alone were they fulfilled.

For the most part the Theses had been ridiculously grandiose, and by the end of 1960 Zhivkov had begun to speak of doubling or trebling not the volume of production but the rate of increase, and in 1961 economic sanity was restored with a return to plan figures which were little different from those of the third five-year plan of 1958. In 1963 the experiments in economic decentralisation were also abandoned, as it was believed that they had contributed massively to the severe food shortages which racked Bulgaria in the early 1960s. By 1964 all that remained of the Zhivkov Theses were the large agrarian units and the liquidation of the surplus labour problem.

Such upheavals inevitably had political connotations. The agrarian amalgamations, the labour decrees and a number of welfare reforms reflected contemporary Chinese practices and led to Sofia's experiments being labelled Bulgaria's 'great leap forward'. Chervenkov had visited China in the autumn of 1958 and this caused some to assume that

Bulgaria's leading Stalinist was aligning with Mao in an anti-Khruschev and anti-Zhivkov bloc. In fact most of the reforms originated not with Chervenkov but with Zhivkov, whose 1959 Theses, his first major initiative in policy-making, had been drawn up before details of the Chinese reform programme had been announced, and the grandiose expansion projects and the administrative reforms were copied from Khruschev, not from Mao.

The major difference between the Khruschev experiments and those of his Bulgarian disciple was that Zhivkov survived their collapse and Khruschev did not. Not without a struggle, however. Yugov had never been in favour of the grandiose design of 1959, and Chervenkov had kept a safe distance from the Zhivkov–Khruschevite camp, especially when the Sino-Soviet split became serious. By the spring of 1961 the tensions could no longer be contained. A number of provincial first secretaries and trade union leaders were removed in the so-called 'coffee-house purge' but the decisive factor proved to be Soviet intervention. At the XXII congress of the CPSU from 17 to 31 October 1961 Khruschev delivered his second and most devastating attack upon Stalin. After such an outburst the Khruschevite Zhivkov and the Stalinist Chervenkov could no longer coexist. Confrontation came quickly. Zhivkov denounced Chervenkov, accusing him of having played Stalin to Dimitrov's Lenin, and in a central committee meeting in November Chervenkov was told he had 'not drawn all the necessary conclusions from the liquidation of the personality cult', indicating that his sins were committed after as well as before the April plenum. Chervenkov had outlived his era and his support in the central committee had by this stage collapsed; he lost his seat in the politburo and soon after resigned as deputy minister president.

The second outburst of destalinisation induced in Bulgaria, as in the Soviet Union, a marked relaxation of cultural controls. By 1965 previously 'untouchable' Western or dissident authors such as Apollinaire, Solzhenitsyn, T. S. Eliot, Kafka, and Ionesco had appeared in Bulgarian translation, and amongst the many talented Bulgarian writers who benefited from this second and more far-reaching thaw were Anton Donchev, Nikolai Haitov, Georgi Markov, Radoi Ralin, and Nikola Lankov whose long narrative poem, *Spomenŭt* (*The Memory*), like Solzhenitsyn's works of that period, touched on the sufferings of the purge victims. There were limits to this new freedom, however, as the reaction to Ralin's *Bezopasni Igla* (*Safety Pins*) showed, but the restrictions were less than at any time in most people's memories, and theatre, art and film – particularly animated film – made much progressive hay during this transitory period of sunshine.

This more open approach to culture won for Zhivkov the sympathy of most of the intelligentsia. In March 1962 he eliminated the opposition from a much more powerful body, the security forces. Since 1951 they had been under the control of Georgi Tsankov, who was now removed from his post as minister of the interior. A number of his nominees in sensitive positions were also removed and replaced by Zhivkovites. Zhivkov received further substantial support in May when Khruschev paid a week-long visit to Bulgaria, his first journey outside the Soviet Union since the XXII congress. Much in the style of the Russian generals of old the Soviet leader toured the country to bolster his chosen political protégé.

The scene was set for Zhivkov's final victory at the VIII party congress which was due to meet in August. It had to be postponed until November, however, because of the plight of Bulgarian agriculture, where the recent upheavals and the dreadful harvests of 1961 and 1962 had reduced food production to a level only slightly above that of 1939. The peasants had to be cajoled and encouraged to increase production, and in the summer of 1962 the Sofia government handed out a large number of concessions to the farmers. Purchase prices for eggs, milk, poultry and vegetables were increased, whilst charges to the collectives for petrol, fertilizers, industrial goods and textiles were lowered; eastern Europe's first minimum wage for collective farm workers was introduced, and the tax burden imposed on the collectives was lightened. There were also increases in general wage levels and in pensions, but these were not sufficient to cover the very substantial increases in the retail prices of meat, poultry, eggs, milk and dairy produce which the agrarian crisis and the concessions to the peasants had made necessary. The government admitted it could only pay for its measures to stimulate agriculture by asking for 'temporary sacrifices on the part of the urban population and the working class'. The urban population and the working class were not pleased. There was considerable unrest in the towns and in August the government introduced tough measures against 'non-productive elements', or black marketeers; in October potatoes, beans, rice and onions had to be rationed and in the same month came an agreement with Canada by which Bulgaria imported at least 100,000 tons of wheat per annum for the next three years.

The summer crisis weakened Zhivkov. In October Yugov voiced strong criticism of Khruschev's policies over China and Cuba, and of the twenty-year plan for Bulgaria's economic development recently drawn up with Soviet assistance. These criticisms were aired in the central committee meeting which preceded the VIII congress. In the middle of the meeting Zhivkov flew to Moscow to hear Khruschev's own account of the Cuban crisis and to secure his backing for action against Yugov. When the central committee reconvened Yugov and a number of his supporters were absent;

those who remained heard Zhivkov announce that Yugov had been removed from the politburo and from his post as minister president. This decision was duly confirmed by the congress, which also voted Yugov off the central committee and expelled Chervenkov from the party. Yugov had been accused of a range of crimes including incompetence, dishonesty, factionalism, violations of socialist legality, cowardice in the war, and opposition to the 'great leap forward'. In 1984, on the eve of his eightieth birthday, the now-rehabilitated Yugov was made a 'hero of socialist labour'.

After the defeat of Yugov Zhivkov took over the minister presidency and strengthened his position in the party by placing two close supporters, Boris Velchev and Zhivko Zhivkov, who was no relation, in the politburo. In 1964 there were also further moves to consolidate peasant support. The leader of the Agrarian Party, Georgi Traikov, was made head of state, and on the twentieth anniversary of the 9 September revolution members of Nikola Petkov's Agrarian Party were among a number of groups granted amnesties; the others included ex-civil servants and royalist army officers.

By the end of 1964 Zhivkov was sufficiently well-entrenched to survive the fall of his Moscow patron. In the following year, however, he had to face what, at the time of writing, was probably the last real threat to his authority. In April 1965 Bulgaria's press agency, BTA, confirmed recent Western press rumours that a number of people had been arrested for conspiring to overthrow the regime. It was also alleged that a military clique, most of whose members had served in the Vratsa partisan units, was associated with the plot, one of whose leaders was general Anev, the commander of the Sofia garrison. There were parallels here with 1886, but the official account of the affair was more concerned with contemporary politics than historical allusions and accused the conspirators of being pro-Chinese, though a more probable explanation is that they were a group dissatisfied with what they thought was Zhivkov's over-reliance upon and supine obedience to the Soviet party; it was to Belgrade or Bucharest rather than to Beijing that the army conspirators looked. They might also have hoped that with the fall of Khruschev Zhivkov would have no real defender, but whatever its motivation, the plot provided Zhivkov with a welcome chance to bring into line the only power factor in Bulgaria which he did not yet totally dominate: the army.

THE ZHIVKOV ERA FROM THE EARLY 1960S TO THE EARLY 1980S

Since the alleged army plot of 1965 there has been no serious threat to Zhivkov's rule. He took swift action to ensure that neither his power in the party nor the party's authority within society was threatened in 1968.

As the danger signals flashed from Prague the Bulgarian party called for the extension of the Fatherland Front's social power by the incorporation into it of organisations at present outside its grasp, organisations as innocent and apparently apolitical as the Slavic committee and the committee for sobriety. At the same time the party wanted supervision of the activities of all organisations dealing with communal–residential, urban and sociological problems, and with the supplying of food and other goods to the population. Within the party there was to be 'iron discipline' and total devotion to democratic centralism; and party cards were called in to weed out the unreliable. The Bulgarian party was not about to succumb to the Czechoslovak disease.

The influence of recent events in Czechoslovakia was still being felt when Zhivkov consolidated his and the party's positions in the new constitution and the new party programme, both promulgated in 1971. In its preamble the new constitution stated that it was based upon the 1944 socialist revolution and the subsequent development of an advanced socialist society and a full people's democracy in Bulgaria. Bulgaria remained a people's democracy but was now also 'a socialist state of the working people in town and countryside headed by the working class'. The party, which had not been mentioned in the Dimitrov constitution, was recognised as 'the leading force in society and the state', and was to direct 'the building of an advanced socialist society in close fraternal union with the Bulgarian Agrarian National Union'. It further stipulated that Bulgarian youth must be educated in the spirit of Communism, and Bulgaria's membership of the socialist camp was also enshrined in the new constitution. Four forms of property were recognised: state, cooperative, that of the public organisations, and private, the latter encompassing real and movable property sufficient for the upkeep of the individual and the family.

The new constitution's most innovative feature was the state council. The new body replaced the praesidium of the national assembly as the supreme organ of state power, and was to exercise both executive and legislative functions. It could initiate legislation, although all laws, though not decrees or resolutions, had to be submitted to the Sŭbranie for approval. In executive terms, in addition to the standard responsibilities for declaring war, signing treaties, etc, the state council also took on some of the *kontrol* or supervisory functions which in most other east European systems are entirely the concern of the party. The state council was to consist of a chairman, who was head of state, and twenty-two members who could be taken from both the political parties and from the mass organisations. The chairmanship of the state council went to Zhivkov, who passed the minister presidency to Stanko Todorov. The new constitution increased the power of the local people's councils by giving them more authority in the administration of local economic affairs, but the councils were also made more responsible to their electorates, to whom they were now required to report at least once a year.

The party structure as defined in the new programme of 1971 was orthodox. Democratic centralism required each party body to subordinate itself to the one above and to eschew any form of 'horizontalism'. In conformity with the 'territorial–production principle' the lowest party organisations were to be based in the workplace but those above were to be territorial, rising through the municipal to the city or regional committees, and finally to the central committee itself. Since 1971 some organisational individuality has been seen in the tendency to convene party conferences in addition to the party congresses which meet regularly every five years.

After routine assertions of loyalty to the CPSU and to socialism's inevitable victory in its struggles with capitalism, 'social democratic illusions' and the opportunism of the ultra-left, the 1971 programme went on to define the party's most important immediate task as the building of an advanced socialist society in which all property and functional differences would gradually disappear; state and collective farms would merge, and in the longer term technological and organisational change would mean that agricultural and industrial labour would become indistinguishable. The nation would therefore become entirely working-class and the party of the working class would be the party of the whole people. During this evolution the systematic application of science and technology would provide the material wealth necessary for gradual progress through advanced socialism to the first stages of Communism.

Ever since assuming full power in the early 1960s Zhivkov has protected his own authority by frequent reshuffles of party and government leaders, generally managing to maintain a balance between conservative and reformist, old and young. Most of these changes involved nothing more sinister than moves from one office or party post to another, but in May 1977 came a substantial change. Boris Velchev was dropped from the politburo, and his removal was followed not only by extensive changes in a number of provincial party organisations, but also by a calling in of party cards in which 38,500 persons lost their party membership. Velchev, it was alleged, had been too ambitious, but there were indubitably more substantial reasons for his ousting, and it is likely that he had developed a penchant for more liberal policies at home and a little more independence in external affairs. His dismissal could also have been intended as a warning to anyone who might wish to associate themselves with the growing unrest which was being felt in Bulgaria, as elsewhere in eastern Europe, during the late 1970s, when the Helsinki accords, and especially the burgeoning of Eurocommunism, had created fresh hopes for liberalisation at home. At the same time the economy was beginning to feel the effect of the upheavals caused in the West by the oil-price hike of 1973; years of encouraging growth were giving way to a more austere period, and, as Poland was soon to show, a disappointed population and a declining economy could prove an explosive mix.

If the disciplining of Velchev was meant to nip growing internal discontent in the bud it failed, and in December 1977, speaking to the third national conference of young writers, Zhivkov made his first ever public reference to dissidence in Bulgaria. In March of the following year there were reports of the clandestine publication of 'Declaration 78', copied from the Czech charter, though never actually signed, and in May came news of an anti-Communist demonstration. The government's embarrassments were intensified by accusations of official complicity in the death of the exiled writer Georgi Markov in London in September and in the attempted murder of another exile in Paris a few weeks earlier.

Against this background came the political earthquake in Poland, to which Zhivkov reacted with considerable skill and subtlety. In 1980 he circulated a letter to district party secretaries, warning them of the significance of events in Poland and calling for a shift in economic priorities and for a more sensitive approach to the public by party officials. Both were granted. The shops were filled with food and consumer goods, and to sanitise the party's image official privileges were reduced, and the 'theses' for the XII party congress to be held in April 1981 were published unusually early to give the public an opportunity to comment upon them, which it did with relish.

In fact the Bulgarian leadership had little reason to fear the Polish contagion. The Zhivkov regime had not lost any of its social power; the Bulgarian economy, though facing mounting hard-currency debts, was not in such dire straits as that of Poland; the Bulgarians did not have the alternative focus of loyalty or national identity which the Roman Catholic church provided for Poles; and the traditional Bulgarian response to a political system which was not liked was apathy and withdrawal rather than opposition and confrontation.

During the tensions of the late 1970s Zhivkov made one of his most interesting political appointments when his daughter, Liudmila Zhivkova, was elected to the politburo. Born in 1942, she was the first member of the leadership who had been raised and educated almost entirely under socialism. That education had been unusually privileged and broad – she had been a graduate student at Oxford – but she quickly established a rapport with the less favoured of her own generation. She had been appointed deputy chairman of the committee for art and culture in 1971, becoming its head four years later; in 1976 she was also given responsibility for radio, television and the press. In 1980 she was made chairwoman of the politburo commission on science, culture and art, but in the same year she began to show in public signs of a private interest in mysticism and non-materialistic ideas such as Buddism and Dŭnovism, a development enthusiastically welcomed amongst some of Bulgaria's younger intelligentsia. More widely appreciated was the strong national flavour which she gave Bulgarian culture. Without any overt hint of anti-Sovietism she emphasised Bulgaria's separate cultural identity and achievement; it was under her auspices that in 1981 Bulgarians celebrated the 1,300th anniversary of the foundation of the first Bulgarian state, and marked the event with, amongst other things, the opening of the new palace of culture in Sofia, which now bears Zhivkova's name. The appointment of Zhivkova, which was initially seen as an instance of nepotism, proved one of the most popular ever made by the Bulgarian party boss.

Zhivkova's popularity owed a good deal to her quiet but firm insistence on Bulgaria's national identity in cultural affairs, but this did not budge her father from his absolute allegiance to the Soviet Union in foreign policy, for his political power had always depended to a large extent upon his being Moscow's most favoured Bulgarian son. In September 1973 Zhivkov remarked that Bulgaria and the Soviet Union would 'act as a single body, breathing with the same lungs and nourished by the same bloodstream', and in major questions such as East–West relations, disarmament, Afghanistan, the Middle East and central America, Sofia's stance has always been all but indistinguishable from that of Moscow. This close association with Moscow brings economic advantages to Bulgaria as well as political strength to Zhivkov, but it is arguable that if he had not adopted such a policy by choice he would at any event have come under considerable pressure to do so, for Bulgaria still occupies a vital strategic position in the Balkans. Its proximity to the Straits remains important, but it is also the only Warsaw pact state to have borders with two NATO countries, Greece and Turkey, in addition to which it is also a neighbour of two socialist states, Yugoslavia and Romania, whose commitment to the Soviet camp is questionable.

Subservience to the USSR is less apparent in Balkan affairs, in which Moscow has taken a less obvious interest since the fall of Khruschev, although it was Soviet dislike of multi-lateral as opposed to bi-lateral agreements which led the Bulgarians to frustrate Greek efforts to increase Balkan solidarity in the mid-1970s. In general, however, the Soviets' relative neglect of the Balkans has enabled the Sofia regime to be more assertive in the diplomacy of the peninsula, a development which helped to make its subservience in other affairs more acceptable to many Bulgarians. Even before Khruschev's fall, Bulgaria had, in June 1964, reached an agreement with Greece, with whom relations had for long been strained by NATO activities in that country and by Bulgaria's settling of Greek Communist refugees along the common border. Good relations with Romania have survived both Ceausescu's coolness towards the Soviet Union and the embarrassments of the continued postponement of joint economic projects, such as the hydro-electric scheme first announced in 1962 and still not started twenty years later. A marked improvement in relations with Turkey was noticeable in the late 1960s. An agreement facilitating the emigration of some Bulgarian Turks was signed in October 1969, and in 1976 Zhivkov became the first Bulgarian leader since the war to visit Turkey. By 1979 50,000 Bulgarian Turks had left under the terms of the 1969 agreement, the non-renewal of which proved to be a pointer to a serious deterioration of Bulgaro-Turkish relations in the mid-1980s.

The most difficult Balkan relationship has been that with Yugoslavia. The conservatives in the Bulgarian leadership had once resented a regime which, they believed, had been responsible for the fall of Chervenkov, and if this emotion was of little relevance after 1962, the Macedonian question remained and was one on which Bulgarians, Communist and non-Communist, could unite. In 1965 the Bulgarians had ceased to recognise 'Macedonian' as a minority race, and further wrangles followed over the legitimacy of Macedonian as a separate language. In 'The Macedonian Problem: Historical-Political Aspects', a pamphlet issued to party members in 1969 and later circulated more widely, the Bulgarians went over to the offensive, claiming that two-thirds of the population of Yugoslav Macedonia were ethnically Bulgarian. In the early 1970s there was some relaxation of tension. Zhivkov, who has always appeared moderate on this issue, made soothing remarks about Bulgaria's lack of territorial ambition, but his moderation was not always reciprocated. In November 1972, in an effort perhaps to ease difficulties in Croatia, Tito reinvoked the bogey of Bulgarian expansionism, telling an audience in Skopje that the Bulgarians must forget 'illusions based upon the distant past'. In the late 1970s, with both states concerned at internal dissent and with their historical consciousnesses sharpened by a string of centennial celebrations, the question flared again, reaching its climax in 1979 when the aged Bulgarian politburo member, Tsola Dragoicheva, claimed in her memoirs that during the war the Yugoslav party had reneged on an agreement that decisions upon the Macedonian issue should be left until after the end of hostilities. The president of the Macedonian Academy of Sciences replied that if the memoirs had not been forged then Dragoicheva was sick. Since this unseemly exchange the dispute has subsided, notwithstanding the occasional academic outburst. Zhivkov has called a number of times for better relations with Yugoslavia, and in 1980 he attended Tito's funeral; Bulgaria made no difficulties at the time of the Kosovo riots in the following year, although a Bulgarian was killed in a frontier incident that summer; trade between the two countries has increased considerably and there has been a series of successful friendship rallies in border towns.

In addition to an improvement in relations between Bulgaria and its neighbours the mid-1960s also saw much more contact with the West. In October 1966 de Gaulle's anti-American France provided the appropriate atmosphere for Zhivkov's first visit to a Western state. In December 1973 full diplomatic relations were established with the German Federal Republic, and another notable turning point came in June 1975 when Zhivkov was received by Pope Paul VI in the Vatican. As a result of this meeting Roman Catholic bishops of the Latin rite were at last sanctioned by the Sofia regime, and in November 1975 a party of Bulgarian pilgrims was allowed to travel to Rome. By 1979 Bulgaria's 70,000 Roman Catholics had their full complement of bishops for the first time since the late 1940s.

Whilst developing its relationships with the West the Bulgarian regime was also establishing links with the Third World. The country has for long received students from this area, though not always with the desired results, for in 1965 Africans studying in Sofia took to the streets to protest at the treatment they were receiving. There has been considerable traffic in the opposite direction, and by the 1980s large numbers of Bulgarian engineers, doctors, nurses and technical advisors were at work in Africa, Asia and Latin America. In 1981 there were over 2,000 Bulgarian medical personnel in Libya, which was by this time Bulgaria's third largest trading partner after the Soviet Union and the GDR. Bulgaria's expanding relations with the wider world were also reflected in the fact that between 1978 and 1983 Zhivkov visited, in addition to all the European Warsaw pact states, Nigeria, Mozambique, Angola, South Yemen, Greece, Vietnam, Laos, Kampuchea, Mexico, Cuba, Iraq, Libya, Malta, Syria – where he was the first socialist leader to meet Yassir Arafat – India, Turkey, Japan, North Korea and Mongolia, in addition to which he received heads of state or other leaders from most of these nations and also from Iran, Ethiopia, Zambia, Afghanistan, Grenada (Michael Bishop), the Congo, Guinea and Algeria.

In domestic affairs the Zhivkov regime has shown more independence and individuality than in foreign policy, and more than has generally been conceded by foreign observers. Zhivkov's consolidation of his hold over the party, the secret police and the army coincided approximately with the completion of the building of Bulgaria's industrial base. Industrial expansion had until then been relatively easy, as collectivisation had pushed masses of displaced peasants into the labour market and the regime had channelled available capital into heavy industry. By 1969 82 per cent of Bulgaria's labour force was employed in industrial production, compared to 37 per cent in 1948. So rapid and massive a social revolution could not have been driven through without enormous dislocation and suffering, nor did the incorporation of unskilled and often unwilling former peasants into the industrial labour force make for efficiency, and economic administration was not made easy by the forced amalgamation of the 6,109 industrial units of 1947 into the 1,650 of 1960. Furthermore, Bulgaria was not immune from the Stalinist *folies de grandeur* which afflicted all east European economies. The huge metallurgical combine at Kremikovtsi near Sofia, which opened in November 1963 and which had eaten up a fifth of the total capital investment in industry during the previous two years, proved a disaster. The nearby reserves of iron ore which the plant was to exploit had long been shown to be inadequate, and both ore and coal have to be imported, with consequent strains upon the railway system and harbour facilities.

After surplus labour had been absorbed and the industrial base completed, further real economic growth had to be sought in increases in productivity. At the same time there was an increasing political need to increase consumer production to reward the nation for its endurance. The commitment of the regime to the latter goal was stated clearly in a resolution adopted by a central committee plenum of December 1972. This statement of economic objectives complemented the recent formulations of the new constitution and the new party programme, and offered an appetising prospect of higher wages, more housing, and greater investment in consumer production.

During collectivisation and the construction of the heavy industrial base Bulgarian policy had followed closely the Soviet model, and in the early 1960s Zhivkov copied Khruschev in devising long-term economic strategies, which were the subject of debate at some 28,000 public meetings. With the fall of Khruschev, however, Zhivkov began to rely more on his own devices and to formulate or improvise more individual policies, which may well account for the frequent experimentation which has affected Bulgarian industry, agriculture and administration since the mid-1960s.

After the 1959 Theses Zhivkov's first foray into experimentation came in December 1965, with the publication of an economic reform programme which was adopted by a central committee plenum the following April. The general principles of the reform were the decentralisation of economic decision-making, greater use of the profit motive, and the tying of wages to production. In practice this meant that individual enterprises were now able to sell both surplus capital and production in excess of that called for in the plan; once items on a government-decided priority list had been produced enterprises were free to manufacture and sell what they thought best, and some were even given the power to deal in foreign currency; the new concept of 'planning from below' meant that enterprises were to draw up their own projects, which would then be coordinated with other plants in the same sector by the central planning mechanism and the forty or so trusts which controlled the various sections of the economy; wages and capital accumulation were to be tied to the profitability of the individual enterprise, and the director of each plant was henceforth to consult with 'production committees' elected by the workers. This was a small step compared to the Yugoslav system of self-management, but it was a great leap forward in the Bulgarian context.

By 1969 the reform scheme had been largely abandoned. A plenum in July 1968 adopted a new approach to national economic strategy, and called for the 'perfection of centralised planning'. In 1970 the economic trusts were given greater authority over constituent enterprises, and were ordered to replace planning from below with the former practice of having plans handed down by the appropriate department of the council of ministers. At the same time the tentative moves towards shop-floor democracy were checked by allowing the established trade unions to dominate the production committees. The reform scheme had fallen victim to two factors; its results, distinctly encouraging at first, had by 1968 become disappointing, and events in Czechoslovakia had made experimentation politically dangerous.

The ending of the reforms did not affect the increasing specialisation in industrial manufacturing which the search for greater productivity had produced. In 1965 an agreement had been concluded with the Soviet Union by which Bulgaria was to assemble automobiles and lorries produced in the USSR, and in the following year a similar but short-lived arrangement was made with France for the assembly in Bulgaria of Renault cars. Bulgaria also developed ship-building and the manufacture of railway rolling-stock and fork-lift trucks; by 1975 one third of its industrial production was in transport goods. By this time Comecon had also begun to move towards the greater international division of labour in the more advanced industries, and under this scheme Bulgaria was to supply eastern Europe with magnetic discs and other important computer parts. By the late 1970s it was also producing complete computers.

Specialisation within the CMEA did not inhibit the search for economic contact with the non-socialist world. Mass tourism, much of it from the West, had made its ugly mark on the Black Sea coast in the 1960s, and by the following decade had become a major earner of hard currency for Bulgaria. In 1975 ten-year agreements on economic cooperation were concluded with Portugal, and, much more importantly, with West Germany. Contracts were also signed according to which Western concerns such as Volvo, Schweppes, Shell, Occidental Petroleum, and, in the early 1980s, Dow Chemicals and Pierre Cardin, were to grant licences for the manufacture and sale of their products in Bulgaria. Links with the West were intended to furnish Bulgaria with the credit and the technological expertise needed to raise productivity and to increase domestic living standards, but association with Western economies also meant exposure to the vagaries of a free market. After the mid-1970s the cost of Western goods, expertise, and above all credit rose alarmingly. By the end of the decade Bulgaria's debts to the West had reached $3.7 billion (US) and were absorbing 38 per cent of its hard-currency earnings. Bulgaria's position was made more parlous by the fact that the only commodities which the West would buy from it were agricultural or processed agricultural goods, the very items which the EEC's common agricultural policy wished to exclude. European protectionism was to some degree overcome by cultivating markets in Scandinavia, North America and Japan, with the result that in 1979 exports to the non-socialist world were 78 per cent higher than for the previous year, and by 1982 the hard-currency debt had been halved and was well under control, thanks in no small measure to the fact that Soviet oil, imported at a favourable price, had been resold for a handsome, hard-currency profit.

Reform of agriculture began in 1968 when new statutes regulating the TKZSs were enacted. The ground rent paid to former owners, which had been declining as a percentage of their income, was abolished. Minimum wages were guaranteed, and workers were to be grouped into permanent brigades which were to have some internal autonomy and which were to cultivate assigned plots of land.

In 1969 more significant changes took place. In the Vratsa area seven TKZSs involving 40,000 workers and covering 38,700 hectares were grouped into a loose federation. Later in the year more such groupings took place, and in April 1970 a central committee plenum approved the general application of this policy. The new units so formed were the agro-industrial complexes, or AICs. This second bout of amalgamation was theoretically voluntary, with the constituent state and collective farms retaining their autonomy, but the AICs rapidly became internally centralised, and by a statute of 1975 many were redefined as 'unified legal entities' and were therefore no longer federations of separate units. Each AIC had its own party group, employed at least 6,000 workers, covered between 20,000 and 30,000 hectares and usually encompassed five or six villages, one of which was nominated as the administrative centre and which had, or rapidly acquired, the amenities of a small town.

The reasoning behind the reform was that horizontal integration based on similarities of climate and terrain would facilitate specialisation in agricultural production, and individual AICs were therefore meant to concentrate on – at the most – three main crops and rear only one brand of livestock. It was also planned, in the longer term, to link AICs closely with manufacturing industry and the trading associations. Zhivkov had told the April 1970 plenum that industrial technology and managerial practices should be introduced to agriculture, and that industrial plants should also be built within the AICs. In 1973 there was a short-lived experiment under which a number of AICs were incorporated into industrial concerns to form industrial–agricultural complexes.

The closer association of agriculture and industry was of great importance. The AICs, if they developed some manufacturing capacity, might help to check urban drift and thus relieve pressure on city housing, but far more important than these possible social benefits were the political implications. The AICs were to merge state and cooperative farms into a new form of public property which did not have the ideological drawbacks of collective ownership; also, if the planned specialisation of agricultural production took place and if it were conducted on industrial lines, then in conformity with the party programme of 1971 agricultural labour would become indistinguishable from industrial. This would be the ultimate defeat of Stamboliiski and his ideas of the land offering varieties of work and saving Bulgaria from the evils of specialised labour and urban life. In fact the homogenisation of Bulgarian society should logically lead to the withering away of the Agrarian Party, for a polity which consists solely of workers would need no other political organisation than the Communist Party. The AICs were in this respect an essential complement to the party programme of 1971 with its aim of creating a 'unified socialist society'.

By the early 1980s theory had not been matched by reality, not least

Table 5 *Planned and achieved growth under seventh and eighth five-year plans*

	Seventh five-year plan 1976–81 planned increase	Achieved increase	Eighth five-year plan 1981–85 planned increase
National income	45%	35%	20%
Industrial production	55%	35%	28%
Agricultural production	20%	12%	18%
Real income	20%	12.7%	15%
Housing provision (units)	420,000	352,000	360,000

Source: Figures compiled from official statements as reported in, *inter alia,* Radio Free Europe Research Bulletins.

because although the AICs had been the organisational core of Bulgarian agriculture for a decade and a half, the 'private' plot had not diminished in importance. The plot, usually between two and five dekars, is not technically private property and may not be sold, mortgaged or worked by hired labour, but its produce is at the disposal of the individual or family which works it. Local collective managers have frequently been ambivalent in their attitude to the individual plots, but in 1979 delegates to a special conference praised its contribution to the national economy and called for greater production of small-sized farming equipment, improved seeds and cheaper fertilizers for use on the plots. In 1981 some of the restrictions on private livestock-raising were lifted, and in 1982 a decree called for private plots to play an important part in the development of marginal land, especially in the mountains. It was not difficult to see why the private plots were held in such esteem. Although they covered only 12.9 per cent of the total arable land they were responsible in 1982 for a quarter of national agricultural output, providing 33 per cent of the vegetables, 51 per cent of the potatoes, and 26.6 per cent of the fruit; though they produced only 2.6 per cent of the total grain crop they grew 21.9 per cent of the fodder grains, all these figures being the more impressive when one takes into consideration the fact that many plots are consigned to the poorer land within a collective. Perhaps here, in their devotion to their individual plots, the Bulgarian farm workers keep alive the national tradition of small peasant farming.

By the late 1970s it was clear that, although the successive reforms had brought about some improvements in living standards, progress had not been as rapid as had been hoped and promised. Plan targets remained largely unfulfilled, and shortages, irregularities in supply and eccentricities of quality had not been eliminated. The leadership, no doubt with an eye on Poland, recognised that in the past too much had been expected of the economy and its workforce, and when the eighth five-year plan was published in 1981 its lower and more realistic target figures showed that lessons had been learnt from the failures of its predecessors (see table 5).

·A more realistic assessment of economic capabilities has not meant the end of the reforming spirit. In March 1979 a central committee plenum endorsed a set of reforms to be applied by the beginning of 1982 and now generally known as Bulgaria's NEM or new economic model. The NEM was to help Bulgaria adapt to current technological changes, to raise levels of productivity, to enhance the quality of goods and services, and to increase the competitiveness of Bulgarian goods in the world market so that trading deficits and hard-currency debts could be eliminated; its overall objective was defined as being to provide 'a new approach to the management of the economy in the scientific–technological revolution'. Its methods were to be based upon decentralisation, democracy, competition, the use of market forces, and self-sufficiency in individual units of production. Decentralisation was to involve a reduction in the power of the central plan, which was now to confine itself to such general tasks as specifying gross profits and foreign currency earnings, overseeing scientific and technical progress, and allocating new capital plant. There was to be no more direct supervision of individual enterprises by the central economic ministries, and the economic bureaucracy was to be slimmed down drastically; in January 1984 a decree removing all administrative levels between the central councils of the AICs and their constituent brigades did away with 11,500 bureaucratic posts at a stroke. There was also a threat that any higher institution which caused economic damage to a lower one would have to pay compensation, even if that compensation had to be found in the higher institution's salary and wages fund. This was a draconian measure intended to tackle the supply problem which bedevils most centralised, planned economies.

Each enterprise was to receive from the central planning authority a state plan, or general guideline, for production during the coming year. Within each enterprise management had to cooperate with the separate work units, or brigades, in deciding the best means for fulfilling the state plan. The brigades, usually between thirty and fifty strong, were given considerable power, with each brigade being required both to decide on its needs for labour, fuel and raw materials, and also to make itself responsible for the disposal of the finished article. Profits were to be retained for reinvestment and for division amongst the workers. The brigades were to become 'the chief organs of self-management' and through them was to be applied the Zhivkov doctrine that whilst the state is the owner of socialist property, the workers' collectives are its managers.

Competition within the NEM was to come through the election of brigade leaders, members of plant councils, and other figures. The elected brigade leader replaced the appointed foreman, in what was a significant departure from Soviet practice in industrial management. Widespread election of responsible persons was to provide the mechanism for what the NEM's proponents referred to as 'mobilisation from below'. Competition was also to determine which units would be allocated new investment funds and new plant. Allocation of the latter, it was stated, would not be made to enterprises which would not move towards adoption of the most modern methods of production, this being one of many examples of how in recent years the Zhivkov regime has become almost frenetic in its determination to push ahead with the 'scientific–technological revolution'.

Under the NEM market forces were to be allowed a much enhanced role. Direct links between producer and consumer were to be established in both the domestic and the foreign markets, and thus the retail trade was to be eliminated, as were a number of trading monopolies. Their disappearance would, it was hoped, mean that the public need no longer tolerate the poor quality and the irregular supplies which the monopolist system had previously imposed upon them; in February 1982 the party newspaper, *Rabotnichesko Delo* (*Workers' Cause*), proclaimed that 'under the new conditions there will be only one master in the domestic market, the consumer'.

The fifth pillar of the NEM, self-sufficiency, was to apply to all production units right down to the brigade. In 1982 the minister president, Grisha Filipov, warned that economic organisations must no longer count on the government for subsidies, which would now be given only in the most exceptional circumstances and then for a maximum of two years. There was also to be a move towards regional self-sufficiency, with local units receiving from beyond their boundaries only those goods which proper research would indicate they might not be expected to produce themselves.

Accompanying the NEM were a number of other efforts to stimulate production and productivity. In 1980 a decree was passed encouraging the establishment of joint ventures financed by both Bulgarian and foreign capital, but so far the results have proved disappointing, with few foreign concerns showing real interest and contracts being signed only with a few Japanese enterprises. Other initiatives have included the promotion of small and medium-sized enterprises which were intended to concentrate on the production mainly of consumer goods and were to employ the latest technology. The new attitudes and the pressing need to increase consumer production and consumer satisfaction also led, in the early 1980s, to a more relaxed policy with regard to private or individual economic activity. The farmers were the most obvious beneficiaries of this relaxation, but there was also talk, though little more than talk, of once again allowing the private restaurateur and the private medical practitioner. Intention was again far ahead of achievement in plans to introduce second-hand stores for certain items, to develop home-delivery services, to open rental shops and to improve the quality of provincial life by establishing department stores in major towns.

That such plans could be considered, however, indicated that the reforms outlined in the late 1970s had produced profound changes of attitude. Indeed the NEM might better be defined as the 'New Economic Mood', and it has certainly been amongst the most far-reaching and radical of Zhivkov's many experiments, and one which led him to proclaim in

February 1985 that 'the economic science of socialism must be pulled out of its present state of simply repeating the formulations of Marx and Engels'. A remarkable evolution has clearly taken place in the thinking of the man who has been the undisputed leader of Bulgaria since the mid-1960s.

BULGARIA IN THE MID-1980s

The 1980s opened in an unparalleled mood of general optimism. In cultural affairs Zhivkova was asserting Bulgarian individuality and allowing some discussion of non-materialist ideas. There was also a more relaxed attitude to the West, with Bulgarians who had sufficient hard currency being allowed much greater, though by no means unrestricted, freedom to travel. At the same time the tourist traffic in the opposite direction was bringing in Western fashion, particularly in the clothes and music favoured by the young, especially after the spread of the cassette recorder. At home the media were allowed to discuss a wider range of issues and were granted more freedom of expression than for a number of years. The law of plebiscites, introduced in 1983, was designed to promote public discussion of selected issues of interest, and, in general, newspapers, radio and television in the early 1980s carried a number of articles and features which would have been unthinkable two decades before.

There was also, in relative terms at least, a more relaxed attitude to the Christian religion. Zhivkov's visit to Rome in 1975 had already regularised the spiritual life of Bulgaria's Roman Catholics. The Orthodox church had always been far too important a national institution and too important a feature of Bulgarian history and culture to be suppressed, but it was no longer subjected to the intense anti-religious propaganda campaigns which had been launched by the government in the 1970s. Protestant sects continued to survive unobtrusively, although, with the exception of the Pentecostalists, they all seemed to suffer a decline in numbers. There were Uniate communities in Yambol, Plovdiv and Sofia, and in the latter there is also a community of Uniate Carmelites, which is still perhaps the only Roman Catholic congregation with its mother house in a Communist state.

In the international sphere Bulgarian sportsmen and sportswomen had raised the nation's prestige, as had Zhivkova's highly orchestrated celebration in 1981 to commemorate the 1,300th anniversary of the founding of the first Bulgarian state. Bulgaria's new sophistication, its cultural self-assurance and that sense of continuity which graces all stable societies, was symbolised by the fact that the Soviet satellite launched in that anniversary year carried Bulgarian equipment not only for the investigation of the ionosphere and the magnetosphere but also for the discovery of archaeological sites in Bulgaria itself. In the field of high politics some observers even detected signs of more independent line, when in 1981 Zhivkov spoke of nominating the Balkans a zone of peace and cooperation – this at a time when Moscow, angered by NATO's decision on Cruise and Pershing missiles, was anxious not to contract the area in which it might deploy its own deterrent.

Most important of all in generating popular optimism, however, were the favourable economic indicators. In 1980 and 1981 the shops were being packed with goods to prevent any spread of the Polish virus, but in addition to that there were other encouraging signs. The NEM had been applied to selected areas of production, primarily in agriculture, and the results had been favourable. It was assumed that the general application of the reforms in 1982 would have equally satisfying results, and long-term expectations were boosted by increasingly enthusiastic reports on what benefits the new methods of production, particularly in biotechnology, would bring.

By the mid-1980s much of this optimism had disappeared. The first blow – and for the intellectuals it was a shattering one – came with the announcement on 21 July 1981 that Liudmila Zhivkova had died of a cerebral haemorrhage; she had not yet entered her fortieth year. Her father promised that her work would continue, but in 1982 his own health was suspect and he could not prevent more conventional spirits reasserting their baleful influence in cultural affairs. Little now remains of Zhivkova's adventurism, and in 1984 the V congress of the Bulgarian Writers' Union called for intensified ideological combat and for a greater degree of 'historical optimism' in literature; the congress said nothing about Blaga Dimitrova's novel, *Litse* (*Face*), an outstanding work which contrasts the heroism and self-sacrifice of the anti-fascist struggle with the self-interest, cynicism and careerism so frequently found in the party today; for such boldness it had been savagely attacked by the literary establishment after which it was quietly banned and then withdrawn from libraries and bookshops.

As unexpected as Zhivkova's demise were the accusations of Bulgarian implication in acts of terrorism and drug-trafficking. The first of these came in September 1982, when it was alleged that the Bulgarian secret service had been involved in the attempt to assassinate Pope John Paul II in May of the previous year. This was followed by further accusations which implicated the regime in other acts, including the involvement of the Bulgarian trading agency, Kintex, in the smuggling of arms and drugs into the West.

The evidence to support Bulgarian involvement in the assassination attempt on the pope on 13 May 1981 is powerful but entirely circumstantial. French intelligence sources are reported to have warned the Vatican of an impending attack, and there was a massive and unexplained increase in wireless traffic between the Bulgarian embassy in Rome and Sofia on the afternoon of 13 May 1981. On that day there was also the extraordinary coincidence of the Bulgarian embassy making a unique request that a TIR lorry should receive customs clearance at the embassy that afternoon; it has been suggested that the vehicle was to provide the means of escape for the two assassins, Mehment Ali Agca and Bekir Celenk, both of whom had spent a substantial length of time in Bulgaria. There can be no doubt that if the Bulgarian secret service were involved in the attempt on the life of the pope then it acted with the approval if not at the instigation of the KGB. And the Soviets in 1981 had sufficient reason to wish to be rid of a Polish pontiff who had threatened to return to his homeland and organise the resistance if the Red Army were used against his countrymen. On the other hand it has to be asked whether a secret service which had disposed so skilfully of Georgi Markov would choose to rely on two unstable, extreme right-wing Turks armed with a small hand gun in a crowd of thousands. And finally it must also be said that no case which relies heavily on the evidence of Mehment Ali Agca can command much respect; if his outbursts in the dock are genuine then surely no clandestine organisation would have employed so unsuitable a person, and if they are feigned he is so brilliant a dissimulator that he will always be able to conceal the truth.

The passage of drugs through Bulgaria occurred in the inter-war period, when IMRO is known to have raised revenue from this activity. Recent allegations, however insubstantial the evidence, allege the involvement of an offical agency, Kintex, which is said to have smuggled drugs into the West and used the proceeds to buy weapons, which were then transported to extremist subversives of both right and left in Turkey and other states which Communist strategists wished to see destabilised. In July 1982 the United States branded Bulgaria as a country engaging in 'state-sponsored terrorism' and suspended cooperation with the Bulgarians on the control of narcotics. The Bulgarians reacted energetically, stressing their record against the smugglers with over a thousand arrests, and, they claim, 30,000 kg of contraband drugs confiscated since 1967; and their case was supported in 1983 at an international conference on trafficking in drugs, in which Interpol had much to say in praise of Bulgaria's efforts to contain this evil.

The optimism of the early 1980s suffered from the death of Zhivkova and from the international opprobrium which the terrorist allegations incurred, but it was immeasurably more damaged by the collapse of hopes for rapid economic expansion and improvements in living standards.

The first signs of disappointment with the NEM came with the failure to improve the quality of Bulgarian produce. Zhivkov tackled the problem in May 1983, in a speech which lacked his customary garnishing of humour and which was broadcast live on radio and television. The leader blasted Bulgarian producers for not improving the quality of their goods; even foreign products manufactured under licence had, he said, been 'Bulgarised' and for this he blamed poor controls, weak labour discipline and a lack of incentive. In the following weeks the press and radio were deluged with complaints about Bulgarian-made items, and in March 1984 the party convened a special conference to discuss the problem. The solutions, it decided, were: to increase investment in scientific development with up to three-quarters of capital expenditure being allocated to the introduction of new technology; to ginger up management by forming élite groups of workers in each enterprise; to extend the NEM further; to make wages dependent on quality; and to give more autonomy to the brigades. There was even talk of consumer protection. As yet, however, little improvement seems to have been made, and by 1985 the quantity as well as the quality of production was far behind the predictions and hopes of a few years before.

The reasons for the disappointing performance of the NEM are varied. In the first place, the government's understandable determination to conquer the hard-currency debt problem inevitably retarded domestic expansion. The import of Western technology had to be curtailed and this slowed down increases in domestic productivity and in the supply of consumer goods, whilst top-quality agricultural produce, despite the judicious stocking of the shops in 1980 and 1981, had to be diverted to the export market. As a result the drive to improve domestic living standards was seriously impaired.

Much more important was the energy problem. Bulgaria has few reserves of good-quality fossil fuels and is therefore more dependent than any other east European country on imported energy. Although Libya and, for a while, Iran have supplied oil, the main source for this and for natural gas and electricity is the Soviet Union, Bulgaria being connected to the Soviet grid since 1972. Soviet expertise was also vital for the construction of the Kozlodui atomic power complex, which opened in September 1974, and, when functioning, now provides about a quarter of the electricity consumed in the country. In the mid-1980s the problem of energy supplies has been greatly complicated by two factors. Repairs to existing nuclear reactors and the construction of new ones are way behind schedule, and thus the nuclear input to the national grid has been greatly reduced; as the Soviet ambassador told a Bulgarian reporter in the summer of 1985, before Chernobyl, 'It seems it is easier to build these things than to use them.' The shortfall in nuclear power production has been compounded by the droughts of 1984 and 1985, the latter being the worst for a century. Reservoirs have been depleted, thus reducing the capacity of the hydro-electric plants which supply about 8 per cent of national consumption. The Bulgarians have not had to endure the privations inflicted upon the Romanians, and they have also had much greater freedom than their northern neighbours to complain about shortages, but the prospects for the winter of 1985–6 are far from encouraging, and by November 1985 electricity supplies were available for only three hours in every six. Few conditions are more demoralising and disruptive of public and private life than the constant interruption of electricity.

A further cause for the disappointing performance of the NEM is that after years of a strict central control which was only occasionally relieved by a bout of short-lived economic or administrative experimentation, local party officials and brigade members in general do not have the expertise, the experience or even the right psychological outlook to cope with the many and varied responsibilities which the NEM seeks to place upon them. And what reason is there to believe that the present reforms, however radical, will be any less transitory than their numerous predecessors?

A long-term problem which preoccupies many Bulgarians is that of demography. According to the 1965 census Bulgaria had more centenarians than any other state, but if this were a cause for self-congratulation, the picture at the other end of the age pyramid was very different. In 1939 population growth had been 1.5 per cent per annum, but in 1974 it was 0.74 per cent and in 1981 a mere 0.3 per cent. If present trends continue Bulgaria will have a zero or even a negative population growth rate by 1995 at the latest. This has been described as a threat to the nation's economic development programme and even to its defence capabilities. There has been a note almost of panic in some reactions to this problem. The deputy chairman of the state council, Georgi Djagarov, writing in an army newspaper, called for an increase in the cost of abortions, higher taxes for bachelors and childless married couples, and extensive provision of clothes, food, free transport and money for large families. In 1983

Grisha Filipov, the minister president, suggested that those who did not marry or have children should be discriminated against in housing allocations and in promotion at work. Some have blamed abortion for the problem – terminations have exceeded live births by as much as 40,000 per annum – whilst a good deal of official comment has focussed upon the instability of marriage. In a revision of the family legal code in 1984, the government proposed to raise the fee for divorce from 100 to 500 *leva*, and to insist on a period of five rather than two years of marriage before separation could be allowed. The plans were the first issue to become a subject for public debate under the law of plebiscites, and came in for heavy criticism; as a result the period before separation could be allowed was to be three rather than five years, although the full and extremely unpopular increase in the divorce fee was retained.

The demographic problem touches upon another issue in which Bulgaria has recently suffered unfavourable publicity: its treatment of the Turkish minority. It is generally assumed that the decline in the birth rate is more marked amongst the Bulgarians than amongst the Turks and particularly the gypsies; in 1970, when the national population growth rate was 0.72 per cent, that in the Tolbukhin province with its large proportion of Turks was 1.21 per cent. Fear of these differential growth rates may have prompted the policy recently introduced by the authorities of insisting that the Turks assume Bulgarian names. In 1940, when Turkish names of towns and villages were Bulgarised, the authorities deemed it unnecessary or unwise to insist upon changes in personal names, but in 1981 national identity was deleted as an item on internal Bulgarian passports, and in 1984, no doubt with the December 1985 census in view, a fierce and often insensitive campaign was launched in areas with a large proportion of Turks to force ethnic Turks to Bulgarise their names; in 1985 perhaps fifty Bulgarian Turks lost their lives in this campaign. Publication of Turkish-language sections in newspapers ceased, and high-ranking party and government officials toured the country making such idiotic assertions as that the Bulgarian 'Turks' had never in fact been Turks, but were Bulgarians who had been Turkified immediately after the Ottoman conquest. Why this policy was adopted is difficult to understand, notwithstanding the 1971 party programme's call for the creation of a 'unified socialist state'. It has been suggested that the elimination of Muslim names will harm Islam, in which name-taking is an integral part of an individual's religious maturation; the desire to weaken Islam, the argument continues, derives from the belief that so conservative a faith will hamper the rapid adoption of the new technology. This argument is less bizarre when viewed in the context of the fervour with which the scientific–technological revolution is being promoted in contemporary Bulgaria. The easy escape from the Turkish minority problem might have been to continue the emigration agreement of 1969, but this was decided against, probably because of the need to retain sources of unskilled manual labour. As matters stand the affair of the Turkish minority seems to have earned the Bulgarian regime a good deal of needless and unwelcome international publicity for little or no apparent domestic purpose.

It has been suggested that discontented Turks were responsible for the extraordinary terrorist attacks which affected Bulgaria in 1984 and 1985. On 30 August 1984 bombs exploded in the railway station at Plovdiv and at the airport in Varna; on that day Zhivkov travelled between the two cities. There were also reports that shortly after the explosions fly-sheets promising 'Forty Years: Forty Bombs' appeared in the streets of a number of Bulgarian cities. On 9 March 1985 seven people died in a suspicious fire on a Bulgarian train, and later in the same month the chief prosecutor, when introducing new and more stringent anti-terrorist regulations, admitted to the Sŭbranie that thirty deaths had been caused by such acts of violence in the preceding year. Apart from the very dubious hints at Turkish complicity there is as yet no indication as to who might be responsible for these outrages.

Until 1984, terrorism, as far as can be ascertained, had been absent from Bulgarian life for a generation. That cannot be said for the problem of corruption in the party and state bureaucracies. Bulgaria's long tradition of centralised, corrupt and extended bureaucracy had created its own version of careerism before 1944, and it was not surprising that this virus thrived in the body politic which the revolution had engendered. Bulgaria's bureaucracy is inordinately large, accounting in 1977 for 13.5 per cent of the total labour force, a ratio more than double that of the other socialist states. Petty embezzlement is widespread, and token measures, such as an order in 1979 that official petrol should be dyed a distinctive colour to limit its illegal sale on the black market, are periodically taken against it. There has also been a number of attacks upon large-scale corruption at the highest levels, but the regularity with which these exposures occur would suggest that the disease has not been eradicated. A particularly venal segment of Bulgarian society has for some years been sports and athletics; in 1979 the ultimate humiliation, defeat by England's soccer team, provoked a major cleansing operation, but in 1985 even more drastic surgery was necessary, with, this time, the complete dissolution and partial reconstruction under new names of two of Sofia's oldest and most popular soccer clubs.

The party's image has suffered from the prevalence of careerism and corruption, and also from the fact that its leadership is thought to be increasingly remote from the population as a whole. Like most ruling parties the BCP is a relatively exclusive body dominated by middle-aged, managerial males. The membership of 826,000 reported at the XII congress in 1981 represents 9.3 per cent of the total population. Industrial workers constituted 42.7 per cent of the total membership, but in 1981 figures for other groups were not revealed; in 1978 industrial workers had formed 41.8 per cent, peasants 22.4 per cent, white-collar workers 30.3 per cent and others 5.5 per cent. The higher echelons of the party show a different composition. In 1981 of the 166 members of the central committee only nine were workers, one was an industrial manager and one an agricultural manager; seventy-nine were government officials, seventy were party officials and thirteen were functionaries of the mass organisations; only eleven were women and there were three Jews, one Turk, one Pomak and no gypsies. Their average age was 57.5 years and only forty-five of the 166 were under fifty years of age.

The latter statistic touches upon the long-felt need to increase the commitment of Bulgaria's youth to the party and its ideals. The IX party congress in 1966 heard calls for greater solicitude for the nation's young people, and in 1967 Zhivkov published his 'Theses on Youth', in which he admitted that the older generation had become symbols of 'conservatism, bureaucracy and fossilisation'. In March 1975 there was a special conference to discuss the anti-social behaviour of minors as seen in such unpleasant phenomena as football hooliganism, and the XI party congress in the following year was marked by particularly severe criticism of the nation's youth. In 1982 Stanka Shopova, the first woman to be made head of the Dimitrov Communist Youth League (the Komsomol), reiterated the strictures which have now become commonplace – the young were too much interested in material acquisitions, pop music, drugs and alcohol, and too little dedicated to work – but neither this nor the numerous calls to the party to propagandise more amongst the young have had much effect. If one studies the remedies which the establishment has advocated one may not be surprised at the persistence of the problem: in 1968 a DCYL statement urged the 'introduction of new military exercises, games and marching songs; and the launching of a cultural programme with concerts, songs and dances in Bulgarian national style'; by 1982 things were little changed, for Shopova suggested that one answer was for 'current political and cultural information to be put over in discotheques'.

The apathy of the nation's youth is but one aspect of the problem of a decline in idealism which, as in most of eastern Europe, has affected even the party itself. The founding fathers of the party and of the Communist system had proved their commitment and constancy before 1944, but that generation is now largely beyond its working life, and its successors are much less interested in ideals than in their own careers. The party is aware of the problem. As early as 1970 an internal inquiry by the Gabrovo Party revealed a distinct lack of interest in ideological work, and subsequent congresses of the party and of the DCYL have heard frequent calls for an increase in ideological activity by party members. The party is having to face the fact that growing numbers of persons of intellect and social conscience are keeping away not only from the party but from its ideals. Just as a substantial part of the intelligentsia which created the nation fell victim to *partisanstvo* after the creation of the state, so the party which engineered the socialist revolution has fallen victim to careerism.

In the country at large, the party's credibility has been impaired not only by corruption and careerism but also by its constant failure to live up to its promises for increases in living standards. The collapse of belief in the party's ideals, both inside and outside the party, does not mean that the power of that body is any the less, but it does mean that the party is seeking means of filling the ideological void. Materialism of the Western type, so popular in the 1970s, has been discredited not only by the failures of the regime to achieve planned growth targets but also by the economic and social difficulties of the West itself; only Hungary remains loyal to this tarnished idol. Organised religion has experienced a powerful resurgence in the non-Orthodox areas, Hungary excepted, but in the Balkans it is the old political warhorse of nationalism which seems set to ride again. Yugoslavia's internal nationality problems in Croatia, Kosovo and Serbia are far from being solved, Greece postures against Turkey in age-old fashion, the Romanian regime glorifies almost all Romanians whatever their beliefs and actions, and in Bulgaria too national pride is encouraged within the general context of proletarian internationalism, though this 'official' nationalism is not to be equated with the assertion of cultural individuality sponsored by Zhivkova. Since 1974 the school curriculum has included the subject 'knowledge of the Fatherland'; there has been a marked stress on historical continuity in the Bulgarian lands, which was marked not only by the 1,300th anniversary celebrations in 1981 but also, in the late 1970s, by the exhibition of the Thracian treasures in Paris, Moscow, Leningrad, Vienna, London, the U.S.A, Mexico, Berlin, Tokyo, Prague, and Cologne; and in April 1985 there was celebration to mark the 1,000th anniversary of the death of Saint Methodius, who was vociferously claimed as a Bulgarian. The 1984–5 campaign against the Bulgarian Turks is a far more sinister expression of nationalism, as are recent developments over Macedonia. The Balkan wars, previously regarded by

Bulgaria's Communist historians as an example of bourgeois expansionism, are now seen as a just pursuit of national aims in which the army played an honourable role. In 1985 new army officers were inducted near the Yugoslav border and dubbed 'the Slivnitsa generation', to commemorate the centenary of the great Bulgarian victory.

The economic failures, the power shortages and the lack of ideological credibility have all sharpened criticism of the present leadership, which has also been weakened by a change in the relationship between the Bulgarian and the Soviet party chiefs. In 1962 Zhivkov had relied heavily on Soviet backing in his contest with Yugov, and during the reigns of Khruschev and Brezhnev he could always be sure of support from the Kremlin. That support is now less secure. Zhivkov made the mistake of supporting Chernenko in 1982, for which he was upbraided by Andropov, and the advent of Gorbachev has widened the gap between Moscow and Sofia. In contrast with Gorbachev and the new generation of Soviet leaders, Zhivkov, who was seventy-four in September 1985, and who since the death of Enver Hoxha in April 1985 has been the longest ruling boss of any party in power, seems like an anachronism. Despite his determination to press ahead with new technology and the Bulgarian NEM, the aura of the corrupt and indulgent Brezhnev era clings to him. When Zhivkov, returning home from an Asian tour, paid his first visit to Moscow since Chernenko's funeral, he had to wait until his second day in the city before meeting Gorbachev. In July 1985 the Soviet ambassador in Sofia told the Bulgarian journal, *Pogled* (*View*), that Gorbachev had told Zhivkov that although the roots of friendship between the two parties were deep and strong, the tree needed watering if it were to bear fruit.

This was an entirely new tone in public Soviet–Bulgarian exchanges, and the cooling of Soviet support together with the manifold internal problems could mean that the Zhivkov era has almost run its course. The power of the Bulgarian Communist Party, however, is hardly likely to be challenged or to diminish.

Suggestions For Further Reading

GENERAL HISTORY OF BULGARIA

John D. Bell, *The Communist Party of Bulgaria from Blagoev to Zhivkov* (Stanford, California, 1986)

Liuben Berov, *Bulgaria's Economic Development through the Ages* (Sofia, 1980)

Georgi Bokov (ed.), *Modern Bulgaria: History, Policy, Economy, Culture* (Sofia, 1981)

Bulgarian Academy of Sciences, *Information Bulgaria* (Oxford, 1985)

Hristo Hristov, *Bulgaria 1,300 years* (Sofia, 1980)

Mercia Macdermott, *A History of Bulgaria, 1393–1885* (London, 1962)

John R. Lampe, *The Bulgarian Economy in the Twentieth Century* (London, 1986) and Marvin R. Jackson, *Balkan Economic History, 1550–1950: From Imperial Borderlands to Developing Nations* (Bloomington, Indiana, 1982)

Charles A. Moser, *A History of Bulgarian Literature, 863–1944* (The Hague, 1972)

Marin Pundeff, *Bulgaria: A Bibliographical Guide* (Washington, D.C., 1965)

Nikolai Todorov, *A Short History of Bulgaria* (Sofia, 1975)

Djenyu Vassilev, *Bulgarian Culture, Old and New* (Sofia, 1965)

BULGARIA BEFORE THE BULGARIANS

R. F. Hoddinott, *Bulgaria in Antiquity: An Archeological Introduction* (London and Tonbridge, 1975)

A. Mocsy, *Pannonia and Upper Moesia* (London, 1974)

A. G. Poulter (ed.), *Proceedings of the International Conference on the Ancient History and Archaeology of Bulgaria* (Nottingham, 1983)

Thracian Treasures from Bulgaria: A Special Exhibition held at the British Museum, January-March 1976 (London, British Museum Publications, 1976)

V. Velkov, *Cities in Thrace and Dacia in Late Antiquity* (Amsterdam, 1977)

V. Velkov (ed.), *Roman Cities in Bulgaria: Collected Studies* (Amsterdam, 1980)

THE MEDIAEVAL EMPIRES

Robert Browning, *Byzantium and Bulgaria: A Comparative Study across the Early Medieval Frontier* (London, 1975)

David Marshall Lang, *The Bulgarians from Pagan Times to the Ottoman Conquest* (London, 1976)

Dmitri Obolensky, *The Bogomils: A Study in Balkan Neo-Manichaeism* (Cambridge, 1948, reprinted New York, 1978)

Dmitri Obolensky, *The Byzantine Commonwealth: Eastern Europe 500–1453* (London, 1971)
Steven Runciman, *A History of the First Bulgarian Empire* (London, 1930)

OTTOMAN RULE AND THE NATIONAL REVIVAL

Stephen W. Ashley, 'Bulgarian Nationalism (1830–1876): The Ideals and Careers of Ivan Bogorov, Georgi Rakovski and Pencho Slaveikov' (Oxford D. Phil., 1984)
James F. Clark, *Bible Societies, American Missionaries and the National Revival of Bulgaria* (New York 1971, reprint of Harvard Ph.D., 1937)
R. J. Crampton, 'Bulgarian Society in the early Nineteenth Century', in Richard Clogg (ed.), *Balkan Society in the Age of Greek Independence* (London, 1981)
Nikolai Genchev, *The Bulgarian National Revival Period* (Sofia, 1977)
Mercia Macdermott, *The Apostle of Freedom: A Portrait of Vasil Levski against a Portrait of Nineteenth-Century Bulgaria* (London, 1967)
Thomas A. Meininger, *Ignatiev and the Establishment of the Bulgarian Exarchate, 1864–1872: A Study in Personal Diplomacy* (Madison, Wisconsin, 1970)
Richard Millman, *Britain and the Eastern Question, 1875–1878* (Oxford, 1979)
D. Mishew, *The Bulgarians in the Past* (republished by Arno Press and the New York Times, New York, 1971)
Zachary Stoyanoff, *Pages from the Autobiography of a Bulgarian Insurgent* (translated from the Bulgarian by M. W. Potter, with an introduction by the translator, London, 1913)
B. H. Sumner, *Russia and the Balkans, 1870–1880* (Oxford, 1937)
Nikolai Todorov, *The Balkan Town, 15th-19th Centuries* (Seattle, Washington, 1983)
Ivan Vazov, *Under the Yoke: A Novel* (translated from the Bulgarian by Marguerite Alexieva and Theodora Atanassova, Sofia, 1976)

FROM THE LIBERATION TO THE END OF THE FIRST WORLD WAR

A. Hulme Beaman, *Stambuloff* (London, 1895)
C. E. Black, *The Establishment of Constitutional Goverment in Bulgaria* (Princeton Studies in History, Vol. I, Princeton, 1943)
H. N. Brailsford, *Macedonia, its Races and their Future* (London, 1906)
Noel Buxton, *With the Bulgarian Staff* (London, 1913)
Stephen Constant, *Foxy Ferdinand, Tsar of Bulgaria* (London, 1979)
Egon Corti, *The Downfall of Three Dynasties* (London, 1934)
  Alexander of Bulgaria (London, 1954)
Richard J. Crampton, *Bulgaria 1878–1918: A History* (Boulder, Colorado and New York, 1983)
I. E. Geshoff, *The Balkan League* (London, 1915)
E. C. Helmreich, *The Diplomacy of the Balkan Wars* (Cambridge, Massachussetts, 1938)
Charles Jelavich, *Tsarist Russia and Balkan Nationalism: Russian Influence in the Internal Affairs of Bulgaria and Serbia, 1876–1886* (Berkeley, California, 1958)
  Russian Policy in Bulgaria and Serbia, 1881–1897 (Berkeley, California, 1950)

George F. Kennan, *The Decline of Bismarck's European Order: Franco-Russian Relations, 1875–1890* (Princeton, 1979)
Victor Kuhne, *Bulgaria Self-Revealed* (London, 1919)
Mercia Macdermott, *Freedom or Death: The Life of Gotse Delchev* (London, 1978)
John Macdonald, *Czar Ferdinand and his People* (reprint edition New York, 1971)
Hans Roger Madol, *Ferdinand of Bulgaria: The Dream of Byzantium* (London, 1933)
Andrew Rossos, *Russia and the Balkans: Inter-Balkan Rivalries and Russian Foreign Policy, 1908–1914* (Toronto, 1981)
Lt. H. Wagner, *With the Victorious Bulgarians* (London, 1913)

FROM THE END OF THE FIRST TO THE END OF THE SECOND WORLD WAR

Elizabeth Barker, *Macedonia: Its Place in Balkan Power Politics* (London, 1950)
John D. Bell, *Peasants in Power: Alexandŭr Stamboliski and the Bulgarian Agrarian National Union, 1899–1923* (Princeton, New Jersey, 1977)
Frederick B. Chary, *The Bulgarian Jews and the Final Solution, 1940–1944* (Pittsburg, 1972)
L. A. D. Dellin, *Trade Unions and Labour Legislation in Bulgaria, 1878–1953* (New York, 1953)
G. P. Genov, *Bulgaria and the Treaty of Neuilly* (Sofia, 1935)
Max Lazard, *Compulsory Labour Service in Bulgaria* (Geneva, 1922)
Geo Milev, *The Road to Freedom: Poems* (translated from the Bulgarian by Edwald Osers, Sofia, 1983)
Marshall Lee Miller, *Bulgaria during the Second World War* (Stanford, California, 1975)
Charles A. Moser, *Dimitrov of Bulgaria: A Political Biography of Dr Georgi M. Dimitrov* (Ottawa, Illinois, 1979)
Nissan Oren, *Bulgarian Communism: The Road to Power, 1934–1944* (New York, 1971)
Stoyan Rachev, *Anglo-Bulgarian Relations during the Second World War (1939–1944)* (translated from the Bulgarian by Stefan Kostov, Sofia, 1981)
Joseph Rothschild, *The Communist Party of Bulgaria: Origins and Development, 1883–1936* (New York, 1959)
Joseph Swire, *Bulgarian Conspiracy* (London, 1939)
Kosta Todorov, *Balkan Firebrand: the Autobiography of a Rebel, Soldier and Statesman* (Chicago, 1943)

BULGARIA SINCE 1944

Michael M. Boll (ed.), *The American Military Mission in the Allied Control Commission for Bulgaria, 1944–1947: History and Transcripts* (Boulder, Colorado, and New York, 1985)
Michael M. Boll, *The Cold War in the Balkans: American Foreign Policy and the Emergence of Communist Bulgaria, 1943–1947* (Lexington, Kentucky, 1984)
J. F. Brown, *Bulgaria under Communist Rule* (London, 1970)
L. A. D. Dellin (ed.), *Bulgaria* (New York, 1957)
Hristo Devedjiev, *Stalinization of the Bulgarian Society, 1949–1953* (Philadelphia, 1975)
George R. Feiwel, *Growth and Reforms in Centrally Planned Economies: The Lessons of the Bulgarian Experience* (New York, 1977)

Paul Henze, *The Plot to Kill the Pope* (London, 1984)

Mito Isusov (ed.), *Problems of Transition from Capitalism to Socialism* (Sofia, 1975)

Georgi Markov, *The Truth that Killed* (translated from the Bulgarian by Liliana Brisby with an introduction by Annabel Markov, London, 1983)

Michael Padev, *Dimitrov Wastes No Bullets: The Inside Story of the Trial and Murder of Nikola Petkov* (London, 1948)

Nissan Oren, *Revolution Administered: Agrarianism and Communism in Bulgaria* (Baltimore and London, 1973)

Atanas Slavov, *The 'Thaw' in Bulgarian Literature* (Boulder, Colorado and New York, 1981)

Claire Sterling, *The Time of the Assassins: The Inside Story of the Plot to Kill the Pope* (London, 1984)

Todor Zhivkov, a collection of his works was published by Pergamon Press, second edition, Oxford, 1985

Liudmila Zhivkova, a collection of her works was published by Pergamon Press, Oxford, 1982

VALUABLE JOURNALS AND PERIODICALS

Bulgarian Historical Review (Sofia)

Problems of Communism (Washington, D.C.)

Radio Free Europe (Munich) research reports and bulletins

Religion in Communist Lands (London)

Southeastern Europe (Tempe, Arizona)

Survey (London)

Survey of World Broadcasts (BBC)

Yearbook on International Communist Affairs (Hoover Institution, Stanford, California)

Index

Adrianople x, 7, 35, 48, 60, 62
Adriatic Sea 4, 6, 93
Aegean Sea 4, 6, 7, 19, 61, 74, 83–4, 92,
    123, 125, 146, 160
Agca, Mehmet Ali 202
Agrarianism, see BANU
Agriculture, 1, 71–5, 107–8, 129, 137–9,
    158, 167–9, 175, 177–8, 182, 184,
    193–7, 201, 203
    collectivisation of 151, 157–8, 164,
      167–9, 172, 174–6, 178–9, 181–2,
      192
AICs 195–8
Albania ix, 8, 57, 59, 60–1, 109, 124,
    139, 141
Alexander Battenberg, Prince of Bulgaria
    21, 24–6, 28, 29–32, 34, 36, 39
Alexander III, Tsar 25, 28–9, 31, 37–8
Alexander, King of Yugoslavia 111, 116,
    120
Allied control commission 145, 153, 156,
    160
Anti-semitism 110, 122, 127, 132
April Plenum, 1956, 179–80, 183
Aprilov, Vasil 12, 14
Armenian massacres 37, 45
Armenians 8, 15, 174
Army 39, 46, 50, 59–61, 64, 66–71, 78,
    85, 93–4, 100, 102–4, 106, 111–12,
    115–16, 123, 126, 129, 155–6, 160,
    185, 192, 209
    Agrarians and 55, 83, 90, 94, 98
    and Ferdinand 33, 36–7
    and Macedonia 27–8, 46, 50, 103–4,
      112
    plots 31–2, 37, 185
    purges of 147, 154–5, 162–3, 173
    Russians and 27–9, 31, 37, 174
Austria 139, 144, 147
Austria–Hungary 16, 19, 30, 34, 40, 45,
    47–8, 50, 52–3, 57, 59, 62, 91

Bagrianov, Ivan 132, 146
Balkan federation 16, 18, 55, 87, 92–3,
    109, 120, 172
    entente 109, 111, 120, 122
    league 58, 62
    mountains 2, 6, 12, 17–19, 26, 76
Banks 25, 27, 44, 75–7, 88, 100, 103,
    113, 141, 158, 166
BANU 61, 64, 69, 71, 82–99, 108–10,
    115–18, 130, 134, 145, 185–6, 195
    and Communists 84–6, 88, 91–4,
      98–101; after 1944, 147, 150–2,
      155–7, 160–3
    divisions in 95, 97, 104–5, 109
    electoral performance 44, 55, 63, 83,
      86, 97, 101, 118, 155, 172
    foundation 43–4,
    ideology 55, 87
    and monarchy 53–4, 98
BDZh, see railways, Bulgarian State
Belgrade 18, 30, 33, 47, 92, 96, 111, 122,
    124, 154
Berlin 124, 208
    conference, 1877, 19
    treaty, 1878, 19, 20, 26–7, 34, 42,
      52–3, 63, 76, 83
Bitolya 35, 65, 67
Black Sea ix, 6, 19, 61, 123, 126, 131,
    194
Blagoev, Dimitŭr 55–6, 69, 101
Bogorov, Ivan 12, 13
Bolsheviks 91–2, 95, 99
Boris III, King of Bulgaria 36, 82, 98,
    101–2, 104, 106, 111, 114–24,
    126–8, 130, 149, 171
    baptism 38, 45
    death 127–8
    marriage 119
Bosnia 19, 52–3, 65
Botev, Hristo 13, 18, 130
Bozhilov, Dobri 128, 131–2

215

Britain 15, 19, 24, 33, 66, 164, 170
Bucharest 15, 18, 92
　treaty of: 1886, 30; 1913, 62–3; 1918,
　　70
Budapest 10, 101
Buddism 188
Bulgaria, relations with
　Austria 16, 19, 30, 34, 42, 45, 47–8,
　　64, 68, 78
　Belgium 78
　Britain 19, 33–4, 66, 78, 91, 103, 112
　　121, 124, 134, 137, 145, 150,
　　155–6, 161
　entente powers 64–6, 68, 70, 82, 85,
　　88, 90, 97–9, 101
　France 42, 64, 66, 78, 91, 112, 143,
　　191, 193
　Germany 34, 41, 64–8, 78, 91, 103,
　　121–2, 123–9, 131–4, 143–4,
　　160, 191
　Greece 11–12, 14, 16–17, 29, 58–61,
　　65, 67, 83, 102, 119–20, 176, 190
　Italy 91, 109, 112, 119, 122, 123, 125
　Montenegro 58
　Romania 11, 60, 62, 65, 69, 77, 83,
　　92, 119, 122, 185, 190
　Russia 15–16, 19, 24–34, 37–9, 45–8,
　　51, 53, 57–9, 61–2, 66, 68–9, 91–2
　　(*see also* relations with U.S.S.R)
　Serbia 49, 57–62, 65
　Third World 191
　Turkey 19–20, 27–30, 34–5, 45, 48–9,
　　52–3, 49, 58–60, 62, 65–6, 78,
　　119–20, 123, 126, 132, 174, 190
　U.S.A 70–1, 82, 91, 124, 134, 145,
　　150, 153, 155–6, 161, 163, 173,
　　176, 202
　U.S.S.R. 112, 121–2, 123, 125–6,
　　128–9, 131, 133–4, 144–6, 148,
　　152, 155, 159, 160–1, 166, 168–9,
　　172, 174–5, 178, 182, 184, 191,
　　193, 203, 209
　the Western allies 122, 128, 131–4,
　　145–6, 150, 152–3, 155–6, 164
　Yugoslavia 83, 87, 92–3, 96–7, 103,
　　106–7, 111, 119–21, 123, 133, 160,
　　171–2, 174, 176, 179, 181, 185,
　　190–1
Bulgarian Academy of Sciences 80, 95
　Agrarian Union, see BANU
　clergy 33, 48–9, 59, 67, 147
　Communist Party 83–6, 88, 91–4,
　　97–102, 104–5, 110, 112, 116–18,
　　123, 125–6, 128–9, 132–5, 145–65,
　　167–8, 171–3, 181–2, 185–6, 195,

　206–9; and army 116, 147, 154,
　　156, 162; congresses, 167–8, 175,
　　177–9, 181, 184–5, 188, 207;
　　divisions within 86, 101, 105;
　　electoral performance 83, 86, 97,
　　101, 107–8, 118, 155; membership
　　130, 146, 172; programme 1971,
　　186–7, 205; purges 170–3, 180;
　　September 1923 rising 100–3; and
　　Soviet Union 84, 91–2, 123, 147,
　　151, 164–5, 179–80, 184–5, 187,
　　202, 209; structure 187
　literature 3, 6, 9, 13, 79, 134, 175,
　　180–1, 183, 201
　National Bank 27, 75–6, 141; National
　　Front 115
　Orthodox church 3–8, 13–16, 24, 55,
　　58–9, 74, 95, 111, 125, 127, 157,
　　170, 173–4, 200
　Revolutionary Central Committee 18, 19
　Revolutionary Social Democratic Party
　　(BRSDP) 56
　Social Democratic Party 83–6, 97–8,
　　101, 105, 107, 110, 117, 130, 134,
　　150–2, 154–7, 163–4
　Workers' Party 103, 105, 107–8, 156,
　　163, 167
　Workers' Union 112, 114, 148
Bureaucracy 39, 42–3, 55, 74–5, 78, 84,
　　94, 97, 113, 125, 129, 144, 169,
　　173, 180, 198, 206–8
Burgas 37–8, 41, 77, 129
Burov, Atanas 96, 157
Buzludja 56

Capitulations 20, 32, 52
Central Committee for Economic and Social
　　Welfare 68
Chervenkov, Vŭlko 171–83, 185, 190
Chesmedjiev, Grigor 130, 145, 150–1
China 182–4
Church and state in Bulgaria 3, 4, 6,
　　14–15, 24–5, 35–6, 38, 58, 95, 111,
　　157, 170, 191
Comecon 166, 194
Cominform 163
Comintern 100, 146, 171
Compulsory labour service 90, 93, 122
Conservatives 21, 24–7, 36, 38, 40
Constantinople x, 6, 7, 11, 13, 15, 16, 19,
　　24, 35–6, 45, 52–3, 58, 60, 65–6
Constitution, Dimitrov 164–6, 186
　Tŭrnovo 19–21, 24–7, 35–6, 53–4, 99,
　　106–7, 113, 117–18, 160
　1881, 25–7, 1971, 186–7

Constitutional Bloc 96–7
  reform 105, 113, 115–16, 118
Cooperatives 54, 75, 87–8, 90–1, 94, 100, 120, 138, 140–1, 166–7
Corruption 38–9, 51, 93, 97, 125, 206, 208
Craiova 123
Croatia 92, 190, 208
Currency 4, 68, 104, 141, 143, 158, 169, 188, 194, 197–8, 200, 203
Cyril, St 3, 88, 125
Czechoslovakia ix, 92, 121, 139, 162, 186, 193

Danev, Stoyan 44, 46–7, 61–2, 83
Danube, 2, 6, 11, 19, 62, 67, 77, 116, 124, 132
Daskalov, Raiko 82, 95, 97, 102
DCYL 207–8
Dedeagach (Alexandroupolis) 40, 62–3, 66
Democratic Alliance 100–1, 104–7, 110
  Party 27, 30, 44, 52, 56, 67, 100, 104, 107–9, 117, 130, 152, 156, 164
Depression 73, 104, 106–8, 137–9
Dimitrov, Alexandŭr 93, 96
  'Gemeto' 105, 150
  Georgi 101, 105, 117, 146, 151, 153–4, 156, 160–1, 163, 171, 174, 183
Directorate of Civilian Mobilisation 123, 143, 158
  for Economic and Social Welfare 68, 79
  for Social Renewal 114–15
  for the War Economy 143
Divorce 205
Dobrudja 43, 63, 65, 67–8, 70–1, 113, 119, 122, 123, 132, 134, 137, 160, 167, 174, 182
Drama 65, 67
Drug smuggling, accusations of 201–3
Dŭnovism 110, 189
Dupnitsa 97, 109

Education 5, 10, 12, 17, 24, 39, 75, 78, 80, 87, 91, 95, 114, 125, 170, 175
Energy supplies 203–4
Enos 61, 65
Esnaf, see Guilds
Exarchate and Exarchists 16–18, 34–6, 48–50, 58–9, 63, 170, 174

Fascism 110, 117, 126, 148–9, 155, 158, 166
Fatherland Front 129–30, 132–4, 145, 150–2, 154–5, 157, 161, 163–4, 186

local committees 147–8, 150, 152, 158, 164
Ferdinand, Prince and King of Bulgaria 53, 57, 60–2, 65–7, 70, 82
  and the army 36
  election of 33
  and Macedonia 45–7
  marriage 35–6
  opposition to 34–5, 51–3, 57–8
  personal regime 38–40, 53–4, 63, 83, 104
  recognition of 33–4, 37–9, 76
Filipov, Grisha 199, 205
Filov, Bogdan 122, 124–5, 128, 131, 134, 149
Firmilian 46, 50
Five-year plans 166–9, 175, 181–2, 197
France 4, 64, 83, 85, 173, 188, 191
Franchise 21, 24–5, 52, 97, 118

Gabrovo 12, 14, 69, 208
Ganev, Venelin 145, 164
General Workers' Trade Union Federation (Narrow) 57, 84
  Workers' Professional Union 148
Georgiev, Kimon 111–14, 130, 134, 145, 153, 156
Germany 29, 34, 41, 64, 66–7, 69, 120, 128, 159, 181–2, 191, 194
Geshov, Ivan 53, 57–61, 67
Gichev, Dimitŭr 105, 117, 132, 150, 152
Gold standard 104, 141
Gorna Djumaya 47, 97, 109
Grain consortium 88, 94, 99, 143
  prices 40, 42, 68, 73
  trade 40, 77–8, 88, 137–8
Greece 1, 29, 58–9, 78, 83, 109, 117, 120–1, 123–4, 129, 140, 160–2, 164, 189–91, 208
Greeks 5, 8, 14, 16, 18, 134
  in Bulgaria 8, 14–16, 36, 51, 63, 74, 125, 135–6
Guilds 10, 12–14
Gypsies 174, 205, 207

Haiduks 9, 24, 101
Haitov, Nikolai 181, 183
Health and medicine 79, 91, 94, 109, 139, 178, 199
Hitler 110, 123–6, 131
Housing 169, 178, 192, 195
Hranoiznos 108, 143, 158
Hungary ix, 84, 86, 123, 131, 139, 147, 162, 180, 208

Ilinden–Preobrazhensko rising 47–50
IMRO 45–8, 50, 92–3, 96–8, 100, 102–3, 106, 109, 112, 119, 202
Indebtedness 42–3
Industry 2, 71, 73, 75–7, 79, 123, 129, 137–9, 144, 159–60, 169–70, 182, 192–5, 199
  in five-year plans 167, 169, 181
  nationalisation of 158–9, 166
  state encouragement of 40–1, 76–7, 137, 139–41
Inflation 75, 93–4, 129, 159
Intelligentsia 7, 8, 12, 17, 21, 43, 48, 51, 74–5, 110, 149, 181, 184, 188–9, 201, 208
Internal Macedonian Revolutionary Organisation, see IMRO
Iran 192, 203
Italy 57, 65–6, 115, 119, 123–4, 128
Ivan Rilski 3, 5

Japan 191, 194, 199
Jews 8, 38, 127, 132, 174, 207

Kalofer 12, 97
Karavelov, Liuben 18
  Petko 25, 27–31, 37, 39, 44, 52, 77
Kaulbars, general 26, 28
Kavalla 65, 67
Kazasov, Dimo 130, 156
Khruschev, Nikita 179–80, 183–5, 189–90, 192, 209
Kioseivanov, Georgi 115–16, 118–22
Kiustendil 6, 97, 109
Kliment, Metropolitan of Tŭrnovo 36
Kolarov, Vasil 101, 105, 146, 151, 153, 156, 171
Koprivshtitsa 12, 19
Kosovo 7, 191, 208
Kostov, Stefan L. 135
  Traicho 156, 171–3, 178–80
Kosturkov, Stoyan 100, 107, 155
Kresna 21, 71
Krŭstev, Krŭstiu 80, 134
Kŭrdjali 62

Labour Bloc 105
Lamsdorff, Count 47, 49
Land holding 71–2, 136–7, 162, 167–9
  reform 88–91, 93–4, 100, 103, 123
Lawyers 88, 94
League of Nations 92, 102–3, 119–20
Legionnaires 126, 128
Lenin 86, 92, 158, 183

Levski, Vasil 18
Liapchev, Andrei 71, 100, 103–4, 106, 108–9, 119, 138–40
Liberal Party (Bulgarian) 21, 24–7, 30, 36, 38–9, 117
  split in 27, 39
Libya 191, 203
Loans 33–4, 41–2, 44, 46, 64, 78, 102–4, 153
Local government 113, 182, 187
Lom 97, 148
London 92, 103, 208
  convention, 1933, 111
  treaty of, 1913, 61
Lukov, general 115, 117, 126, 128–9
Lulchev, Kosta 150–2, 154, 163–4
Lule Burgas 59, 62
Lyaskovets 12, 15

Macedonia 1, 10, 16, 17, 19, 21, 24, 33, 45, 49, 58, 62–3, 67, 74, 92, 124–5, 146–7, 160
  Greece and 34, 45, 48–9, 51, 58, 63
  Serbia and 33–4, 45–9, 58, 63
Macedonian question in Bulgarian politics 27–30, 34–8, 41, 44–50, 53, 58–60, 63, 65–7, 70, 83, 92–3, 95–9, 102–7, 109–10, 112, 120–1, 124–5, 146, 160, 171–2, 174, 190–1, 208–9
  refugees 27, 36, 49, 74, 87, 92
Malinov, Aleksandŭr 52–3, 57, 70, 100, 104, 107, 117
Maritsa 7, 26
Markov, Georgi 183, 188, 202
Marseilles 111, 120
Methodius, St 3, 88, 125, 208
Mexico 191, 208
Midia 61, 65
Milan, Prince of Serbia 29, 33
Military League 94, 96, 98, 100, 106, 114–15
Monasteries 3, 5, 7–8, 10–13, 51, 89
Montenegro 59
Morava 19, 67–8
Moscow 151, 153, 164, 169, 171, 184, 208–9
Muraviev, Konstantin 133–4, 150
Mushanov, Nikola 107, 152, 156–7
Muslims 7, 9, 24, 38, 42, 63, 71, 170, 205–6
Mussolini 91, 93, 119, 122, 124
Mutkurov, Sava 31, 36

Narodniks 18, 135

National Alliance 96, 98, 100
  Liberal Party (Stambolovist) 39, 54, 107
  Library 80, 171
  Party 53, 83, 96, 100
  Social Movement (NSM) 110–11, 115, 117
  Theatre 51–2, 80, 135
NATO 189–90, 201
Nazi–Soviet pact 121, 128, 161
Nazis 109, 117, 120, 126–7, 149
Neichev, Mincho 145, 154
NEM 197–200, 203–4, 209
Neofit Rilski 12, 14
Neuilly-sur-Seine, treaty of 83–4, 87, 90, 92, 94, 119–21
Nish 15, 17, 33, 121
  convention 93, 97–9

Obbov, Alexandŭr 104, 151, 156–7, 163
Ohrid 4, 5, 14, 15, 35, 65, 68
Omarchevski, Stoyan 91, 94–5, 175
Orange Guard 85, 90, 94, 96–8
Orthodox church 3, 6–8, 14–17, 24, 36, 59, 111, 157, 173–4
Ottoman conquest 7–8, 205
  empire 7–11, 14–16, 17, 20, 29, 34, 44, 45

Paiisi Hilendarski 10, 12
Panitsa 34–5
Paris 42, 44, 92, 208
  peace negotiations, 1918–19, 83, 85; 1944–7, 155, 159
Partisanstvo 38–9, 43, 74–5, 108, 149, 208
Patriarchate, Bulgarian 3, 174; Greek 3, 7, 14–7, 34
Peace treaty after Second World War 146, 149, 153, 155, 159–60, 168
People's Bloc 107–10
  Constitutional Bloc 117–18
Pernik 51, 64, 86, 101, 103, 140
Petkov, Nikola 52, 130, 145, 150–7, 160–4, 166, 170, 179, 185
  Petko 47–52, 104
Petrich 92, 97, 102–3, 112
Petrograd 66, 69
Petrov, Racho 36, 47–51
Pladne Agrarians 109, 117, 150–1
Pleven 12, 19, 43, 98
Plovdiv 7, 15, 18, 29–30, 32, 52, 74, 80, 96, 100, 116, 122, 129, 135, 176, 178, 200, 206,
Poland ix, 9, 92, 115, 129, 139, 149, 162, 180, 188, 197, 201–2

Police ix, 84–5, 93–4, 118, 148, 160, 173, 177, 184, 192
Pomaks 7, 207
Pope John Paul II 201–2
  Paul VI 191
Popular Front 105, 117
Population 71, 75, 92, 136–7, 204–5
Porto Lagos 63–4
Portugal 115, 194
Prague 92, 102, 186, 208
Progressive Liberal Party (Tsankovist) 44, 83, 100
Proportional representation 52, 63, 106, 118
Protestants 15, 170, 200
Protogerov, general 82–3, 102

Radical (Democratic) Party 69, 100, 106–7, 117, 155, 157, 163–4
Radomir 82
Radoslavov, Vasil 31–2, 54, 62–7, 69–70, 83
Railways 20, 28, 30, 40, 42, 51–2, 63, 68, 74, 77, 85, 101, 139, 141, 159, 169, 192
  Bulgarian State 27, 76
  Burgas–Yambol 38, 42
  Oriental Railway Company 40–2, 53
  parallel 41
  Russe–Varna 27, 31, 34
  Sofia–Danube 25–6
  Sofia–Kumanovo 58
  Vienna–Constantinople 26, 38
Rainov, Nikolai 80, 135
Rakovski, Christian 56
  Georgi 13, 18
Ralin, Radoi 175, 180, 183
Red Army 130–4, 145–7, 153, 160, 164, 202
Refugees 87, 90, 95, 100, 102–3, 119, 136
Reichstag 69, 117, 161
Resen 13, 49
Resistance in Second World War 129–30, 146, 149
Rila monastery 3, 8, 95, 149
Roman Catholic church 9, 16, 170, 173, 188, 191, 200
Romania ix, 11, 13, 38, 54, 62, 67, 78, 83, 92, 109, 120, 123–4, 132, 139, 153, 162, 189, 208
Rose oil 169, 172
Rumelia, Eastern 19–21, 25–6, 28–30, 38, 41, 45, 52–3, 74

Russe 15, 32, 135
Russia 11, 15–16, 19, 24–6, 28–30, 32, 33–5, 38–40, 44–8, 50, 54, 57–9, 61–2, 65–6, 84
Russian navy 37, 123
  provisional administration 21

St Petersburg 44, 46, 61
Sakŭzov, Yanko 56, 82
Salonika 33, 48, 59–60, 71, 82, 121
Samokov 12, 15, 69, 97
San Stefano, treaty of 19, 20, 38, 50, 129
Sarafov, Boris 45–6
Savov, general 62, 82
Science and technology 187, 197–201, 203, 205–6, 209
September rising, 1923, 100–1, 105
Serbia 6, 7, 10, 11–12, 16, 18, 27, 29, 33, 40, 59, 62, 65–6, 78, 208
Seres 15, 65, 67
Shipka pass 19, 46–7
Shumen 2, 32, 96
Simeon II, King of Bulgaria 128, 154
Silistra 32, 37, 60
Skopje 15, 35, 46, 49, 125, 190
Slaveikov, Petko 79, 80
Sliven 18, 51, 56, 69
Slivnitsa 30, 62, 209
Sobolev, general 26, 28
  deputy commissar 123
Soccer 122, 206, 207
Socialism 44, 55–7, 61, 63–4, 71, 85
Socialists: Broad 56–7, 83–4 (*see also* Bulgarian Social Democratic Party); Narrow 56–7, 66–7, 69, 83 (*see also* Bulgarian Communist Party)
Sofia ix, 2, 6, 7, 15, 18, 21, 24–5, 30, 31, 43, 45, 47, 50–1, 59, 62–3, 69, 75, 80, 82, 84–5, 90, 92–4, 96–9, 101, 106, 108–9, 114, 122, 123–4, 134, 136, 144, 146, 150, 153, 161, 164, 171, 189, 200, 206
  bombing 128–9, 131, 144, 159
Sofronii Vrachanski 10, 11
Stalin 122, 133, 176–7, 179, 183
Stalingrad 128, 130
Stamboliiski, Alexandŭr 53–5, 66, 69–70, 74–5, 82–99, 104, 109–10, 117, 119, 133, 138–9, 154, 158, 179, 182, 195
  Asen 156, 162, 179
Stambolov, Stefan 29, 31–7, 39, 40, 44, 92
Stambolovists 45, 49, 51–2, 54, 59, 65

Stoilov, Konstantin 37–45, 67, 76, 137
Straits 120, 123, 189
Strikes 51–2, 56, 84–6, 94–6, 100–1, 116–17, 133–159
Struma 47–8, 53, 59–60, 62
Stürshel 175, 180
Supreme Macedonian Committee 44–50
Svishtov 12, 14, 15, 25
Svoboden Narod 154, 157
Switzerland 69, 78, 154, 163
Synod 24, 58–9, 95, 157

Tariffs 20, 33–4, 42, 49, 52, 76–7, 139–40
Taxation 5, 11, 15, 42–4, 57, 74, 76, 90, 103, 108, 144, 158, 175, 184
Teachers 12, 43, 48–9, 56, 75, 91, 94, 112, 147
Textiles 1, 10–12, 76, 79, 139, 141
Thrace 1, 2, 6, 16, 29, 48–50, 58–60, 62–3, 65–7, 70, 83, 92, 121, 123–5, 146, 160
Tito 147, 170–2, 179, 190–1
TKZSs 157–8, 167–8, 175–6, 194
Tobacco 42, 44, 74, 78, 104, 116, 137–8, 143, 146, 159, 169, 176
Tolbukhin province 205
Tomov, K. 95, 97, 105
Topencharov, Vladimir 180–1
Tourism ix, 194, 200
Towns 8, 10–11, 13, 43, 56, 70, 74–6, 84–5, 87, 90, 93–4, 99–100, 107–8, 136, 144, 184
Trade 7, 8, 10–11, 77–8, 123, 143–4, 169, 175, 181, 191, 194, 197
  unions 56–7, 100–1, 103, 112–13, 157, 161, 163
Truman doctrine 160, 164
Tsankov, Alexandŭr 100–5, 107, 109–10, 116–19, 126, 128, 135
  Dragan 16, 24–7, 33, 35, 37, 39
Tsankovists 30, 44
Turkey 109, 120, 132, 189, 191, 202, 208
Turks in Bulgaria 38, 42, 63, 71, 73–4, 76, 123, 135, 174, 190, 205–8
Turlakov, Marko 85, 95, 97
Tŭrnovo 6, 7, 14, 15, 17–19, 21, 27, 52–4, 96, 98

U.S.A. 69, 82, 139, 153, 160, 170, 202
U.S.S.R. 123, 139, 145, 159, 168–70
Unemployment 107, 159
Uniatism 16, 24, 35, 63, 200

Union of Bulgarian Priests 170
  with Rumelia 29–30, 31, 34, 36, 38, 79
  Writers' 181, 201
United Radical Party 152
University of Sofia 51–2, 68, 78, 91,
  94–5, 125
Usury 42–3, 54, 73, 75, 88

Vardar 19, 61
Varna 32, 37, 51, 63, 77, 98, 129, 131,
  135, 206
Vatican 173, 191, 202
Vazov, Ivan 14, 79, 80, 134
Velchev, Boris, 185, 187–8
  Damian 111–16, 134, 145, 154, 163
Vidin 6, 7, 15, 17, 176
Vienna 10, 42, 102, 124, 208
Vrabcha Agrarians 105, 107–9
Vratsa 15, 18, 100, 185, 194
Vŭlkov, general 104, 179

Wages 56, 76, 84, 100, 107, 123, 129,
  151, 159, 178, 192–4, 203
War: Balkan 59–63, 73; first Balkan 57,
  59–61; First World 64–71, 73–5,
  77–8, 80–1, 123, 129, 132, 143,
  151; Greek–Turkish 1897 45, 48;
  Russo–Turkish, 1806–12, 11, 17;
  1828–9, 17; 1877–8, 19;
  Serbo–Bulgarian, 1885, 29–30, 38;
  second Balkan 62–3, 74, 93; Second
  World 95, 99, 121–34, 138, 143–4,
  151; Spanish civil 128, 173
Warsaw 66, 92, 163
  pact 166, 189

Western allies 126, 131–2, 146, 149–50,
  153, 156
Women 69, 90, 118, 125, 157, 163, 207
World council of churches 170
Wrangel, general 87, 95–6
Working class 56, 84–5, 93, 107, 130,
  159, 184, 187

Yalta conference 151
Yambol 38, 97, 200
YMCA 110–11
Young Turks 52–3, 57, 59
Youth 103, 114, 125–6, 150, 157, 163,
  207
Yugoslavia ix, 83, 109, 119–20, 124, 129,
  139, 149, 160, 181, 189, 193
Yugov, Anton 145, 151, 156, 177–9, 181,
  183–5, 209
Yurukov 157, 162

Zadruga 74
Zemedelsko Zname 55, 151
Zhivkov, Todor 179, 183–209 *passim*; rise
  to power 177, 180–1, 184–5; and
  Soviet Union 180, 183, 185, 189–90,
  209; Theses, 1959 182–3, 193; on
  Youth 207
  Zhivko 185
Zhivkova, Liudmila 188–9, 200–1, 203,
  208
Zlatev, general 114, 120
Zveno 106–7, 111–12, 114, 115, 130,
  134, 147–8, 154–7, 162–4, 166

DR
67
.C73
1987

Crampton, R. J.

A short history of
modern Bulgaria

$14.95

© THE BAKER & TAYLOR CO.